I0868181

IN THE NEIGHBORHOOD

In the Neighborhood

Women's Publication in Early America

Caroline Wigginton

University of Massachusetts Press
Amherst & Boston

Copyright © 2016 by University of Massachusetts Press
All rights reserved
Printed in the United States of America

ISBN 978-1-62534-222-5 (paper); 221-8 (hardcover)
Designed by Jack Harrison
Set in Adode Caslon Pro with Monotype Bell Display
Printed and bound by Sheridan Books, Inc.

Library of Congress Cataloging-in-Publication Data
A catalog record for this book is on file at the Library of Congress.

British Library Cataloguing-in-Publication Data
A catalogue record for this book is available from the British Library.

For Kerry

And for my grandmothers,

Georgia Ball Curtis and Helen White Hopkins

CONTENTS

ACKNOWLEDGMENTS

It takes a neighborhood of readers and colleagues, friends and family to make a book, and this one would not have been possible without the many gracious and smart people who helped me in the process. Throughout, Lisa Moore and Joanna Brooks could not have been more wise and inspirational. I consider them my mentors, collaborators, and, best yet, friends. They cast long and lovely shadows. At the University of Texas, William Scheick as well as James Cox, Jennifer Wilks, and Carolyn Eastman offered support and inspiration. Catherine Bacon, Layne Parrish Craig, Naminata Diabete, Molly Hardy, Michelle Lee, Aména Möinfar, and Laura Smith gave encouraging critiques along the way. Phil Barrish, Cole Hutchinson, Martin Kevorkian, and Michael Winship also offered answers and guidance. Members of the Native Literatures Reading Group—Jim Cox, Kirby Brown, Katy Young Evans, Lydia Wilmeth French, and Amanda Moulder—provided engaged and rigorous conversation. I am indebted as well to the unforgettable Matt Cohen, who showed me in which direction I actually was moving.

At Rutgers University, I found a new neighborhood of friendship and support. My special gratitude to my colleagues Louise Barnett, Sylvia Chan-Malik, Jeff Decker, Nicole Fleetwood, Allan Isaac, Lou Masur, Ben Sifuentes, and Andy Urban. I am grateful as well for the exchange of ideas that took place in the Public Knowledge and Formalisms seminars at the Rutgers Center for Cultural Analysis, led by Meredith McGill, Jonathan Kramnick, and Jonah Segel.

The University of Mississippi has been a collegial and welcoming new home. Thank you to Lindy Brady, Erin Drew, Chi Elliott, Cristin Ellis, Derrick Harriell, Ivo Kamps, Marc Lerner, Peter Reed, Dan Stout,

Ian Whittington, and Jay Watson for feedback and support, and to Brad Cook for helping me with the Latin.

My gratitude also goes to the virtual neighborhood of early American studies scholars, who only occasionally gather in person but whose comments and ideas permeate the book. First and foremost are the members of my writing group, Angie Calcaterra, Travis Foster, Greta LaFleur, Michele Currie Navakas, Wendy Roberts, Kacy Tillman, and Abram Van Engen. At conferences, formal and informal discussions with Kelly Wisecup, Dennis Moore, Sari Altschuler, Gordon Sayre, Kathleen Donegan, Michelle Burnham, Vin Carretta, Katy Chiles, and Crystal Lake have been especially invaluable. Josh Piker gave me thoughtful and important advice on chapter 1.

The editorial staff at the University of Massachusetts Press has been gracious and enthusiastic throughout the process. The book has benefited immensely from the assistance of Clark Dougan, Carol Betsch, and Dawn Potter. I am grateful to my readers Kelly Wisecup and Lisa Brooks for their perceptive and robust feedback.

Part of chapter 1 appeared in an earlier form as “In a Red Petticoat: Coosaponakeesa’s Performance of Creek Sovereignty in Colonial Georgia,” in *Native Acts: Indian Performance in Early North America* (2011), 169–93. Thank you to the University of Nebraska Press for permission to reprint and to Laura Mielke and Joshua David Bellin for their editing of that essay. A version of chapter 2 appeared as “Vexing Motherhood and Interracial Intimacy in Sarah Osborn’s Spiritual Diary,” *Early American Literature* 47, no. 1 (2012): 115–42. I thank *Early American Literature* for permission to reprint it, and Sandra Gustafson, Catherine Brekus, and an anonymous reader for their helpful comments.

The research for this book has been supported by a New Faculty Fellows Award from the American Council of Learned Societies, funded by the Andrew W. Mellon Foundation. It has also been funded by a McNeil Fellowship from the Historical Society of Pennsylvania; an Ellen Clarke Temple Graduate Award in the Study of Women in History from the Center for Women’s and Gender Studies at the University of Texas at Austin; a Presidential Excellence Postdoctoral Fellowship at the University of Texas; and the College of Liberal Arts and the Department of English at the University of Mississippi. Additional research was conducted at the American Antiquarian Society, the American Philosophical Society, Brown University’s John Carter Brown Library, the Connecticut Historical Society, Haverford College's Quaker and Special Collections, the Library Company of Philadelphia, the Massachusetts Historical Society, the Newport Historical Society, and Yale University's Beinecke Library. I thank their welcoming and helpful archivists and librarians.

Finally, I am deeply grateful to my early teachers for inspiring me: Debra Moddelmog, Chadwick Allen, and the late Nicholas Howe. My father, Joseph Hopkins, mother, Sara Hopkins, and stepmother, Prudence Hopkins encouraged my education. My grandmothers, Georgia Ball Curtis and Helen White Hopkins, offered models of lifelong learning and unapologetic feminism. I wish I could share this with them. My brother, Thom Hopkins, made sure I looked up from my books occasionally. Maureen Young has been the best of friends. My children, Luke, Georgia, and Aubrey, were (relatively) patient with the many "mommy minutes" that I asked for; Aubrey in a way is a part of the book, as I drafted chapter 3 on Phillis Wheatley's elegies for children while pregnant with her. And my husband Kerry has been both patient and supportive about my at times incomprehensible pursuits. Thank you.

IN THE NEIGHBORHOOD

Introduction

In early America, women navigated a landscape of Massachusetts townships, Creek *talwas,* and Quaker meeting houses. They stepped into each other's kitchens and shops and fields. They delivered each other's children, tended each other's bodies, bought and sold each other's labor, occupied each other's land. Together they prayed, sang, celebrated, stitched, and read. They shared news, sent letters, kept diaries, passed along commonplace books, petitioned their grievances, and wrote verses for the dead. In short, they resided in neighborhoods that spanned public and private, religion and politics, likeness and difference. These neighborhoods enfolded the daily interactions that occurred within and between people who lived alongside each other. They were supple, heterogeneous, and pervasive.

In the Neighborhood tells the story of the new American publics created in women's quotidian intimacies and exchanges. Even as certain men fostered the nation through republican print, women of diverse racial, religious, and class backgrounds were engendering and reforming what was for them a more pressing scale of affiliation, the neighborhood.[1] Bringing together textuality, material culture, and performance, their publication practice communicated revised territories of bondedness. Confined to neither print nor the home, they paired composition with circulation to choreograph the neighborhood's asymmetrical relations and map them across and beyond a local geography. The neighborhood by turns complemented and counterbalanced the emerging nation, mooring imagined communities to daily life.[2]

What distinguished these women's practice was its retention of particularity. Eschewing republican print's constitutive fraternal anonymity, it was rooted in material intimacies and enacted a vision of relationality. Women's intertwined roles as mothers, wives, friends, slaves, trading partners, and parishioners offered readily available repertoires of particularized intimacy. Their practice did not resolve or expunge difference among neighbors; rather, publication rearranged its dynamics. Indeed, particularity—racial, gendered, religious, class—pervaded the neighborhood, and its presence animated women's reimaginings of expression and association. Transnational trading partners became kin, dutiful citizens were friends, and aspiring converts were daughters and sons. By altering quotidian bonds, women's publication fomented the transformation of early American neighborhoods.

Relational Publication and Early American Neighborhoods

To give a sense of how women's publication reconstituted the neighborhood, I turn to a pair of examples, separated by more than half a century. In 1728, James Le Tort, a Euro-American trader, heard rumors of hostilities in the Pennsylvania backcountry and abandoned plans for a northwest voyage. He sought confirmation from his French-Algonquin expedition partner, Isabelle Montour, and was told that the unrest had originated with a grieving mother.[3] According to Montour, a Lenape woman, inconsolable over a Shawnee's murder of her son, turned to the leader Manawkyhickon, also Lenape, and presented him with "a Long Belt of black Wampum of twelve Rows, Desiring that by means thereof her Tears might be wiped away."[4] To Manawkyhickon, this substantial belt woven entirely from valuable black beads signaled a demand for vengeance.[5] Mourning the loss of a kinsman executed by colonists, he too longed for retribution. He dispatched the belt to the Haudenosaunee, or Iroquois, who in turn sent it to the Miamis.[6] Along with the belt was delivered "a message desiring to know if they would lift up their Axes, and joyn with them against the Christians."[7] When Manawkyhickon learned that the Miamis had agreed, he supplemented the original belt with four replicas, which he sent to hunters "abroad," "ordering them quickly to return home." After imparting this news to Le Tort, Montour hastened him back to Philadelphia to relay a warning about the impending violence.[8]

Sixty years later, a Delaware Valley *salonnière* named Elizabeth Graeme Fergusson transcribed her pre-Revolution poem "The Dream" into her bound manuscript collection, *Poemata Juvenalia* (see plate 1).[9] The poem recounts a vision in which the waters of the Atlantic part to reveal a "haughty" Albion "claim[ing] Dominion" over recalcitrant Pennsylvanian subjects. In response, long-dead founder William Penn appears on a "lucid Cloud" and reminisces about carving a colony from the wilderness wherein "Manly Liberty and virt[u]ous Peace" would reign, threatened only by faction. He then hands a scroll to the dreamer. Rather than read it herself, she consigns it to a young man in the crowd who is, a footnote reveals, John Dickinson, author of *Letters from a Farmer in Pennsylvania,* a tract collection that had roused colonists to rebellion in the aftermath of the Stamp Act crisis.[10] In Fergusson's vision, it is Dickinson who delivers the reminder of rural Pennsylvania bounty and self-sufficiency contained in Penn's scroll, thus recalling the colonists from their subservient and divisive pursuit of British commodities. Once the scroll has been read aloud, a "buzing murmur of Applause," gradually increasing in volume, spreads through the "Neighboring Ground" and causes the dreamer to awaken to the violence of an approaching storm.

Both examples involve the transmission of a publication, one that could be relayed in a series of deliberate and interpretive exchanges that retained without transfixing their origins. Both center on a realignment of communal affiliations and partitions, local and transnational. The Lenape mother's wampum belt is a material communication, which Manawkyhickon replicated and dispatched to other Native nations in tandem with a shifting spoken message. He activated widespread Haudenosaunee protocols, which required belts for condolence rites as well as diplomatic interactions. Participants, would have retained or passed them on as living archives of their conversations. In other words, the belt functioned as a statement of grief and a plea for resolution that Manawkyhickon embedded within his own wampum circulations.

Fergusson's scroll is a celestial communication, dreamed by her, delivered by Penn, and transferred from Fergusson to her chosen messenger, John Dickinson, thereby obliquely attributing his real and influential patriotic "letters" to a white female source. The scroll calls on Pennsylvanians to turn from England toward each other to become self-sufficient. Its passage from hand to hand and its oral delivery summon them to a collective gathering on "Neighboring Ground." This imagined summoning mirrors the real summoning Fergusson performed through belletristic exchange. She sent copies of "The Dream" to Dickinson and to the prominent London physician John Fothergill "within a year after it was Composed."[11] Most likely, she also presented early versions and pieces of the poem, if not all seven hundred lines in their entirety, at her own literary salon. Fergusson's heterosociable gathering, now considered to have been America's first salon, included such luminaries as Dr. Benjamin Rush, Reverend Jacob Duché and his wife Elizabeth, Dr. John Morgan and his wife Mary, the harpsichordist Francis Hopkinson and his wife Ann, the poet Annis Boudinot Stockton and members of her family, the musician James Bremnar, the sculptor Patience Wright, the landscape painter Betsy Pyle, and occasionally Dickinson himself.[12] Circulated via her literary network, Fergusson's poem envisions communal change through a message about neighborly interdependence, the sharing of labor and harvest.

What connects these examples is the way in which they moved through a series of exchanges, shedding and accreting meaning while remaining linked to their authors and still addressing a specific audience. As acts of publication, they circulated through interpersonal relations, and relationality motivated their composition and form. Together, content and distribution reinforced, revised, and extended a neighborhood of bonds. They ask us to rethink publication in light of the relational quality of the real and virtual neighborhoods inhabited by early American women.

Here, I use publication to mean something other than printed words on a page. Eighteenth-century print transformed conceptions of public bonding, yet many early Americans could not or would not turn to it as an expressive vehicle. Moreover, the printed page, especially when circulated in a local geography and among intimates, articulated with other forms of public knowledge and visibility. In *The Networked Wilderness,* Matt Cohen reasons that a "broad" approach that "insist[s] on . . . performative elements" may be more true to early American materials. Rather than publication, he opts for "publication event," which he defines as "an embodied act of information exchange," one that "presumes that its participants are aware that an act of communication is intended (though they may not be aware of the customs and rhetorics shaping it)."[13] "The event," he continues, "is also constituted by its retransmissions subsequent to the original publication moment, some anticipated by the participants and some beyond their control." His reconsideration of publication rests at the convergence of early American and Native studies, which has recently been reconceiving of publication, literacy, text, and writing to do justice to the period's Native authors and actors. As Abenaki scholar Lisa Brooks explains, wampum in early America was part of an "indigenous writing system" that, like birch-bark scrolls and pictographs, sought to connect people across time and space.[14] Native peoples' European colonist and enslaved African counterparts brought their own histories and literacies to North America. Studies of early American textual and print cultures have shed light on such subjects as the interconnection of the spoken and written word in the public sphere and black Americans' keen interest and involvement in book production as laborers, consumers, and authors.[15] All shared an imperative to read and write in a new landscape of communications, performances, and material productions. As Sandra Gustafson concludes, "integrative, multimedia histories of the verbal arts provide better accounts of the past—and a better view of the future."[16]

In this integrative sense, a publication *makes public* an expression of its author, invites a reading, submits itself to circulation. In early America, wampum belts and manuscript verse as well as petitions (oral and written), spiritual diaries, costume, and gestures were just as much acts of publication as novels and political pamphlets were. The accompanying material and performative circumstances are fundamental to their interpretation. By calling a publication an expression of its author, I am reading authorship itself generously, as a shorthand for the varied ways, including collaborative, that early American women made public rather than as a synonym for *writer*.[17] A narrower view of publication risks falsely limiting women to the margins of early American literary and cultural histories, bound by a model that rarely serves their interests.

In this light, print may not be the best avenue via which to approach the relational quality of early American women's publication. Because both the Lenape mother and Fergusson were familiar with publication as the circulation of a message, I turn instead to epistolarity to foreground early American women's familiarity with the interdependence of textuality and bondedness. For many, epistolarity is synonymous with letter writing. For those who lived prior to the invention of telecommunications, letter writing, as William Merrill Decker reminds us, was "a discursive practice to which people of nearly every class and level of literacy had recourse." Through letters, correspondents sought to "bridge the geographic and interpersonal spaces that separated people."[18] Thus, early Americans were nimble epistolarians, experienced at using letters to affirm and order relationality.

In turning to epistolarity to consider the publication repertoire of the Lenape mother and Fergusson, I signal not letters per se but rather their constitutive particularity or what Janet Gurkin Altman calls "pronominal relativity." In *Epistolarity: Approaches to a Form,* her important formal inquiry into the eighteenth-century epistolary novel, she observes that epistolarity pertains to the mediation of meaning through relationality. In words that mirror Decker's, she notes that letters first indicate interpersonal "distance" and then "bridge" that distance; exchange transpires across that bond.[19] "Pronominal relativity," or the "particularity of the *I-You,*" governs this exchange.[20] For her, novelistic epistolarity assembles particularity in addition to letters and collates interpersonal relations in addition to narrative events. Thus, the quotidian relational practices of neighborhoods articulate with publication practices, altering the production of meaning. If we think about this relationship between medium and content in the terms of media theory and Marshall McLuhan—who argues that "the 'content' of any medium is always another medium"—we observe that relationality itself functions as a medium.[21] Pushing this idea further, we can say that letters and epistolary novels remediate relationality, where remediation is "the representation of one medium in another."[22] Letters represent particular interpersonal bonds, which may be created or transformed through their representation.

Approaching early American women's publication through epistolarity directs us not to form but to the retention of particularity. The practices of the Lenape mother and Fergusson retained and reconfigured (in other words, remediated) the dynamic and uneven bonds of early America. As with letters, their publication practices were inextricable from quotidian exchange and invested in its adaptation and extension. But unlike letters, neither inscribed a salutation or a signature. Here, the epistolary model highlights the dynamics of interpersonal exchange, and I coin the term *relational publication* to name their practice. Not bound to letters, relational publication could mobilize a variety of technologies—scriptive, print, performative, material—to negotiate and reimagine a neighborhood's particularities.[23] Recall that the Lenape mother's black wampum belt (a material, symbolic, and performative message) activated recollections of specific moments of loss and reorganized regional affiliations. Fergusson's "The Dream," a manuscript poem that was circulated in a literary coterie and whose subject is the circulation of a celestial letter, amplifies geographic particularity by elevating Pennsylvania's bounty and history. In it, the vagaries of local climate and landscape guide regional and transatlantic exchange. For these two women, publication altered the dynamics of bondedness, and they arranged and rearranged structures of affiliation through composition and circulation.

Early American women's relational publication was a counterpoise to republican print, whose emergence and spread has long been theorized as a precursor to democratic origins.[24] Accounting for the rise of the modern democratic nation-state, Benedict Anderson famously and influentially concludes that "print-as-commodity is the key to the generation of wholly new ideas of simultaneity" required for national consciousness.[25] Similarly, Jürgen Habermas (theorizing the emergence of the bourgeois public sphere) and Michael Warner (intent on early American republicanism) find evidence in print.[26] In their models, print is the medium via which people felt akin to each other. Before widespread literacy and printshop proliferation, parochial concerns consumed isolated individuals. In contrast, a reader awash in periodicals, broadsides, and books imagined himself perusing the page alongside others who resembled himself. Relational publication was like republican print in that it forged and extended bonds between early Americans. Yet it differed in its reliance upon particularity. In expositions of republican print, anonymity is indispensable. Warner emphasizes that "the meaning of public utterance . . . is established by the very fact that [print] can be read and participated in by any number of unknown and *in principle unknowable* others."[27] The nation, aligned as it was with a "republic of letters" determined to be co-extensive with print, effaced particularity in the service of an imagined "fraternity" of "deep, horizontal comradeship."[28] The republican model conceives of a temporal progression whereby the nation superseded and subsumed provincial identities.[29] With its emergence, the reader transformed into the democratic citizen who felt his kinship with those anonymous fellows who were ostensibly just like him. Republican print disseminated a sense of belonging alongside shared values—liberty, reason, republicanism, literacy—thereby distinguishing citizens from noncitizens. Republican print was for the virtuous citizen.

These studies more or less concede that republican print hinged on a masking of gender, class, and racial difference in the service of a normative formulation of the reader-citizen as male, property-owning, and white.[30] Eighteenth-century women could participate in this fraternity only insofar as they could efface their gender—a partial exercise at best.[31] For them, republican citizenship was impossible: their gendered bodies were stubbornly present, and they were relegated ideologically to the domestic sphere.[32] Even Elizabeth Maddock Dillon, who in *The Gender of Freedom* insists on the presence of women as authors and subjects in the public sphere, distinguishes between a literary and a political public sphere and concludes that women's presence in the literary (not political) public sphere worked to circle the "concerns" of that sphere back onto the "intimate sphere rather than the state."[33] Thus, women remained ideologically confined to the intimate or domestic and did not enter the fraternal realm of the political.

But alongside the emerging fiction of a national fraternity, the early American neighborhood endured as a space of particularity. There, women circulated promiscuously between house, church, farm, and business. Neighborhoods are geographic spaces where diverse people live by choice and chance alongside each other, their borders permeable and hazy. Neighbors reside in intimate proximity among a shifting web of relations.[34] Never static, neighborhoods are also a virtual spaces, traced through the circulations of texts, objects, and people. The itinerancy of a preacher, the crossroads of a trading post, and the serial passing on of a letter offer focal points for mapping routes of bondedness that some neighbors never walk. As both geographic and virtual spaces, neighborhoods are subject to interdependence, disparities in power, and vulnerability. Speaking specifically of antebellum slavery, Anthony E. Kaye explains that "neighborhoods served as the locus of all the bonds that shaped the contours of [slaves'] society."[35] Along these same lines, the early American neighborhood indexed quotidian relations. Reimagining the neighborhood transformed those bonds of interdependency, disparity, and vulnerability.

A focus on print and nation has masked women's occupation with this different scale of community, this different kind of transformation. Whereas republican print facilitated the republic, relational publication concerned itself with the neighborhood. It demanded particularity as it was functionally and formally distinct from the flattening and authorizing impulses of republican print.[36] The former engaged and extended difference, the latter uniformity. Relational publication capitalized on and adapted the ineluctable intimacy of daily life, presenting new and revised visions of bondedness and mapping lines of exchange and interdependency. By reimagining geographies of bondedness, women's relational publication transformed early American neighborhoods, sometimes in revolutionary ways.

The word *neighborhood* recurs frequently in the period's writing.[37] A quick search of the database *Early American Newspapers, Series 1,* limited to before 1800, returns more than 34,000 hits for *neighborhood.*[38] European and Native diplomats alike turned to *neighbor* and its cognates to conceptualize transnational geography. For example, the Middle Plantation Treaty of 1677, between Virginia and the Powhatan Confederacy, differentiated between "Foreign" and "Neighbour" Indians. The purpose of the treaty was to "conclud[e] a good Peace with the Neighbour *Indians.*"[39] Among its other provisions, it required that any "Foreign" Indian must be accompanied by a "friendly neighbour *Indian.*"[40] Several "Articles of Agreement" made in 1701 between Pennsylvania and Native diplomats, including Onondaga, Shawnee, and Susquehanna, claimed that "hitherto there hath always been a good understanding and Neighbourhood between the sd. Wm. Penn & his Lts, since his first arrival in the said Province, and the Several Nations of Indians inhabiting in and about the same."[41] Some twenty-five years later, Haudenosaunee and Susquehanna representatives came to Philadelphia to discuss several issues. After reiterating their desire to continue with the colonists as "one Body, one Heart & one Blood to all Generations," they "take Notice that both the French & the English are raising Fortifications in their Country and in their Neighbourhood, . . . the meaning of which they doe not very well conceive."[42] Colonial treaties and provincial council minutes abound with such examples.

The shared term *neighborhood* resonates with indigenous conceptions of spatialized association and communication. The Haudenosaunee wood's edge—the place outside a village where visiting diplomats paused to announce their arrival—indicated a predisposition to friendly negotiation and assent to diplomatic protocols.[43] Native cartographers of the colonial southeast might "manipulat[e] distances and directions" to "graphically evoke degrees of ethnic relatedness, limits of political control, and networks of cooperating or competing groups."[44] For both Natives and colonists, the neighborhood was uncertain, a confluence of

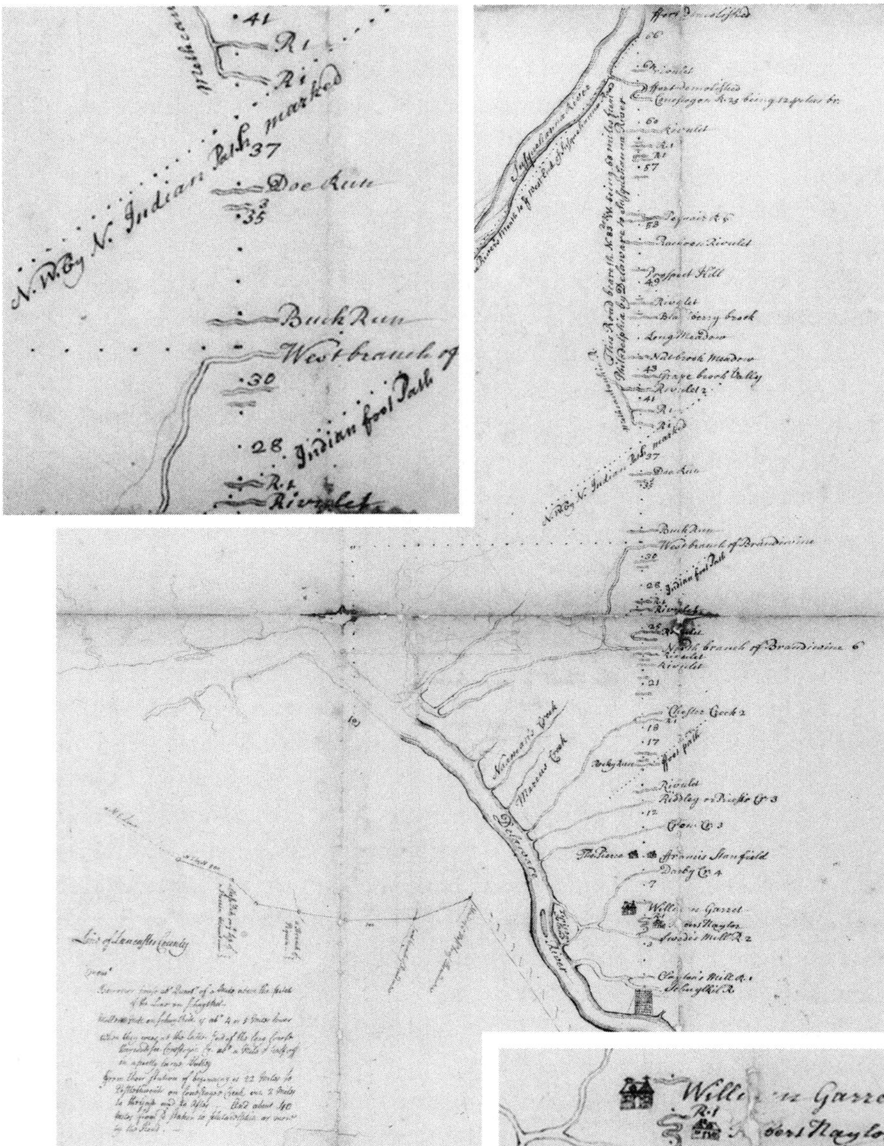

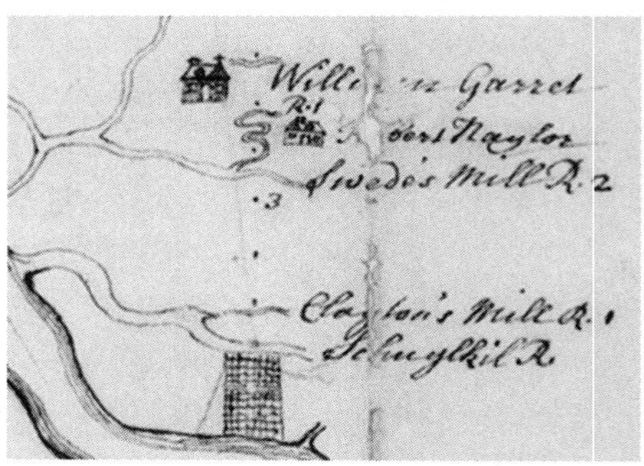

FIGURE 1. An early eighteenth-century map of the Lancaster line and the Susquehanna and Delaware rivers. The presumably Euro-American surveyor included drawings of fellow colonists' houses and mills and marked "Indian foot Paths." The back reads "Survey [?] from Philad.a to Susquehanna and The Line of Lancaster Coun[ty]." See Norris Manuscripts, Scrapbook of Surveys and Indentures (Oversize), p. 71, Historical Society of Pennsylvania. Image courtesy of the Historical Society of Pennsylvania.

the new and familiar, friends and enemies (see fig. 1 and plate 2). Residents were in flux, "meaning[s]" obscure. In a neighborhood, Native-European co-residency demanded ongoing interpretation and negotiation to maintain accord and regulate exchange.

Other early American documents attest to a concern with the neighborhood as a space of difference and discomfort. Even the title of Cotton Mather's account of the Salem witch trials conceives of witchcraft as a disturbance in the neighborhood:

> The Wonders of the Invisible World. OBSERVATIONS As well *Historical* as *Theological,* upon the NATURE, the NUMBER, and the OPERATIONS of the DEVILS. Accompany'd with, . . . Some Counsils, Directing a due Improvement of the terrible things, lately done, by the Unusual & Amazing Range of EVIL SPIRITS, in Our Neighbourhood: & the methods to prevent the *Wrongs* which those *Evil Angels* may intend against all sorts of people among us; especially in Accusations of the Innocent. . . .[45]

The *Pennsylvania Gazette* for 5 March 1750–51, prints clauses from two acts of assembly that seek to alleviate "the great Annoyance and Danger to the Neighbours" of disorderly "Negroes, and other Blacks."[46] In *Letters from an American Farmer,* J. Hector St. John de Crèvecoeur dissertates on, among other things, environmental evolution in a neighborhood. In the case of "back settlers," "by living in or near the woods, their actions are regulated by the wildness of the neighbourhood."[47] They transition from the "plough" to the hunt, the "chase render[ing] them ferocious, gloomy, and unsociable," more savage than the "Indian natives." Nearby, another "mixed neighborhood" develops into a "strange religious medly" as people of varied roots and sects intermarry or experience their fellow colonists' foreign forms of worship.[48]

The early American neighborhood retained the difference that republican print sought to elide. Indeed, it included a strange mixture of black, white, and Native individuals who interacted daily. Demographically diverse, they associated by way of frequently violent and unequal relationships. Bondedness and exchange often transpired contrary to desire and across undisputed divisions, such as those of race and religion. The neighborhood spanned the domestic and the public.[49] It was forged in the interactions within and among households, businesses, trading posts, farms, churches, and towns. To borrow Kaye's distinction, it was "pervasive but not uniform." His discussion of antebellum slave neighborhoods focuses on their fluidity and ubiquity:

> In some locales, neighborhoods marked the field of discipline or terrain of marriage and family life, the dominion where a coterie of old folks held sway. In others, this was the circuit worked by slave preachers, where seekers repaired to their praying grounds and convened for religious meetings. In some precincts, neighborhoods were the quarters of every kind of fraternizing. The geography of kinship, work, sociability, and struggle overlapped with neighborhoods in different ways in different regions. Neighborhoods might encompass some of these social relations or all of them and more. Everywhere neighborhoods covered different geographic areas.[50]

Like those of antebellum slaves, early American neighborhoods reflected the varied intimacies engendered by quotidian proximity: neighbors knew each other's habits and moods, smells and noises.

Bodily intimacy, then, helps distinguish between the nation and the neighborhood. Republican print ideally produced a horizontal fraternal kinship, or an abstracted intimacy of likeness, among anonymous citizens. America aspired to be an "affect-nation," but encounters with difference insistently disrupted the feeling of likeness.[51] This inability to expunge their particularity and feel absolute likeness disabled citizens from permanent communion with the nation and each other.[52] The anxiety of unwanted attachments still haunts explanations of national intimacy, which persists as vital yet fleeting, terrifying, and unsatisfactory.[53] As Lauren Berlant speculates, "virtually no one knows how to do intimacy."[54] Perhaps this dubiousness about intimacy's sustainability results from the links that Berlant and others perceive between the nation, the public, and anonymity. It does seem impossible to be intimate with those one does not know. And even the *counterpublic*, Warner's term for the virtual space where those who are subordinate to the public collect, "comes into being through an address to indefinite strangers."[55] In the neighborhood, however, there is little chance for anonymity, and intimacy is persistent and transactional.[56] Instead of an elusive product of republican print, intimacy among early Americans was a precursor to and product of relational publication. It arose from the daily familiarities and exchanges that occurred because of geographic proximity and interdependency. It arose in the physical touching, smelling, tasting, and seeing of objects and bodies; the hearing of voices; and the witnessing of circulation. Intimacy permeated the neighborhood.

Relational publication drew on that intimacy—the quotidian interpersonal fabric of practice and idiom—to revise and reimagine the neighborhood. Through composition and circulation, women rearranged bondedness to advance their communal visions and desires.[57] The reimagined neighborhood might have been geographically localized, but it also might have been diffuse, linked in terms of embodied and textual circulation. Changes in the neighborhood countered, paralleled, complemented, and co-evolved with a nascent national community. The Lenape mother's wampum belt affected Conestoga, a diplomatic crossroads where Natives and Europeans congregated to negotiate the protocols of occupying an uneasy neighborhood. Her message relied on preexisting bonds to catalyze a shift in the neighborhood's personal and transnational alliances, as the white trader perceived hostility where once he saw friendship and rushed homeward. Similarly, Fergusson's "The Dream" takes place on "Neighboring Ground," a geographic space that transforms to reflect the points of her vision.[58] Rather than a contest between men, her poem refigures the Stamp Act crisis as a concern among neighbors, a moment to capitalize on local bounty and labor, thereby imagining an inclusive, if idealistic, future. It arranges a space for all Pennsylvanians, including women, in a well-ordered colony in which each contributes according to his or her skill. In both instances, publication originated with the individual and then circulated beyond the authors and initial recipients, promoting alternative modes of affiliation that depended on the particularity, not anonymity, of the neighborhood and its inhabitants. They capitalized on and reconfigured the intricacies of daily bondedness.

Hand in Hand: From Letter to Relational Publication

As I have discussed, a turn to epistolarity makes us attentive to the ways in which particularity buttressed early American women's relational publication. Indeed, the widespread practice of letter writing schooled many women in how to use publication to reconfigure real and virtual neighborhoods. Letters, through the expected progression of salutation, body, and signature, textually represent a relationship and an exchange that is avowedly particularized. Furthermore, they call to mind the protracted material processes of writing: the production of ink, the filling of the inkpot, the scraping of the sheet, the shaping of the quill, the rasp of pen on paper, the folding and sealing of the letter. Among early Americans, these activities might have occurred in designated spaces such as a writing closet or a desk, where supplies were readily at hand. A writer may have sent a completed letter via the mostly coastal post system or entrusted it to a traveling surrogate.[59] An at times circuitous itinerary that was vulnerable to delay, misdirection, and destruction linked the location of composition to the recipient's site of reading. After delivery, the recipient would have broken the seal, unfolded and touched the same page, beheld the dips and sweeps of the writer's hand; the letter may have felt alive, an embodiment of the correspondent.[60] The letter itself concatenated a relationship by enacting contact, separation, migration, and reunion.

Letter writing is sensuous, material, architectural, and geographic; it envelops informational, interpersonal, and physical exchange.[61] We should not be surprised, then, to learn that the practice relates to communal formation. A host of scholars have scrutinized its alliance with class and its engendering of exclusive community through tools and conventions.[62] Their work emphasizes that letter writing can eliminate distinctions yet also confirm or configure imbalance. Its conventions demand the performance of subservience and dominance, and its transmission functions as a technology of colonization and empire. For example, when still in her teens and unmarried, Eliza Lucas took charge of her family's South Carolina plantations during her father's military deployment, and her correspondence reports familiar and business matters, including her "vegitable" experiments.[63] In about July 1740, she noted in her letterbook: "Wrote my Father a very long letter on his plantation affairs . . . ; On the pains I had taken to bring the Indigo, Ginger, Cotton and Lucerne and Casada to perfection, and had greater hopes from the Indigo (if I could have the seed earlier next year from the West India's) than any of the rest of the things I had tryd."[64] The confluence of "pains" and "I" when referring to her experiments suggests that they were labor-intensive and entirely her own, not her father's, whose absence had distanced him from the requisite labor and knowledge. Yet she would not have performed the physically demanding and extended agricultural process of indigo cultivation alone, especially as she had an alternate source of labor at hand: slaves.[65] Her letter's use of "I" subsumed the slaves' "pains" and claimed their particularity for herself. It seems enslaved men and women were, for her, physical resources, less important to mention than seeds were. The same instances of "I" also marked her useful and individual presence in the world of "plantation affairs." In effect, she wrote herself into the landscape of imperial trade through commodity experimentation, locating herself as the node through which a distant father and hidden enslaved Africans had to relate to the plantation and its products.

While such examples affirm that eighteenth-century American letter writing advanced colonization and increasingly indicated and reproduced a new white middle class, the form was nevertheless supple and democratic. Indentured servants, for instance, inscribed or dictated letters to ameliorate their hardships. Countering the elision enacted in business letters such as Eliza Lucas's, they conveyed their experiences and desires, asserting the presence of particular laboring bodies in a mercantile neighborhood. Elizabeth Sprigs, addressing her estranged father in England in 1756, complains of living worse than "many Neagroes," nearly naked and barefoot.[66] She quotes her master's insult, "You Bitch you do not halfe enough," and goes on to relate that he then bound and whipped her. Appealing to her father's "Bowels of Compassion," she requests clothes and reverses the customary close: "Your undutifull and Disobedient Child." In acknowledging her past filial misbehavior, Sprigs performed subservience even as she claimed a continuing unruliness and implicated her father in the brutality of mastery.

Like their Euro-American counterparts, some Native women used letters for class mobility.[67] Narragansett mother Sarah Simon placed five of her children with Reverend Eleazar Wheelock at Moor's Indian Charity School. In a 1767 letter, she asked him to "take" one son to his "Self" till he be "Capabel of Bisness" and receive a younger son who "is calld to be a publeck man."[68] The letter bestowed flattery and gratitude so that her grown sons did not have to. At his school, Wheelock instructed Native students in humility and subservience via letter writing. At times his students performed like good disciples; at others their epistles evince uneasy discipline. In one missive to her schoolmaster, Sarah Simon's daughter, also named Sarah Simon, muses on a pious future in service to her "Parishing Brethren" but elsewhere admits that she has avoided pastoral counsel, finding Wheelock's teachings impotent against "weickid thoughts."[69] As in Sprigs's letter, the correspondence of these impoverished and marginalized women enacted and denied affinities by insisting on particularity, thereby prefiguring autonomy.

Petitionary correspondence embedded structural features of the letter within a more formal setting.[70] For persons otherwise "refused . . .

the technical machinery of political expression"—women and persons of color especially—the petition presented a significant, if imperfect, opportunity to air and resolve grievances.[71] Doubly distanced, the aged African Belinda addressed the Massachusetts legislature in 1782, seeking an allowance from her Loyalist former master's confiscated estate. In her petition, she slips back in time to her childhood, before her abduction. Her sequence of sensations progresses from idyll to horror: she enjoyed "the happy temperature of the air" and "the fragrance of her native groves"; she entered a "sacred grove" to pray with her parents; "an armed band of white men . . . rushed into the hallowed shades"; "tears, . . . sighs, and supplications, bursted from the tortured parental affection"; she fruitlessly lifted "her supplicating voice" and was "ravished from the bosom of her country," her too-old parents left behind.[72] Having engaged the sympathies of her audience, her next words enact the disorientation of the Middle Passage:

> Scenes which her imagination had never conceived of, a floating world, the sporting monsters of the deep, and the familiar meetings of billows and clouds, strove but in vain to divert her attention from three hundred Africans in chains, suffering the most excruciating torment; and some of them rejoicing that the pangs of death came like a balm to their wounds.
>
> Once more her eyes were blest with a continent: but alas! how unlike the land where she received her being! How all things appeared unpropitious. She learned to catch the ideas, marked by the sounds of language, only to know that her doom was slavery, from which death alone was to emancipate her.[73]

The legislators who heard Belinda's words were transported into slavery, her petition momentarily suspending their difference. They continued to listen as the petition returned to the present, when she was "marked with the furrows of time, and her frame feebly ben[t] under the oppression of years." Separate again, her conspicuous singularity demanded that the legislators grant her fiscal justice. And they did.[74]

The writings of all of these women attest to the constitutive relational particularity of letter writing. The practice activates and performs an interpersonal bond and then revises that bond through the composition and circulation of an individual epistle. This formulation can make letter writing seem tangential to the neighborhood and only occasionally of impact, but early Americans and their transatlantic counterparts understood that letters might be structural to a neighborhood, especially those that were geographically diffuse. The structural potential is borne out in institutional examples such as the Society of Friends. The Society transacted its organizational structure by way of an entangled exchange of documents—letters, reports, testimonies. Each district's main representative governing body, the Yearly Meeting, would annually communicate its messages to the regional Quarterly Meetings through official epistles. The Quarterly Meeting might transcribe and retransmit all or part of the epistle to its local Monthly Meeting affiliates, along with its own messages and queries.[75] The epistles offered pious greetings and instructions and requested qualitative and quantitative information about the spiritual status of the community. Business meetings at every level were generally segmented into men's and women's, each holding complementary, often monitory, functions. Additionally, there were meetings for worship, preparation, discipline, and sufferings. Within this tangled hierarchy, epistles moved laterally as well and provided encouragement and reports of their own on the present state of the Society.[76]

The Women's Yearly Meetings in Philadelphia and London exchanged epistles throughout the American Revolution, and the Philadelphia minute book archives the experience of transmission and receipt.[77] An anxious silence troubles the 1778 epistle from Philadelphia, which begins: "Altho' we have not been favor'd as heretofore with the receipt of an Epistle from you, yet we trust you were not unmindful of us under manifold exercises & trials."[78] With some relief, the writers of the 1779 Philadelphia epistle report "the receipt of your acceptable Epistles for 1777 & 1778."[79] They effusively continue: "But trust we are as epistles written in each others hearts, in that fellowship, which time, distance, nor death itself will lessen or impair."[80] The unbreakable epistolary connection between the transatlantic Meetings permanently inscribed that bond within their communities, but the Philadelphia authors also note that the bond was supported by their knowledge of specific itinerant London Friends whose past visits were "still fresh in [their] minds" and "near to [their] spirits." Personal familiarity combined with letters to link minds and souls to hearts. Their communications bridged distance and stood in for the geographic proximity of a spatial neighborhood, forging a virtual neighborhood materially bound by letters. The writers acknowledged their experiential difference, but that difference justified correspondence, for the London Meeting could serve as a concerned body of neighbors who would witness and encourage. Their sense of closeness grew through iterative correspondence and circulation.

Within the Society's network, still more epistles, communicating the counsel of esteemed leaders, flowed from Meeting to Meeting, read and reread aloud, copied and recopied into the minutes when old exhortations became fresh and urgent again and when messages for a local community were deemed worthy of elevation. Women's Meetings set aside time to recall the words and testimonies of deceased Friends. In 1781, in response to continued requests, Elizabeth Smith's farewell 1772 epistle to the Burlington Quarterly and Chesterfield Monthly Meetings was "revived among [them] to [their] refreshment & comfort": "it was recommended to be read in each of our Monthly Meetings, and directed to be transcribed in the Minutes of this Meeting."[81] The clerk would have duplicated the epistle in her neat script, once into the minute book and again for each of the Monthly Meetings, her labor mirroring that of the compositors and pressmen who printed the epistles of Society luminaries such as Samuel Fothergill, Anthony Benezet, and John Woolman. Smith's epistle was published within a neighborhood of Women's Meetings, while those of Fothergill, Benezet, and Woolman were published throughout the American colonies and the British Isles.[82]

As deft epistolary cartographers of bondedness, Quaker women ported their practices into the sociable realm. In the mid-eighteenth century, for instance, three Philadelphia-area women sustained a correspondence.[83]Addressing Fidelia (the well-known pseudonym of Hannah Griffitts), Sophronia (that is, her cousin Hannah Harrison) reviewed her recent settlement near Fairhill, the country estate of their uncle Isaac Norris.[84] Sophronia hinted at her desire for admission to a rumored all-female "Band of friendship," of which she believed Fidelia to be the "head" and Sophia and Fellicia (Norris's daughters, Mary and Sarah) members. Initiation to such an inner "Rural-Circle" would have permitted Sophronia to situate herself among her new neighbors:

> I should like to be Tête à Tête with you now & then, —but would beg the Liberty to [be] Conversant with all my Reputable Neighbours, for as Members of Society, we are dependant upon one another, & tho our capacities, Education, & Stations may differ, yet it may be in the power of the meanest to be of Service or diservice to us. Therefore I would chuse to be civil to all, & to have but few Intimates.

Granting the exigencies of association among diverse neighbors, she nevertheless aspired to regulate exchange by identifying a more exclusive and "polite" conversational circle, free of "unpolish'd" gentlemen. Fidelia rebuked Sophronia for so hastily dismissing the neighborhood's rural residents, especially their widowed uncle, predicting that "when the Acquaintance is improv'd into an Intimate friendship, you will own I have not flatter'd them, but That the Originals, far exceed the Painting." "If you would have the Saucy Sex keep Their Proper Distance," she continued, "ever preserve your own proper Dignity." In parallel letters, Sophia and Fidelia weighed Sophronia's inclusion. Fidelia, who had a prior acquaintance, summarized Sophronia's character and charms: "Nature has Thrown but a very few grains of Gravity in her Composition, she is (when w[ith] her female fr[ien]ds) a livly & agreeable Companion, she has a sprightly wit, a pretty understandg, & a Ludicrous Notion of men & things." Suggesting that her faults were environmental, the result of an urban upbringing neglectful of women's education, Fidelia alluded to potential improvement in their society. "Indeed, my D[ea]r," she concluded, "she will be an agreeable Addition to our Circle."

Provoked by a new arrival, this correspondence assessed the contours of interaction and intimacy within a geographic neighborhood. It conjectured that prolonged acquaintance breeds familiarity; one must arrange proximity, selecting whom to invite to come closer and whom to hold at a distance, in order to manage exchange within a shifting population of diverse neighbors. As they iteratively considered such subjects, the correspondents assembled a cartography of present and future associations. For instance, one letter relates an anecdote in which Sophia encountered a man "Beat[ing his wife] in an Unmerciful manner." Confronted by his "Inhuman[ity]," she was nonetheless reassured that his "scotch dialect" proved that he was "not the disgrace of our Country." Though she was unable to banish or reform the husband and his "wretched" wife, she was able to textually locate these foreign neighbors as her inferiors.

Here are letters *qua* exhortations, testimonies, supplications, confessions, conversations, and judgments. They call to mind archaic practices (to borrow Linda K. Kerber's descriptor for petitions) grounded in oral performance.[85] This archaic realm respects hierarchy and ceremony, which are reflected in eighteenth-century epistolary conventions that demand expressions of service and duty. Letters, though, are not only orality made incarnate. Orality requires proximity, but letters signal absence too; they are autonomous by virtue of their materiality.[86] In early

America, letters were often circulated beyond their original audience. The expectation of redirection and redistribution produced pleasure and anxiety.[87] A letter providing longed-for news might be passed around, read aloud, or forwarded, so correspondents kept extended audiences in mind.[88]

As practiced letter readers and writers, early American women had long been familiar with how one might trace bondedness through the circulation of a text. A study of their letters divulges an impulse to arrange and delimit exchange and to reimagine their neighborhoods. We can discern this impulse in other acts of publication, such as the Lenape mother's wampum belt and Fergusson's poetic dream scroll. Surveying them collectively moves us from letters' structural components to a more capacious analytic that foregrounds function. The term *relational publication* alludes to a practice that emerged within and between early America's uneven bonds, one that evolved and persisted alongside republican print and was suited for those who could not or would not be anonymous citizens. Women's relational publication varied across scenes and occasions, depending on the particularities of the neighborhood, its residents, and the author herself. It called on a shifting and contingent array of formal features, performative gestures, materiality, and protocols of exchange. For scholars, the identification of early American relational publication is not so much a sorting process—this is relational, this is not—but a practice in and of itself. To read for relationality is to note how a neighborhood's bonds and communicative repertoire motivated and structured publication practice, to see how interpersonal exchanges made circulation possible, and to trace the resulting rearrangement of the neighborhood's communal cartography.

Founding Neighbors

Scholars have long acknowledged male authors' predominance in early American literary studies, often ruefully figuring women authors, usually elite and white, as exceptions. When the field treats republican print as virtually synonymous with publication in the eighteenth century, it preemptively excludes the kinds of publication in which women actively engaged. The collapsing of the distinction between the two obscures early America's robust publication repertoire and curtails our understanding of how publication inflected American association. It skews our thinking about relationality in postnational public life, long tied to the republican print model and its emphasis on intimate anonymity among citizens.

Consider Benjamin Franklin, a founding father of republican print but also a serial cross-dresser, at least on the page. A scrutiny of his earliest authorial forays—which habitually invoke the neighborhood and women's communication—reveals the copresence of relational publication and republican print. In 1728, Franklin was an ambitious young man whose greatest assets were his printing experience and a newly acquired press. After entrusting the wrong confidant with his "Secret" intention of introducing a second Philadelphia newspaper, he watched with "resent[ment]" as another city printer, Samuel Keimer, filched his idea and began his own.[89] Luckily for Franklin, Keimer soon imprudently reproduced an encyclopedia entry on abortion. Shortly thereafter, Philadelphia's senior paper, the *American Weekly Mercury,* published two letters of complaint—one signed "Martha Careful," the other "Cælia Shortface." Careful excoriates Keimer for "Expos[ing] the Secrets of our Sex, in That audacious manner" whereby they will be "read in all *Taverns* and *Coffee-Houses,* and by the Vulgar."[90] She warns that if he "Publish any more of that kind," she and other women "are Resolved to run the Hazard of taking him by the Beard, at the next Place we meet him, and make an Example of him for his Immodesty." Shortface, a Quaker matron, reports that "Thee, and *Thy Indecencies*" have been the "Subject of . . . Discourse" among her "Acquaintance[s]" and "that if thou proceed any further in that *Scandalous manner,* we intend very soon to have thy right Ear for it."[91] Ironically, Keimer's failure was one of reckless dissemination.[92]

A week later, a new *Mercury* correspondent, "the Busy-Body," accepted the implicit mandate of these letters and set himself up as a "*Censor Morum*" to make "Remonstrances" and "Reformation" of the community.[93] He would "publickly expos[e] . . . Private vices": "However, let the Fair Sex be assur'd, that I [unlike Keimer] shall always treat them and their Affairs with the utmost *Decency* and Respect." His subsequent essays offered advice on proper manners and incorporated women's letters, such as one from "Patience," a shopkeeper and single woman who complained of a "certain Neighbor . . . with whom I have had an Intimacy of some Time standing."[94] This woman "makes her Visits so excessively often," rendering it impossible to hold onto the "little Secrets and

Privacies that are not proper to be expos'd even to the nearest Friend." Patience asked the Busy-Body to "talk a little against such unreasonable Visiting in your next Paper."[95]

These paper barbs, of course, were not launched by Martha Careful or any other of their purported authors but by Franklin himself.[96] His employment as the printer of the *Mercury* abetted such mockeries, and an earlier successful experiment in authorship (for his brother's Boston paper under the guise of "Silence Dogood") had schooled him in the pleasures and liberties of pseudonymous critique. In the eyes of many scholars, these transparent personae emancipated Franklin's intellect from a limiting, singular embodiment. In such moments, he learned that self-as-editable-text could roam, revise, and proliferate. Print gave him a disembodied anonymity that became constitutive of the public sphere and the imagined community of democratic nationhood. Franklin helped disclose "print—not speech" as "the ideal and idealized guardian of civic liberty" in the new American republic.[97] In short, his personae functioned as a formative step in personal and national self-fashioning.

Yet a paradox persists: Franklin devised an ideology of disembodied republican print by resorting to femaleness.[98] The tale of Keimer's misguided reprinting of the abortion entry and Franklin's iterative repurposing of female personae remind us that he twice inaugurated his newspaper career—first in Boston, then in Philadelphia—under the guise of women letter writers. Even while counterfeit, these personae conspicuously rely on gender. They signal a concern with communal demarcations and regulating the circulation of bodies and discourse in a system composed of irreconcilably particularized constituents. Careful berated Keimer, not because abortion was wrong or secret but because he had shifted that information and its discussion from the conversational circles of women and the "Learned" to the "Vulgar" realms of "coffee-houses" and "taverns."[99] When objecting to the "*Indecen[t]*" encyclopedia entry, Shortface did not call for the obliteration of abortion knowledge, just its removal from promiscuous circulation. She suggested that Keimer should "Sell [the encyclopedia] at Thy next Luck in the Bag," thereby transferring its contents to a more limited and thus knowable circle.[100] Even the single shopkeeper Patience wanted to delimit zones of "Intimacy" between neighbors. She complained that her eager neighbor's children "mix" together her stock of variously sized nails, forcing her to sort them out again after the children leave.[101] She cast careless mingling as undesirable and inefficient and sorting as harmonious through deliberate, repetitive labor.

Franklin's serial cross-dressing expressed a desire to reorder affiliations within a localized geography. Though fabricated, his periodical letters were motivated by a neighborhood's relationships, ones that crisscrossed among coffee and meeting houses, taverns, bedrooms, and shops. They relied on the local newspaper to circulate their content, their pseudonymous veneers transparent among neighbors. Thus, while Franklin's early writings foreshadowed republican print, they also exploited the particularity of letter writing, which was suited to regulating localized public life because it engaged with the dynamics of difference rather than facilitated anonymity.

Franklin's facile female personae attest to the entanglement of relational publication and the origins of republican print. They served different ends—sometimes complementary, sometimes competing, sometimes entirely separate. In 1728, Philadelphia witnessed Franklin's intervention into conversational protocols as well as the aftereffects of the grieving Lenape mother's wampum message. Decades later, Franklin and Fergusson also occupied overlapping belletristic circles; perhaps they even exchanged drafts of "The Dream." The eighteenth-century publication repertoire was multitudinous and interdependent, much as the neighborhood was. Franklin, it seems, could not imagine a nation without also considering the neighborhood. He could not embark on republican print without also conjuring relational publication. A relational publication model attends to the persistent sites of particularity, the practices and places in which women, before and after nationhood, interrogated and revised the intimacies of public life. The abstraction of a fraternal national imaginary resolves into the quotidian materiality of complementary and competing neighborhoods.

In the Neighborhood compiles its archive from the publications of early American women of diverse racial, spiritual, and social backgrounds. It examines letters but more often other kinds of communications and performances, public rituals, material objects, occasional verse, legal and diplomatic documents, commonplace books, and diaries. My abiding concern is with moments in which a woman's publication practice imagined a transformed neighborhood, a momentous if not always successful or expected alteration in its structures of association and exchange. In such cases, print, too, may have served a relational function: even when publishing in print, an author may have known rather than imagined a community of fellow readers. Moreover, neighbors might have circulated a printed text among themselves even as it also circulated beyond the neighborhood's borders and concerns.

Temporally, *In the Neighborhood* glances at the seventeenth century and then steadies its gaze on the middle decades of the eighteenth century, approximately 1730 to 1785. My goal has been to elude artificial demographic partitions and offer an account that stays true to the strange crucible of early American culture. Thus, the book predates the American Revolution and republican print, accounting for revolutions in the neighborhood before and with the national and imperialist frameworks delineated in other studies. Because relational publication persisted as copresent with republican print, it permits us to discern a scale of community formation and adaptation that the alignment of print with an anonymous, masculine public sphere fails to grasp.

In the Neighborhood is methodologically indebted to practices of close reading and contextualization. The object of close reading includes more than words on a page. Modes and routes of circulation, material production, oral and embodied performances, sites of consumption are all constitutive of the text. Additionally, while literary in approach, the book draws context from religious, book, and regional histories as well as anthropology, media, and performance studies. Each chapter situates its central example in a performative and relational context, emphasizing the particularity of a woman's practice, situation, and vision. At crucial points, the texts themselves guide the refinement of key concepts, such as what a Creek diplomat meant by circulation and what a disowned Quaker pacifist meant by composition. Because relational publication negotiated uneven bonds that arose by way of force, proximity, and power, the book maps a crooked path across the early American affiliatory terrain rather than smoothing the contradictions and discomfort of the neighborhood.

While each chapter stands on its own, they are connected by themes of communal revolution, revival, and exchange. Chapter 1 revolves around Coosaponakeesa, a mixed-blood Creek diplomat and interpreter who was at times seen as the savior and destroyer of Savannah. Examining her diplomatic journeys and legal documents from the 1730s and 1740s, the chapter considers how Creek and English models of kinship, dress, and circulation facilitated a spatialized performance of publication and affiliation. Through a dynamic practice of relational publication, Coosaponakeesa mapped and remapped the political and economic bonds of her colonial southeastern neighborhood, which included both European and Native neighbors.

Turning from Coosaponakeesa's spectacular publication practice to a more intimate but nevertheless turbulent example, chapter 2 narrates a spiritual crisis and resolution documented in the 1760s diaries of Sarah Osborn, a poor, pious schoolteacher from Newport, Rhode Island. The crisis arose when Osborn invited her "female society" to pray over the pending sale of Bobey, a young man whom Osborn and her husband owned. After Bobey's enslaved mother Phillis—not owned by the couple but present at the meeting—refused to acquiesce to the sale, Osborn used her diary communications with God as a pathway to rerouting the affective, filial bonds in her household and neighborhood. Her alteration of affiliation catalyzed a transformation in her view of herself as spiritual mother, which in turn led to purposeful communal nurturings and eventually contributed to the burgeoning New England abolitionist movement. Here I counterpose the neighborhood with the most private of relational publications, a diary addressing God, to attest to the unruly effects of intimate exchange, especially in a cross-cultural context.

Chapter 3 traces the revised neighborhood mapped by poet Phillis Wheatley's 1770s funeral elegies for children and presents a contrast to the first two by examining how relational publication could repeat its transformative reimaginings through its circulation beyond the neighborhood. Shared by mourners and read aloud in their households, the elegies were rooted in neighborly exchanges and addressed to a multivalent audience that included enslaved Africans and bound servants. In locating herself as a transcendent inflexion point between the mourning and the dead, Wheatley offset the traumatic dislocation of enslavement by articulating a prophesy of redemption grounded in the disorientation of circumatlantic circulation.

Chapter 4 reappraises the climactic moment of republican print discourse, the American Revolution, through the lens of Delaware Valley Quaker women's textual productions. Geographically isolated by the rebellion, Milcah Martha Moore gathered the writings of her intimates into a commonplace book, thereby countering faction through relational publication. Juxtaposing poetry and protest, the book articulates a vision of affiliation grounded in piety, reciprocity, and temporality.

The afterword surveys relational publication in the new nation. As women's postnational letters, histories, poetry, novels, basketry, and needlework suggest, the modern democratic nation-state co-evolved with the neighborhood. I touch on the correspondence of Cherokee beloved woman Katteuha, Deborah Norris Logan's salvation and arrangement of William Penn's and James Logan's colonial correspondence, Annis Boudinot Stockton's epistolary critique of Mary Wollstonecraft's *Vindication of the Rights of Woman,* and the role of letters in Hannah Webster Foster's epistolary novel *The Coquette.* Looking also at material objects and contemporary art, I explicitly connect the chapters to a conversation about postnational American public affiliation, one that begins where I end.

For too long, women have been seen as peripheral to the story of early American communal transformation. *In the Neighborhood* accounts for the capacious flexibility of publication and its material intersections with women's quotidian associations—those that arose as they moved among each other's kitchens, shops, and fields, as they touched, wounded, and exchanged—in order to make plain their vital presence. Their concerns and intimacies are as much a part of our foundations as are those of Ben Franklin and his founding brothers. Women's prayers and celebrations, complaints and desires achieved traction where asymmetrical relations held sway. Our understanding of communal transformation and the persistence of particularity must attend to the neighborhood, that peculiar, motley, uncomfortable territory where we all reside.

1

Coosaponakeesa's Colonial Neighborhood

August 1749 was a tumultuous time in Savannah, Georgia. The Creek diplomat and trader Coosaponakeesa, then going by the name "Mary Bosomworth," came to this port town to board a ship for England.[1] Tired of waiting for colonial administrators to recognize her long-standing land claims and reimburse her for her substantial economic and diplomatic services to the colony, she planned to cross the ocean and press her claims in person before the board of trade. Back in the Lower Creek Nation, however, news of her pending departure brought to a boil long-simmering rumors that colonists were planning to detain and deport her for debts and treason. When a large contingent of Lower Creek men, women, and children led by her professed kinsman Malatchi, the powerful *mico* of Coweta, arrived in the colony, Mary Bosomworth marched with them from her nearby plantation into Savannah.[2] Leading the "Parade" were her third husband, Englishman Thomas Bosomworth, clothed in Anglican vestments, and his brother Adam, with Mary Bosomworth and Malatchi just behind.[3] The Creek warriors saluted Savannah with volleys of gunfire, thereby discharging their weapons while also reminding the Georgians of their military might.

Georgia's council cautiously welcomed Malatchi and the other Lower Creek micos. Inviting them and translator Mary Bosomworth into President William Stephens's house, they inquired about the purpose of their visit. Malatchi admitted "they had no Talk to deliver."[4] After relating the rumors circulating in the Nation, he declared that if the colonists intended to send Mary Bosomworth to England "in Irons," he "would untie her." To ensure that the colonists understood her importance to friendly diplomacy, he added that she "was to give and receive all Talks from them and us." At this point, Bosomworth stopped translating and began to speak on her own behalf. She declared that she was "Empress and Queen of the Upper and Lower Creeks, and that She could command every Man to follow her."[5] When the council asked, "Was [she] not a Subject of the King of Great Britain? She answered, She owed no Allegiance otherwise, than in Alliance, being herself a Sovereign." After several more "contraverted points," Bosomworth abruptly left, taking Malatchi and half of the other micos with her.

This scene's confluence of spectacle, procession, and words marks a vivid moment in Bosomworth's practice of relational publication, one that relied on her deft interweaving of both Creek and European repertoires. During the march on Savannah, the presence of Malatchi and the other Creeks signaled her enduring dependence on Creek kinship in making claims to power. It also suggested her willingness to guide the Creeks' circulation between the colony and the Nation. Her English husband's position in the "Parade"—marching in front of her and Malatchi—and his peculiar decision to wear vestments four years after he had left active ministry called attention to her intimacy with European ritual and authority. Later, her translation of Malatchi's words and its reliance on the language of exchange—"deliver," "give," "receive"—when discussing the "Talks," cast diplomacy as material and textuality as reciprocal. And her transformation from translator to "Empress"—a performance that utterly reconfigured her affiliations—suggested a radical desire to alter the region's neighborhood, making her not only a "Sovereign" self but a sovereign power that reconciled and united disparate interests.

The march on Savannah signifies a dynamic practice of relational publication, one that emerged from Coosaponakeesa's experiences as a Creek diplomat and trader facilitating the contours of the Southeast's evolving colonial neighborhood. She continually transformed Native and European repertoires of kinship, authority, and communication to advocate for her vision of a peaceful and mutually prosperous neighborhood, even as she advanced her own interests. Circulation was at the heart of her practice because the physical movement of bodies, of goods, and of paper was integral to the Southeast's politics and economies and because it made bonds tangible and visible. Those bonds were often personal but also transnational, as the neighborhood, before and after colonization, included an array of nations, indigenous and European.

Coosaponakeesa was a product of just such a personal and transnational union. Born early in the eighteenth century, she was the daughter of Edward Griffin, a Euro-American trader, and a Tuckabatchee Creek woman.[6] After spending her early years among the Creeks in Coweta, she moved to Pon Pon, South Carolina, to live with her father. When colonists arrived in 1733 to establish Georgia, Coosaponakeesa, then known as Mary Musgrove, and her first husband, the mixed-blood Creek John Musgrove, were operating a new trading post on a bluff overlooking the site of the first settlement, Savannah.[7] She played an active role in Georgia-Creek relations during James Oglethorpe's tenure in command and a somewhat less active but still prominent role under subsequent leaders. In addition to interpreting and helping Oglethorpe relate to the local Yamacraw Indians and the region's larger, more powerful Creek confederacy, she ran a series of trading posts and plantations with three successive husbands, assisted during trade and land negotiations, and helped enlist (or delay) Creek military support for British struggles with other indigenous Nations and European powers in the region.

Coosaponakeesa had influence and standing throughout the neighborhood. Her avowed matrilineal relationship to prominent Lower Creek leaders in Coweta, a relationship that she told the colonists made her a "Rightfull and Natural Princess," added to her influence.[8] As Mary Musgrove, she stabilized Creek *talwas,* or towns (the main political unit of the Creek confederacy), and expanded trade by helping to negotiate treaties and produce written versions of land claims and schedules of prices for traded goods. Lower Creek micos trusted her during treaty talks to relate and explain the contents of English-language documents. Ultimately, various Lower Creek micos (though not all) rewarded her by approving her territorial claims to several coastal islands—Ossabaw, Saint Catherine's, and Sapelo—south of Savannah and at the fringes of Creek territory.

These islands became the focus of a long legal battle between Coosaponakeesa and Georgia's administrators. In the mid-1740s, shortly after marrying her third husband, Thomas Bosomworth, she filed the first of many memorials with the colonial government requesting restitution for her services to the colony. The "Bosomworth Controversy," as historians of Georgia know it, occupies much paper and archival space. In addition to these memorials, Mary Bosomworth and her husband filed copious articles of documentation, including transcriptions of colonial records, letters, and government journals as well as affidavits from Creek leaders, fellow translators, and Indian traders. It was during this legal fight that she led her march on Savannah, thereby implicitly threatening Georgia's existence. In the mid-1750s, after many years of battling, she reclaimed her Creek name, signing her final memorials as Coosaponakeesa rather than Mary Bosomworth. Eventually, Governor Henry Ellis settled, giving her the proceeds from the sale of two of the islands as well as the deed to Saint Catherine's. Coosaponakeesa died soon thereafter.[9]

A sifting of colonial archives uncovers numerous documents bearing Coosaponakeesa's various signatures and names as well as unsigned diplomatic texts.[10] In addition to the documents related to her restitution efforts, she left behind letters, interpreter reports, and the translations of talks and treaty conversations. She fascinated colonial archivists and record keepers, who cataloged her dress, her migrations around the region, her speeches, and their readings of her performances. As a result, we can trace the shifting visions of affiliation that she embedded in treaties, letters, and legal documents as well as her transnational and transatlantic circulations. She drew on Native and European modes of circulation and communication—performative, visual, textual—to form a relational publication practice that continually reimagined and enacted her vision for the transnational neighborhood that was the colonial Southeast.

Coosaponakeesa's practice is emblematic of a broader history of Native women who responded to colonial encounter by uniting new, and at times European, practices of publication with indigenous affiliatory and communicatory models.[11] By creating a partnership among performance, textuality, and embodied circulation, they, like Coosaponakeesa, restructured their colonial neighborhoods' networks of relations. America's indigenous women had long been involved in diplomacy and politics, and European colonization compelled them to use, augment, and adapt their skills.[12]

Historically, scholarly comparisons of Native women's power before and after colonization have presented a declension model. In contrast, more recent work has refused to see power as "absolute and measurable," instead focusing on "how women's political rights, economic roles, and individual freedoms changed."[13] Though the earliest European colonizers made scattered references to the Native women leaders they encountered (Hernando de Soto, for example, met a woman he called the Lady of Cofitachequi, and John Smith mentions Opossunoquonuske, "Queen of Apamatuck"), later records attest to the ways in which many Native women persistently led via sociocultural authority even when colonization had curtailed more direct forms of political and military leadership.[14] Through interpersonal bonds and shrewd adaptations of new and old communicatory practices, they formed and strengthened alliances and stabilized their communities. By means of relational publication, Native women could fashion and extend quotidian bonds across increasingly disperse and expansive geographies and thereby mold colonial neighborhoods according to their visions. Coosaponakeesa's march on Savannah, then, was a significant but not singular scene of relational publication within a broader history of Native women's practices.

I begin with the spectacle of Coosaponakeesa's march rather than her writings to emphasize that where, what, and how she made public exists within and shaped colonist-authored texts. Notably, she wrote some of the earliest Native-authored texts in the English language, a fact that few literary scholars have remarked. However, her writings altered the colonial neighborhood in concert with other elements of her publication practice. Often, colonists recorded her acts of publication, and their documentation in the colonial archive means that the archive is part of a Native literary history. Moreover, nonscriptive moments such as her march demonstrate that early American publication was not imported whole cloth but arose before and within the fabric of encounter. It was as much a product of indigenous peoples as it was North America's new European and African residents.

Native Women As Cultural Remediators

When we think of Native women who changed the course of early American colonial encounter, the woman known as Pocahontas often comes to mind.[15] Of all the marks she left on the archive, the most immediate is her portrait, Simon van de Passe's *Matoaka als Rebecca,* which she sat for in 1616 during her sole visit to England (fig. 2). The young Dutch-German engraver portrayed her in costly clothing and accessories, including a lace ruff and a pearl earring.[16] On her head she wears a high capotain, and in her hand she holds a white three-feathered fan.[17] An oval inscribed with her pedigree encloses her image, and the caption reads: "Matoaks al[ia]s Rebecca daughter to the mighty Prince Powhatan Emperour of Attanoughskomouck al[ia]s virginia converted and baptized in the Christian faith, and wife to the wor[thy] M.r Joh: Rolff."[18]

The twin statements of pedigree align this portrait with the other engravings of royal figures that van de Passe produced while he was in London.[19] Of those, *Matoaka als Rebecca* closely resembles not only Anne of Denmark's picture but also van de Passe's engraving of Anne's husband, James I, king of England at the time of Pocahontas's visit (figs. 3 and 4). Both James and Pocahontas wear feathered brimmed hats and high collars, a similarity that suggests a parallel between these two state figures. Pocahontas's clothing borders on the masculine, though her femininity and foreignness are belied by her breasts and hairless cheeks, her shaded skin and pearl earring. The portrait marks her as a figure of Powhatan royalty, one whose modes of diplomacy and influence are not entirely familiar or legible, even though they are cloaked in the vestments of British authority.[20]

Knowing that the engraving would be printed and distributed as part of the publicity surrounding her visit to England, Pocahontas undoubtedly participated in its production and design.[21] As Camilla Townsend suggests, she may have insisted on the name "Matoaka" rather than the childish yet famous "Pocahontas."[22] Van de Passe probably did not choose the unusual hat, and the costly clothing reveals only her face and hand, hinting that she was "well aware of what was said about naked savages."[23] (For comparison, see the low-cut neckline of Anne of Denmark in figure 3.) We can view this portrait as Pocahontas's sartorial performance, a printed artifact by which she collaboratively circulated her affiliation with a foreign indigenous authority and likened them through juxtaposition ("al[ia]s") to more familiar British terms.

We may regret the voicelessness of her portrait, but her visible, silent presence can also be understood as an act of publication. Silence appears to have been one of Pocahontas's first lessons in diplomacy. In the spring of 1608, she visited Jamestown with her father's warrior-messenger as part of negotiations for the release of several Native hostages. That same year (more than a decade before she became a celebrity in England), John Smith mentioned her in print for the first time:

FIGURE 2. *Matoaka als Rebecca* (1616), engraved by Simon van de Passe, from *Baziliωlogia: A Booke of Kings.* This portrait was included in John Smith, *The Generall Historie of Virginia, New-England, and the Summer Isles* (London, 1624), II. Image courtesy of Houghton Library, Harvard University (STC 13581).

FIGURE 3. *Anna Dei Gratia Magnæ Britanni[æ] Franciæ et Hyberniæ Regina Etc* [Anne of Denmark] (1617), engraved by Simon van de Passe, from *Baziliωlogia: A Booke of Kings.* Image courtesy of Houghton Library, Harvard University (STC 13581).

FIGURE 4. *Potentiss: Iacobus D.G. Magnæ Britanniæ Galliæ et Hiberniæ Rex Fidei Defensor* [James I] (ca. 1618), engraved by Simon van de Passe, from *Baziliωlogia: A Booke of Kings*. Image courtesy of Houghton Library, Harvard University (STC 13581).

> Powhatan understanding we detained certaine Salvages, sent his Daughter, a child of tenne years old, which, not only for feature, countenance, and proportion, much exceedeth any of the rest of his people, but for wit, and spirit, the only Nonpareil of his Country: . . . [Powhatan's warrior-messenger] with a long circumstance told mee how well Powhatan loved and respected mee, and in that I should not doubt any way of his kindnesse, he had sent his child, which he most esteemed, to see me; a Deare and bread besides for a present: . . . his litle Daughter hee had taught this lesson also: not taking notice at all of the Indeans that had beene prisoners three daies, till that morning that she saw their fathers and friends come quietly, and in good tearmes to entreate their libertie.[24]

According to Smith, Pocahontas was sent from her village, Weramocomoco, to Jamestown to facilitate a negotiation. Unlike the gifts of bread and deer, she was not offered for consumption, nor was her visit seen as permanent. Her presence marked "how well Powhatan loved and respected" Smith while implying that his continuing esteem would be contingent on future exchanges. Yet Pocahontas was not an object on loan; she served as an active diplomat on behalf of her nation by "not taking notice at all" of the "prisoners" until the arrival of "their fathers and friends." According to Smith, she ably followed her father's lead in diplomacy.[25]

In this light, Pocahontas's portrait takes on new significance. The curved lines on her bodice and sleeves draw attention to the jagged, wavelike markings in the background border. Unlike the elaborate curlicues and symbols in the engravings of James and Anne, which circumscribe the frame and thus suggestively circumscribe their domain, these more subtle and uniform details indicate the expansive fluidity of her personal affiliations, the ways in which they entail movement and presence, sight and silence. The juxtaposition of names—Matoaka with Rebecca, Attanoughskomouck with Virginia—along with the references to her father Powhatan and husband John Rolfe underscore that these affiliations must be translated into a new linguistic and relational environment. As an act of publication, the portrait archives her transnational and transoceanic circulations.

These particular relations were the fabric of the strange new neighborhood that included Jamestown and Weramocomoco. Smith included the portrait in his popular *The Generall Historie,* which by midcentury had been reprinted multiple times and by late century was appearing in collections such as Oxford University's Bodleian Library and the personal library of John Maitland, Duke of Lauderdale (1616–82).[26] Thus, her presence proliferated and endured. Persisting alongside her fantastical salvation of Smith, the portrait resists the intangibility of her mythologization and inscribes her illegible reality. We cannot read her, but we can read the transnational relations that her portrait structures and publishes.

Texts such as *Matoaka als Rebecca* indicate that Native women's relational publication practices were coterminous with encounter and colonization. Indeed, they suggest that we cannot fully account for the emerging contours of colonial neighborhoods without attending to Native women and their communicatory responses. Other scholars agree that Native women are integral to colonial history. For example, Clara Sue Kidwell's seminal essay "Indian Women As Cultural Mediators" (1992) foregrounds the often unremarked but fundamental role they played in colonial encounters: "While men made treaties and carried on negotiations and waged war, Indian women lived with white men, translated their words, and bore their children."[27] In their capacities as "wives and mistresses, they counseled, translated, and guided white men who were entering new territory," thereby "mediating . . . meaning between the cultures of two worlds." For Kidwell, Pocahontas as well as other Native women such as Nanye'hi/Nancy Ward (Cherokee) and Sacajawea (Shoshone) are mediators because they used their work and their intermediary position between cultures to facilitate communication.

By referring to Indian women as mediators, Kidwell also implicitly invites us to think about their interventions in terms of media and communication technologies.[28] Because indigenous media existed prior to and continued after contact with Europeans, Native women's uses of media after colonization—even those that relied on European models—were not entirely new. Some women were *re*mediators, authors who repurposed both European and Native media.[29] As I noted in my introduction, Jay David Bolter and Richard Grusin define *remediation* as "the representation of one medium in another," and they remark on its long history and cite medieval and early modern examples.[30] In their introduction to *Colonial Mediascapes,* Matt Cohen and Jeffrey Glover underscore that remediation was multidirectional, with indigenous forms appearing in European media and vice versa.[31] Yet we should not think of media only in terms of product, the static results of printing and engraving. We also should think of it in terms of practice, of making public. For Native women, making public might have included trading and gift giving, wampum weaving and other craftwork, marriage and divorce, dress, and vocal or silent attendance at a treaty talk. To make public, these women might have leveraged old and new kin ties, followed old and new paths across the landscape.

The concept of remediation foregrounds Native women's relational publication as a continuous and dynamic practice. Of primary interest here is not that English-language texts represented precontact Native media or that new Native media represented English-language technology. Rather their practice was an ongoing and accretive translation that turned to, devised, and transformed a spectrum of communicatory and circulatory modes. Women's acts of publication were relational in that they drew on and revised the shifting terrain and interpersonal bonds of a colonized North America. At the same time, women enacted relationality in the form of their publication practice, determining how to mediate among these disparate modes. In this light, *Matoaka als Rebecca* remediated Pocahontas's dress, royal parentage, marriage, and transatlantic crossing into an expression of transnational bondedness without submitting Weramocomoco to Jamestown and London.

My thinking about remediation and the repurposing of bondedness builds in part on Abenaki scholar Lisa Brooks's important analysis of Native literary and writing traditions. In *The Common Pot,* she relates how seventeenth-century Wabanaki children developed their own writing systems and wrote down the Lord's Prayer on birchbark. Those scrolls, containing "new knowledge," circulated through various villages using an "extant system of communication."[32] According to the French Jesuit missionary Chrestien Le Clercq, who witnessed the children's creation of *awikhiganak* (writings on birchbark), that system functioned at least in part via kinship ties, as "the son teaches his father, the mother her children, the wife her husband, and the children the old men."[33] Thus indigenous "writing tradition[s]," exemplified by awikhiganak and wampum, were spatialized and represented a network of temporal, geographic, and familial relationships. Brooks explains: "The graphic symbols used in both forms represented the relationships between people, between places, between humans and nonhumans, between the waterways that joined them. The communal stories recorded on birchbark and in wampum would even connect people with their relations across time, bringing the past, present, and future into the same space."[34] She concludes that the letters, petitions, treaties, histories, and journals that emerged from this traditional system constitute an "indigenous American literary tradition" and asks readers to understand the indigenous publication repertoire as coterminous with affiliation, grounded in communal bondedness.[35] Though Brooks hones in on Native writing, *Matoaka als Rebecca* reminds us that there were other ways of making public—including dress, visual representation, travel, naming, and marriage.

Like remediation, affiliation can be a practice. For indigenous peoples, kinship is the vital affiliatory model. As Cherokee scholar and author Daniel Heath Justice explains, "kinship isn't a static thing; it's dynamic, ever in motion. It requires attentiveness; kinship is best thought of as a verb rather than a noun, because kinship, in most indigenous contexts, is something that's done more than something that simply *is*."[36] In colonial North America, Native women often enacted their economic, political, and religious influence through kinship networks. In the Southeast, for example, Cherokee, Creek, and Choctaw communities were matrilineal. When a man and a woman married, the man moved into the woman's household or compound, and any children resulting from their union belonged to the wife's matrilineage and, by extension, her clan.[37] While fathers retained much material responsibility and emotional connection to their children, the wife's male relatives in her matrilineage, especially her brothers, were the most important male figures in the children's lives. Matrilineages directly and indirectly governed cropland distribution, residences, inheritances, hunting territories, justice, social responsibilities, leadership, and marriages through kinship and clans. Through the resulting network, women influenced political and economic decisions. In the Northeast, the women of the matrilineal and matrifocal Haudenosaunee wielded a political structure that complemented the men's: they selected tribal leaders, ratified treaties, acted as judges, decided citizenship, and declared war and peace.[38] Even among the male-centric Ojibwe nations, women could fight in battle and become religious leaders.[39] The assumption of typically masculine roles occurred through their kin ties, as they fought alongside or instead of their husbands and gained knowledge of sacred writing when male *mide* (medicine) shamans employed their women relatives as amanuenses.

Enfolding the fluid practices of affiliation and remediation, Native women's relational publication was, like kinship, "ever in motion" as it intervened in the shape of colonial neighborhoods. Consider these early examples. Thanadelthur (circa 1695–1717) was a young Chipewyan woman captured by the Cree. She and another woman captive seized an opportunity to escape, hoping that the "wondrous" European trade goods seen in the Cree camps meant that a trading post refuge existed nearby.[40] Soon Thanadelthur found herself lost and alone. Scavenging what she could from a harsh and cold land, she followed the tracks of Hudson Bay Company goose hunters until she found their camp.[41] There she met Governor James Knight who, believing trade would expand with peace, enlisted her help in negotiating a truce between the Crees and the Chipewyan.[42] Thanadelthur journeyed back to the Cree and Chipewyan communities with gifts from Knight, and eventually her "perpetuall talking" and "Scold[ing]" reluctantly convinced the enemies.[43] She returned to Knight with a party of Chipewyans that probably included her brother.[44] Her circulations made peace and trade possible among these different groups, and her steps traced those affiliations on the landscape just as the company hunters had left their marks on it. She made public her importance as she journeyed and mapped a neighborhood of new transnational alliances, shifting her own role within the Chipewyan society, which placed little value on women, from margin to center. European trade goods, hunters' tracks, diplomatic gifts, kinship ties, relentless speech: all were contained within her relational publication practice; all were fodder for her remediation.

Other women's remediations paired indigenous rhetorics of kinship with English legal documents. In 1792, an Oneida woman, Sally Ainse (circa 1728–1823), presented an affidavit to the land board in Detroit documenting that Ottawa leaders had reserved certain lands for her and had not deeded them to the English as part of a larger land cession:

> The Chiefs Agushaway and three others of the same Nation, doth hereby declare that the Indians of River la tranche, when they sold the Lands at River la tranche, that they told Captain McKee that there was a tract of Land that they gave their Sister Sally Ainse, which they would not sell, as she had always used them well and likewise they gave Colonel McKee a string of wampum, and he the said Colonel McKee told them that she was a good woman and received the wampum, saying that he would do all he could and speak to the Commanding Officer about it; this was before they had signed the deed for the Land.[45]

Seven chiefs, including Agushaway, had signed this affidavit with their marks, which for the most part resemble animals and probably identified their clans.[46] Along with this document and her petition for recognition of her legal possession (and her right to remove Euro-American settlers), Ainse included deeds and a receipt showing that she had paid for the land.[47] All of the documents were duly recorded in the minutes or filed.

By traveling to the land board and presenting it with this collection, Ainse inserted into the record a network of relations between the chiefs, their "Sister," their clans, and the land, a move that further implicated the sympathetic Euro-Americans who had witnessed the original and subsequent transactions. Ainse was Oneida and therefore part of the Haudenosaunee confederacy; here she acted as a *gantowisas,* or "Indispensable Woman," whose "duties were frankly political, economic, judicial, and shamanic."[48] Her documents delineated a neighborhood among three nations—the Ottawa, the United States, and the Oneida—that included a marked domain for her and perhaps, by extension, the Haudenosaunee. Her relational publication practice remediated textual inscription, wampum exchange, and kinship to involve those around her in a neighborhood bound by their recognition of her rights to her land.[49] In these examples, Native women's relational publication occurs as they circulate across the landscape, thereby producing and making public diplomatic affiliations and treaties.

A Diversity of Paths

The relational publication practices of Pocahontas, Thanadelthur, and Ainse helped to revise the bonds in their colonial neighborhoods and increasingly enfolded the production of visual and scriptive texts.[50] Yet the traces of their lives and acts of relational publication are fragmentary, scattered tracks across the landscape. In contrast, the archive related to Coosaponakeesa is much more substantial and offers a rich opportunity to analyze Native women's early American relational publication. Like them, she was reared in a particular Native context and was well aware that powerful women must be agile remediators of a range of affiliatory and communicatory practices, Native and non-Native, if they wished to influence the shape of their neighborhoods.

As a Creek woman raised in Coweta and Pon Pon, Coosaponakeesa would have been sensitive to modes of circulation. At that time, the Creek confederacy was organized into two groups, the Upper and Lower Creeks. These designations related to geography: the Upper Creek talwas were along the Alabama and Coosa rivers, and the Lower Creek talwas were along the Ocmulgee, Flint, and Chattahoochee rivers. Incorporating new talwas and tribes into the confederacy typically involved establishing a community along one of those rivers or their tributaries. Sometimes older talwas shifted location as proximity to Europeans' colonial settlements became more or less desirable and sustainable. Creek talwas participated in a larger southeastern Native trade network that increasingly involved the French, Spanish, and English as well as the colonists' African slaves. The result was a transnational colonial neighborhood that entailed intimacy among diverse peoples and languages.[51] Thus, governance, diplomacy, and affiliation went hand in hand with circulation and translation.

A few extant eighteenth-century deerskin maps illustrate how Native peoples conceptualized the relationships between nations and geography. Native cartographers in the Southeast graphically denoted relationships between nations, both Native and European, as paths (plate 2 and fig. 5).[52] They used circles to mark locations in a transnational indigenous network of friends and enemies, varying the size of each circle to suggest relative importance. On these maps, scale has to do less with geographic orientation and distance than with diplomacy and affiliation. Because Native leaders might present these maps to colonial leaders during diplomatic conversations, the cartographers sometimes included Euro-American forts and cities (in one instance using right angles that evoke a colonial settlement's grid) but always locating them on the periphery. The maps demonstrate that colonists situated places such as Savannah and trading posts in already extant and active Native neighborhoods.

The paths on these maps stress southeastern Native nations' spatial conception of affiliation. According to John Juricek, these paths, which could occur only between "societies at peace," were linear bonds, "both physical and metaphorical": "A 'path' was a track beaten into the soil by innumerable human feet and animal hooves, the durable record of a two-way flow of people, animals, and goods between English and Indian towns."[53] Even after the establishment of Georgia, the main path between British colonists and the Creeks connected Charleston, not Savannah, to Coweta. A traveler needed to diverge from the main path at Fort Augusta on the Savannah River to reach Georgia's main settlement. Such paths mapped the region's economy and marked its depen-

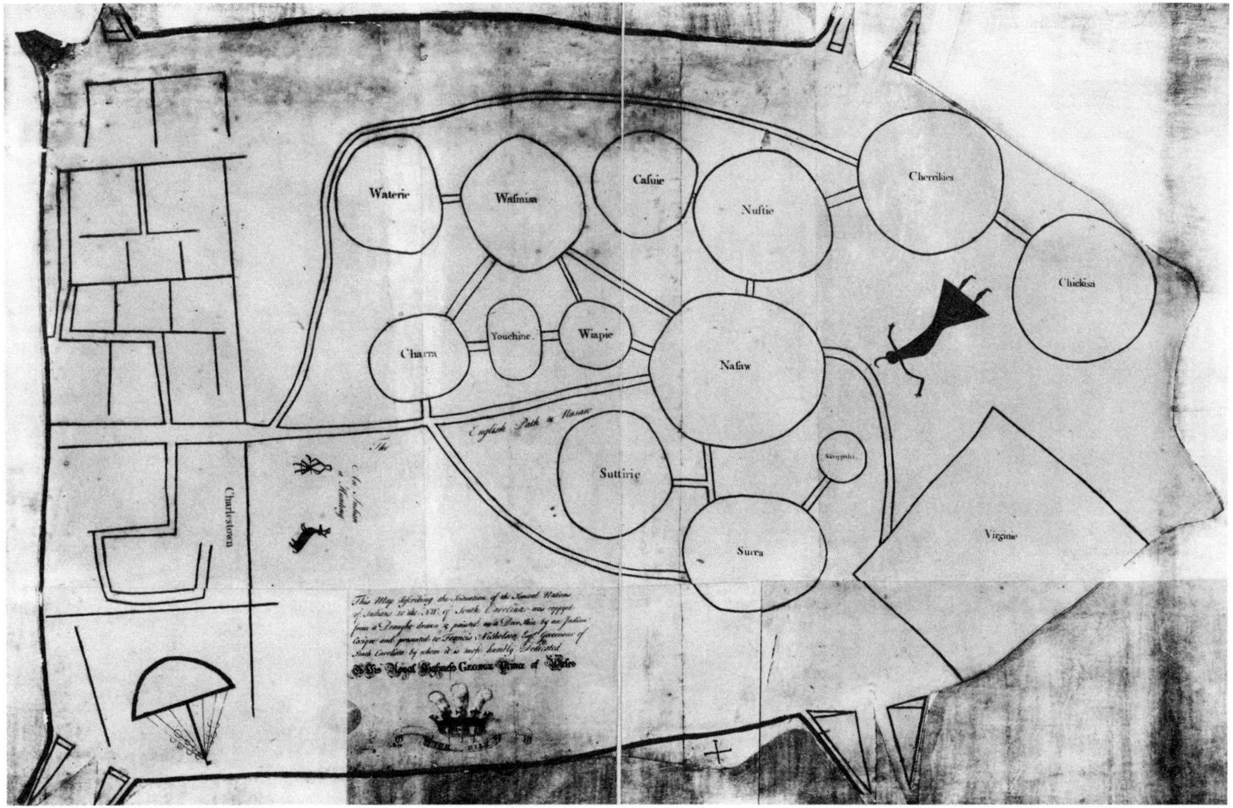

FIGURE 5. Catawba map of 1721. The caption reads, "This Map describing the Scituation of the Several Nations of Indians to the NW of South Carolina was coppyed from a Draught drawn & painted on a Deer Skin by an Indian Cacique and presented to Francis Nicholson Esqr. Governour of South Carolina by whom it is most humbly Dedicated to His Royal Highness GEORGE Prince of Wales." The vast majority of the lines are red, while the text is black. Image courtesy of the Library of Congress, Geography and Map Division (call no. G3860 1724.M2 1929).

dencies. When moving from talwa to fort and trading post, from trading post to colonial settlement and other Native town, travelers enacted bonds and delineated colonial neighborhoods as the confluence of networks of circulation. New relationships and new sites demanded new paths and new circles, creating offshoots or even superseding old ones.

From her earliest days, Coosaponakeesa witnessed the Creeks' considered interventions into the routes and contours of the Southeast's shifting paths. Her fluency with colonial circulatory repertoires was similarly intimate, lifelong, and practiced. As the daughter of an English trader who lived by turns in Creek talwas and colonial trading posts, she was well versed in the flow of goods. The deerskin trade was the prosperous Southeast's economic linchpin. A series of cattle plagues in Europe during the early eighteenth century had led to severe restrictions on English cowhide importation. As a result, the demand for Native-sourced American deerskins rose sharply.[54]

Native hunters in the Southeast began bringing deerskins to trading outposts to exchange for manufactured goods. In response, Creek economic systems changed drastically. Previously Creeks had depended on hunting and agriculture for their needs, but their partnership with Europeans produced what Kathryn E. Holland Braund calls a complex mixture of "power and dependence": "By the eighteenth century, cloth and metal tools had become essentials. Guns, bought with deerskins, made the Muscogulges [Creeks] the preeminent power in the Southeast. . . . The deerskin trade—more than ancient traditions, lifeways, and alliances—became the dominant force in Creek destiny."[55] As Braund makes clear, the Creeks were invested in trade with the English. By trading deerskins, they could acquire items such as copper pots, cloth, and guns. To expand their trading capabilities and acquire larger numbers of deerskins, they reorganized their hunting patterns. Women's traditional role in processing deerskins ensured their importance in the trade and meant that some women traveled with their husbands on hunting trips. While European colonists were not a daily part of most Creeks' lives, the cultural adaptations encouraged by the deerskin trade were omnipresent, making the use of paths and the circulation of goods a pervasive component of colonial life.

Coosaponakeesa witnessed both sides of this exchange, and her plantation and trading posts became essential nodes in the network of paths and sites through which exchange occurred. At the same time, she realized that Europeans used the circulation of texts and persons of authority to enact cultural influence—a lesson she learned, at least in part, from the activities of Christian missionaries. Coosaponakeesa's first sustained contact with Christianity probably occurred when she moved to Pon Pon, South Carolina, to live with her father. Missionaries would have provided her with an education in ciphering and English literacy, skills that became crucial to her future as a trader, diplomat, and interpreter.[56] She herself recalled that Pon Pon was where she was "baptized, Educated and bred up in the Principles of Christianity."[57] During the early 1700s, the Society for the Propagation of the Gospel in Foreign Parts (SPG) sent missionaries to South Carolina to minister to the colonists and baptize and educate ostensibly willing Natives and Africans, most of them enslaved. The SPG instructed its missionaries and schoolmasters to use the Book of Common Prayer, the Bible, and Jean Frédéric Ostervald's catechism, though the society also supplied a list of other appropriate texts and some funding for their purchase. The SPG provided specific morning and evening prayers for children to recite in schools and at home. It also offered missionaries advice about record keeping and correspondence, and urged them to maintain communication with their fellows and to minister to their entire regions rather than preach from a single church or chapel.[58]

In the Southeast, SPG proselytization among Natives and Africans was largely abandoned in favor of ministering to and educating the European colonists. Most schools for Native children were unsuccessful, likely because of student absenteeism or inaccessibility, cultural differences, and pedagogical inexperience. Coosaponakeesa's statement about her education as well as her alphabetical and numerical literacy suggest that she was one of the few Native students who received an education. While we can only speculate about what that instruction looked like, it was almost certainly steeped in catechizing.

SPG instructions suggest which specific "principles of Christianity" were promoted among Native children. Beginning in 1706, the group's "DIRECTIONS for Catechists for Instructing Indians, Negroes, &c." told ministers to convey first the nature of God and then the Bible as source of spiritual knowledge and history:

> But forasmuch as our Knowledge of God, and of his Will, is imperfect, shew them farther, How He has made Himself, and his Will known to Men, by a certain Book, called the *Bible,* which was written by several holy Men, to whom God made known Himself and his Will, that they might teach others.

> For a Proof of this, shew them, That this Book contains Things worthy of God, that the Men, who wrote it, in several Places of it, do foretel Things, which none but God could make known to them; and that they did many wonderful Works, which none but God could enable them to do; and give them some plain Instances in both Kinds out of the Bible.
>
> Shew them farther, That this Book called the *Bible* has been carefully preserved, and handed down to us from Generation to Generation, and has all the Marks of Truth and Sincerity in it.[59]

As this excerpt makes clear, the Bible as authoritative text was a central tenet of the SPG's pedagogical practices. In the society's view, the Bible manifests God's existence and God's will. "Heathens" could perceive the wonder of God's existence, not by witnessing wonders themselves but through their inscription and circulation. The repetitious circulation of the missionaries through the region's large but sparsely populated parishes would have reinforced this aspect of divine authority.

In the 1730s, Coosaponakeesa deepened her familiarity with Christianity when several evangelical Christian sects established settlements in Georgia and, perhaps more significantly for her, the SPG appointed missionaries to the new colony. Two of those missionaries were John Wesley and Charles Wesley, the young founders of Methodism who had come to Georgia to convert the Indians. Almost immediately, the Wesleys determined that their companion, Benjamin Ingham, would spend half the week at Coosaponakeesa's plantation outside Savannah, learning to speak Creek from her and teaching her children to read. He would spend the other half of the week in Savannah, transmitting what he learned to Charles Wesley and the Moravian leader, David Nitschmann.[60] John Wesley appears to have baptized at least one of Coosaponakeesa's children during his tenure.[61]

During the 1730s and early 1740s, George Whitefield, an evangelical celebrity, intermittently visited the southeastern colonies, preaching before enthusiastic urban and rural crowds.[62] When not there, he stayed in epistolary contact with his supporters, who recirculated his letters with each other and penned their own, thereby maintaining and extending his network.[63] In the early 1740s, he established an orphanage that became Georgia's largest civil employer, educating not only children and other potential converts but "organiz[ing] ritual burnings of books considered heretical."[64] When Coosaponakeesa's future husband Thomas Bosomworth arrived in the colony, he found Whitefield's followers so disruptive that he wrote a letter to the trustees denouncing them as "Desperadoes."[65] In South Carolina, Whitefield used his writings to publicize slave owner Hugh Bryan's support for Georgia's poor but faithful evangelicals; then, in 1742, Bryan was arrested for fomenting a slave uprising.[66] Such incidents attest to the visible threat of evangelical fervency.

As this background suggests, Coosaponakeesa was familiar with Christianity, had persistently experienced proselytization, and had heard missionary rhetoric.[67] Moreover, she had witnessed the power of charismatic itinerant preachers to command followers and alarm colonial administrators and the central role that textual inscription, interpretation, and circulation played in Christianity. This knowledge articulated well with her understanding of Creek geographic sensibility and colonial economic exchange. For her, relational publication was not about printed words produced by a press on paper. Instead, it was about the movement of goods, people, and manuscripts along shifting paths. It was about sartorial choices, oral words and written marks, and engagement in tangible and visible acts of alliance and exchange. Publication could serve her vision of the colonial neighborhood's bonds but also her vision of her own influence and location in its network of relations.

Coosaponakeesa's Relational Publication

Long before her 1749 march on Savannah, Coosaponakeesa had an opportunity to use sartorial performance and other modes of relational publication to shape a momentous wave of neighborhood alterations. The trigger was British determination to establish the new colony of Georgia. In 1732, at the request of both the Yamacraw band and the governor of South Carolina, Coosaponakeesa, then known as Mary Musgrove, and her first husband, John Musgrove, stationed a trading post on a bluff overlooking the Savannah River. Thus, she was well positioned to greet James Oglethorpe in January 1733 when he arrived to scout the area, and she convincingly argued in favor of locating Georgia's first settlement in Yamacraw territory. In March, the first colonists arrived, and the Yamacraws "saluted [them] with a voly of their small arms."[68] The settlers returned the greeting. The two groups, led by Oglethorpe and the Yamacraw mico Tomochichi, approached each other and had the first of many friendly diplomatic conversations.[69]

From the perspective of Oglethorpe and the other colonists, Mary

Musgrove "then appeared to be in mean and low Circumstances, being only Cloathed with a Red Stroud Petticoat and Osnabrig Shift."[70] Her clothing accentuated that she was a woman, but an Indian one. As garments typically worn by English women, the petticoat and shift were familiar signs of femininity. Yet English women usually wore them as undergarments and, because she was also bareheaded, she looked strange and perhaps improper.[71] Moreover, her outfit evoked the economic motivations behind the colony, which was to extend Britain's mercantile empire. Stroud was a woolen rag cloth usually used to make blankets for trade with Indians. By wearing it as a petticoat, she demonstrated that she, as a trader and a woman, was willing to exchange for British-made objects and to adapt them for her own purposes.[72]

Written by a colonist sixteen years after the establishment of Georgia, the account attests to the vividness of the moment even as its dismissive insistence on Musgrove's "mean and low Circumstances" couches her difference in terms of poverty and inferiority. The colonists had encountered a woman who was attired in the objects of European commerce, fluent in English and Muskogee, experienced as a trader, and recommended to them by South Carolina's governor.[73] They may have read her as an embodiment of their hopes for the new colony, a figure of raw potential awaiting the adornment of prosperity. After all, they depended on her skills and her opinion throughout their early years in Georgia, even when they found her motives suspect.

Yet this image of Musgrove in her spare, unusual clothing spoke of more than Georgia's promise. To the Yamacraws, a band composed mainly of Creek exiles, her choice of the color red recalled southeastern indigenous diplomacy. Creek cosmology centered on dualities and balance, and the confederacy structured political relationships around the red and white (roughly translated as *war* and *peace*) duality.[74] Both the main Creek political unit, the talwa, and individual male leaders identified as red or white. During local and national councils, those who were red argued from a red stance, and those who were white argued from a white stance, regardless of individual beliefs. Additionally, a man could identify himself as on the red or white path in terms of a relationship with another person or group.[75] Unlike men, women maintained balance in the cosmos "behind the scenes," even as they also belonged to a red or a white talwa.[76] Although red and white alignments structured political engagements, women's "considerable impact" on political matters derived from their private influence on public opinion, using "tears, ridicule, and other methods to persuade husbands, brothers, uncles and sons. This was especially true of matters of war and peace."[77]

By choosing a red petticoat, Musgrove boldly donned the Creek diplomatic male color of war. To Yamacraw eyes, she was the opposite of the exploitable poor female subject the Georgians read in her strange apparel. Yet her color choice should not be seen as a declaration of war with the colonists. In explicating Creek duality, George E. Lankford explains that balance instead of competition defines the relationship between dual categories: "As seems to be true of most dual oppositional thought, the goal is to maintain a workable balance between the opposing forces or worlds. The opposition is not one which is envisioned as temporary, with one to become a victor over the other, but a permanent tension of opposites which need to be kept in balance."[78] As Joshua Piker explains in his discussion of the Red Coat King, a civil leader of the Upper Creek talwa Okfuskee, "peace and kinship were never far removed from war and death. Townspeople invoked the white to ward off the red, while showing a willingness to use the red to restore the white."[79] Even though Musgrove chose a red petticoat, her willingness to mediate between Tomochichi and Oglethorpe and to facilitate a colonial settlement in Yamacraw territory stressed her readiness to adapt her behavior to an evolving terrain, to use red for white and white for red. Indeed, her attire signaled that she would be a deft diplomat because the red petticoat itself was a balance of Yamacraw and Creek diplomacy and English fabric.[80] Her position on the bluff accentuated this ability to navigate the neighborhood's new and shifting paths, a performative foray into a relational publication practice that welcomed Yamacraws and colonists alike to an evolving colonial neighborhood.

Mary Musgrove's Creek-Georgian Diplomacy

One component of Coosaponakeesa's early forays into relational publication was her active participation in determining how Creeks and Georgians would share residency in the neighborhood. What was at stake was the formation of mutually prosperous bonds in the absence of shared kinship and nation. From the Creek perspective, the way forward rested in part on the translation of Creek kinship for non-Native neighbors, a translation that Mary Musgrove facilitated. For example, in 1733, she helped negotiate "Oglethorpe's First Treaty with the Lower

Creeks at Savannah" through her role as diplomat and interpreter. These "Articles of Friendship and Commerce" formalized the trade affiliation between Georgia and the Lower Creeks and involved promises on both sides.[81]

While most of the treaty is an adaptation of treaties with South Carolina, the land settlement clause specifically addresses British territory acquisition and is unique to this agreement.[82] The land settlement clause is also unique in the context of the treaty as a whole. The other clauses have more clearly identifiable goals and fewer references to Creek beliefs. They include price schedules and provisions for criminal justice, treaty violations, and runaway slaves. In contrast, Creek kinship and understandings of land form the logical foundations of the land settlement clause. As the chief interpreter during this portion of the negotiation, Musgrove chose the English translations that encapsulated what the Lower Creek leaders wanted to embed in the contract.[83] The clause reads as follows:

> Fourthly. We the Head Men of the Coweta and Cussita Towns in behalf of all the Lower Creek Nation being firmly persuaded that He who lives in Heaven and is the occasion of all good things has moved the hearts of the Trustees to send their Beloved men among us for the good of us our Wives and Children and to Instruct us and them in what is Streight do therefore declare that we are glad that their People are come here, and though this Land belongs to us the Lower Creeks yet we that we may be instructed by them do consent and agree that they shall make use of and possess all those Lands which our Nation hath not occasion for to use and we make over unto them their Successors and Assigns all such Lands and Territories as we shall have no occasion to use, Provided always that they upon Settling every New Town shall set out for the use of ourselves and the People of our Nation such Lands as shall be agreed upon between their Beloved Men and the head men of our Nation and that those Lands shall remain to us forever.[84]

Echoing the spoken sentiments of the Oconee mico Oueckachumpa, the clause begins by expressing satisfaction about contact between the Georgians and the Creeks, especially Creek women and children, and a hope that those contacts will continue. The article then formalizes an agreement that the colonists may occupy lands that the Lower Creeks "hath not occasion for to use" so long as colonial settlements continue to reserve an adjacent portion, to be agreed on by the Georgian and Creek leaders, that "shall remain to us forever."[85] This opening underscores interpersonal relationships and therefore implies that sustainable trade arises from the kind of personal knowledge that defines mutually beneficial communitarian interaction. By moving from relationships to the topic of land, the clause subtly connects relationships and trade to quotidian geographic proximity—in other words, the neighborhood.

The nature of these envisioned neighborly connections pointedly articulated with Creek culture. By emphasizing that the whites were "among us," including "Wives and Children," the clause documents that the colonists were moving into Creek homeland. Recall that Creek culture, like that of many other southeastern Native nations, was matrilineal. From this perspective, then, the reference to "Wives and Children" in the land settlement clause demonstrates that the Creeks were already beginning to claim a form of modified kinship (what the treaty calls "friendship") with Georgians because some settlers had been in contact with their women and children, the units through whom kin attachments were made and claimed. In calling for continued contact with women and children and for portions of land to be set aside for Creeks alongside Georgian settlements, the clause institutes a mechanism through which this friendship would continue. Out of proximity would emerge friendship, and friendship would be the primary bond of a peaceful and prosperous colonial neighborhood.

Interestingly, the land settlement clause also establishes a difference between land that "belongs to us the Lower Creeks" and the "possess[ion]" of land. The implication here is that the land will *always* belong to the Creeks even if Georgian colonists temporarily possess and use it.[86] This distinction seems to place colonists in the position of Creek husbands, whose contributions to the community never gain them full right to their wives' matrilineages but whose entrance into already established Creek territorial divisions helps bind clans, families, and communities. In other words, as a Creek woman, Musgrove participated in producing a written English-language treaty that modifies Creek kinship and formulates relationships that seem markedly female.

Ultimately, the clause argues that proximity is a crucial component of stable, prosperous trade. Proximity leads to personal acts of exchange. Personal acts of exchange lead to familiarity. Familiarity leads to friendship. The desired neighborhood adheres in these daily interactions, arising from the quotidian production of friendship rather than the moment of signing a treaty. This trajectory toward friendship would have seemed clear and reasonable to Musgrove, a mixed-blood woman who had spent significant portions of her life residing at colonial trading posts and in culturally and linguistically diverse areas such as Coweta and Pon Pon. Building on Creek kinship models and English diplomatic technology, the clause made public a practice by which the region's colonial neighborhood could flourish.

Another document from this period articulates how friendship could structure the neighborhood's obligations. On July 17, 1734, Musgrove wrote a letter to Oglethorpe about a diplomatic discussion between a band of Choctaws and the English colonists. According to the Choctaws, trade with the French had stagnated, so they were looking for a new European trading partner. Because the Choctaws had been trading with and militarily supporting the French for decades, these talks appeared to be a crucial turning point in the region's balance of colonial power.[87] Oglethorpe could not be present at the talks because he was in England, reporting to the colonial trustees and shepherding Tomochichi and other Yamacraws on a state visit. However, Musgrove's reason for writing the letter is unclear.[88] Perhaps it is the only survivor of a series of letters she wrote to Oglethorpe to keep him informed during his absence.

Musgrove began the letter by establishing an intermediary position for herself: "I make bold to acquaint You that Thos. Jones is returned from the Choctaws and according to your Honours Desire he has brought the Choctaws down and they have received great favours."[89] Her position as writer and communicator was clear: she was "acquaint[ing]" Oglethorpe instead of acting on either his or an indigenous nation's behalf. The letter's opening sentence lends a tone of impartiality and implies that her comments were disinterested.

The remainder of the paragraph, however, ridicules the Choctaws, elevates the Creeks, and flatters the colonists. This process begins with a description of the Choctaws' happiness in talking with the English: "The Choctaws are so glad that some white People whom they call'd their Masters has taken such Care of them as to send for them and they was very glad of the opportunity to come for they lived very poor before and now they are in good hopes to live as well as the other Indians do, for they had nor have no Trade with the French and their Skins lye by them and rot."[90] Through her authorial choices, Musgrove characterized the Choctaws as weak. According to her, they had admitted their inferiority to the colonists by "glad[ly]" calling them "Masters." By choosing these words, she underscored the lack of value in this potential connection, admitting their dependence but not their friendship. Friendship arises from proximity and reciprocity; without friendship, there is little or no obligation. Thus, when she subsequently claimed that the Choctaws needed someone to care for them, she implied that the English, being under no obligation to fulfill their need, could choose whether or not to do so solely on practicality. As she went on to suggest, it would be impractical to trade with the Choctaws—who, unlike other Indians, "live very poor" and, in perhaps their greatest transgression, had ineptly negotiated in trade and were so unaware of the value of their commodity that their deerskins "lye by them and rot."[91] Musgrove's meaning was clear: while she acknowledged Oglethorpe's "Desire" to establish friendly ties with the Choctaws, she urged him to deny his desire due to the Choctaws' unworthiness and untrustworthiness.

At the same time, the letter attests to Oglethorpe's wisdom in maintaining a primary trade relationship with the Creeks. Musgrove began this argument with her observation that the Choctaws did not "live as well as the other Indians do."[92] In Savannah, the principal Indians were Creeks, and the fact that they lived well demonstrated that the current trading partnership was a prosperous one. A few sentences later, she directly established a distinction between the Choctaws and the Creeks: "The Choctaws are all amazed to see the Creeks drink as they do, and they think the Creeks are saucy to the white People."[93] Her reference to her fellow Creeks' behavior sounds boastful; but such a tone, especially in light of the previous sentence, creates a nuanced contrast: the Creeks did not consider the English colonists to be their masters and therefore were capable of maintaining a friendship with them, with its mutual and binding obligations, in ways the hapless and subordinate Choctaws could not.

The remainder of the letter is crucial to a full understanding of how these subtle distinctions between the Choctaws and the Creeks became an argument for a continued trade relationship between the Creeks and the Georgians.[94] In the second paragraph, Musgrove abandoned the topic of the Choctaws and emphasized her connection to Oglethorpe: "The Colony is in good health and I hope your Honour and all your family is in good health and my Husband is the same, and I beg your Honour will take great Care of him."[95] The textual proximity of the various references to familial components—"I," "your Honour," "all your family," "my Husband"—highlighted the real proximity of Oglethorpe's family and her husband. The phrases located Oglethorpe and her husband within the quotidian bonds of friendship, despite their physical distance from the geographic neighborhood. And because exchange and reciprocity characterize friendship, the sentence reminded Oglethorpe of his obligation to care for her husband. In other words, by writing the letter, Musgrove had honored her obligations and provided him with information, and now, presumably, he was obliged in return.[96] In moving from the topic of Choctaws, Creeks, and Georgia to the familiar, even intimate, language of family, the letter implies that primary trade between Creeks and Georgians was not only practical but obligatory due to their ongoing friendship.

Like the memorable red petticoat she donned for the arrival of the colonists, both the treaty clause and the letter were acts of publication that suggest Musgrove was well versed in translating Creek and Georgian repertoires to facilitate a colonial relationship that would be prosperous for all involved, including herself. As with diplomacy, that relationship required an ongoing and supple performance, adhering in geographic proximity and exchange and present in friendly interpersonal bonds. These examples point to the broader affiliatory adaptations of Native persons and nations in the Southeast. European colonization of the Americas had long since disrupted precontact political and economic structures, and the relatively young Creek confederacy flourished by capitalizing on its pliable affiliatory model and its emphasis on kinship, obligation, and consensus.[97]

Unlike the petticoat, the treaty clause and letter also took advantage of European scriptive technologies even as they made use of Creek kinship. Paper texts could reside and circulate in tandem with or instead of individuals, offering a new mode through which to perform inter- and intracommunal attachments (or perform and remind another of mutual obligations). Compared to the fluid connections that the Creek confederacy rebalanced in response to persistent local and regional fluctuations, texts could lead to more rigid alliances. In a colonial context, Georgian officials were adept at manipulating texts to their own ends, and they combined inscription with circulation and preservation to heighten their authority.[98] Coosaponakeesa borrowed from both Native and European models to respond to an expanding and resource-hungry colony and to insist on the need for friendship and mutual obligation to sustain a prosperous neighborhood for Creek and Georgian residents alike.

Friendship Betrayed

More than a decade later, Coosaponakeesa's relational publication practice no longer evinced such confidence in friendship. The respectful and friendly Governor Oglethorpe had returned to England. Seeking compensation for her years of diplomacy—which in addition to promoting the peaceful settlement of Savannah had included eliciting Creek military support for Oglethorpe's war with Spain over Florida—as well as recognition of her property rights to several coastal islands, she petitioned the colony's new leaders. Writing memorials in support of her claims, she again wielded her pen as well as the other tools in her repertoire to insist on her central role in the neighborhood's ideally peaceful bonds.[99]

As Mary Bosomworth, Coosaponakeesa produced the first extant memorial on August 10, 1747. She wrote to a sympathetic Lieutenant Colonel Alexander Heron and inscribed a narrative of colonial affiliation that continued to adapt Creek kinship and appeal to the need for peaceful relations to support mutual prosperity.[100] Bosomworth began by formalizing her kinship to the leaders of the Lower Creek Nation. She next emphasized the Creeks' past loyalty to the British and the continued importance of Creek friendship "to the British Interest."[101] After reminding Heron of her centrality in establishing and maintaining that friendship, she provided a detailed personal history that mentioned her childhood, marriages, and various services to Georgia. In the context of this history, she noted her financial investments and frequent losses, often incurred after sacrificing personal interests to British interests. She then tallied her exact investment at "Five Thousand Seven Hundred and Fourteen Pounds Seventeen shillings and Eleven pence sterling" and requested remuneration.[102] At this point, Bosomworth suggested how Heron could help, justified her anger and indignation at Britain, and concluded with a not-so-veiled threat to disally the Creeks from the British, leaving Savannah and other Georgian settlements open to attack by hostile Native and European nations.

The rhetorical linchpin of this document is the fact that friendship constituted the Creek-Georgian bond. Now in a contentious dispute with an unreceptive administration, Bosomworth chose to undermine that friendship by casting it as tenuous. Her first step was to align herself, through untenuous kinship, with the Creeks. Her opening paragraphs explain that she "was born at the Cowetaw Town on the Oakmulgee River which is a branch of the Alatamaha and the Chief Town of the Creek Indian Nation. That She is by Descent on the Mothers Side, (who was Sister to the Old Emperor) of the Same Blood of the Present Mico's and Chief's now in that Nation, and by their Laws, and the Voice of the Whole Nation is esteemed their Rightfull and Natural Princess."[103] Not only did she declare her familial relationship to Creek leadership, but she underscored that the kinship was through her matrilineage.[104] She reminded Heron that the "Friendship and Alliance" between the Creeks and the Georgians was based on "Several Treaties," contrasting these constructed paper documents with the "Natural" relationship she claimed with the Creeks and the land.[105]

Significantly, in the next paragraph, when Bosomworth threatened the British government by reminding Heron of the importance of the Creek alliance in maintaining the regional balance of power with the French and Spanish colonial forces, she asserted that these forces "have for some time past, and are at this Juncture, Labouring by all the Artifices Imaginable to seduce that Nation from their Alliance with his Majestys Subjects, which will certainly be a great Addition and Increase of Territory Strength and Power to his Majestys Enimies."[106] The allusions to "Artifices" and "seduc[tion]" suggest again that the colonists were like husbands entering a matrilineage's settlement, where their right to remain was tenuous. As Charles Hudson explains, "among the Creeks as among other matrilineal people, marriages were somewhat fragile and divorce was rather common."[107] Like a husband, the colonists' right to reside on the land could last only so long as they maintained a mutually contented relationship with their Creek partners.

Despite her threats to erase the paths between Creek talwas and the colonial settlements, Bosomworth still insisted that the paths could be repaired. Though by natural law she was a Creek, she reminded her reader that "your Memorialist by the Laws of Great Britain is a Subject of that Crown."[108] She then substantiated Britain's responsibility to her by listing in detail the "many Signal Proofs of her Zeal and Loyalty."[109] Throughout, she was careful to note how her services to the neighborhood had negatively affected her personal assets while contributing to Georgia's peace and safety.

In the next, most crucial section, Bosomworth invoked British abuse of her friendship to justify her current paper war and a possible military war between nations, promoted through her Creek influence:

> AND Lastly your Memorialist cannot Help repeating with an equal Mixture of a Real Grief of Heart, and Indignation; that her Injuries and Oppressions have been such, as she believes; have been scarce paralleled under a British Government. Language is too Weak to Represent her present Deplorable Case; She at present Labours under every sence of Injury; and Circumstance of Distress; Destitute of even the Common Necessaries of Life, being Insulted, Abused, contemned and Dispised by those ungratefull People who are indebted to her for the Blessings they Injoy.
>
> The Only Returns she has met with for her past Services, Generosity, and Maternal Affection (she has at all times shewn for the whole Colony) has been injust Loads of Infamy and Reproach; Branded and Stigmatized with the Odious Name of Traytor, for Making any Pretensions to those Rights she is Justly entitled to by the Laws of God and Nature (as her ancestors were the Natural born Heirs Sole Owners and Proprietors of every Foot of Land which is now his Majestys Colony of Georgia,) tho she has in Vain made Application for a Grant from the Crown, and is Desireous and Willing to hold What Posesions she is there entitled to by the Laws of Nature and Nations, as a Subject of great Britain.[110]

Through these words, Bosomworth initiated a relational shift between herself and Georgia. Her "Real Grief of Heart, and Indignation" personalizes Georgia's abuses and indicates that they were no longer wrong merely because of an abstract understanding of British justice. Her description of language as "too Weak" implies that words gain force through material embodiment. Her use of "Labours" in the next sentence—suggesting not only work but childbirth—insinuates that Britain's abuses of her as a woman were particularly atrocious. Her statement that the people of Georgia were "indebted to her for the Blessings they Injoy" helps categorize the colony as her child, the result of her "Labour." This claim widens in the following paragraph, when the document mentions the "Maternal Affection" that "she has at all times shewn for the whole colony." British violations of the "Laws of God and Nature" now appear to be acts of matricide—a heinous crime in a matrilineal culture. In committing matricide, Bosomworth declared, the colonists had dishonored their obligations under friendship with the Creeks and deserved to be treated as outcasts. Their only recourse was a return to the obligations of friendship.

As Creek scholar and author Craig Womack contends, "When Creek people assume they have the inherent right to interpret their own literature and history," it "is an important exercise of sovereignty."[111] Bosomworth's memorial is an expression of sovereignty. It tells her own history and narrates and justifies her anger; its storytelling meshes with the political, for the author's public presence on the red path might restore friendship and make it white.[112] This memorial displays an intensifying willingness to reinterpret affiliation and to publish a history of circulation and alliances that serves personal interests. In this case, a peaceful and prosperous colonial neighborhood could not arise solely from co-residency. Proximity and exchange were no longer sufficient for friendship. Rather, such a neighborhood was constituted by a purposeful and ongoing performance of friendship's obligations. Bosomworth's memorial presents a history that attributes past successful performances of those bonds to her efforts; it suggests that the neighborhood's future rested on a reinvigoration of those bonds. By acceding to her Creek kinship and her contingent submission to the British Crown, Georgian colonists would not only reengage with the ongoing performance of neighborly bonds but also recognize that Bosomworth was essential rather than incidental to the neighborhood.

Remapping the Bosomworth Controversy

The notorious march on Savannah occurred two years after Coosaponakeesa sent her memorial to Alexander Heron. Though he had supported her petitions, he could not satisfy her requests, and the march and its aftermath were part of her ongoing efforts to fulfill them. As such, the events evince a relational publication practice that continued to adapt and that enfolded circulation, both embodied and textual, to make public her insistence on her vital place in the neighborhood.

The spectacular nature of Coosaponakeesa's practice appears most visibly in the contrast between her stationary red petticoat performance as Mary Musgrove and the elaborate procession that she orchestrated some sixteen years later as Mary Bosomworth. With her English husband in front of her in his Anglican vestments, her kinsman Malatchi at her side, and a train of fellow Creeks behind her, she performatively communicated the narrative she had presented in her 1747 memorial. Malatchi's presence announced his support and protection, and her husband's vestments suggested that the Anglican church had consented to her leadership role. The presence of a group of Creeks firing their guns behind her suggested that she was not making idle threats. Bosomworth blazed a trail from talwa, to her plantation, to Savannah, mapping a transnational neighborhood that required her presence and was under her control. Later that day, during a diplomatic discussion, she declared herself "to be Empress and Queen of the Upper and Lower Creeks, and [said] that She could command every Man to follow her." Thus, the march on Savannah retrospectively resembled a coronation and an ordination, making her a "Sovereign" who owed "no Allegiance" to any king, any mico, any husband.[113]

Bosomworth's efforts to alter affiliation intensified during the visit. During the first evening, she stood before the president's door and, in front of Creek and Georgian witnesses, threatened "the destruction of the Colony, through her influence with, and command over the Indians."[114] She caustically announced, "You talk of your White Town, your General [Oglethorpe] and his Treaties, a fig for your General, you have not a Foot of Land in the Colony, and Stamping with her Foot on the Ground impudently said, Th[is] very Ground [is mine]."[115] Six days later, she had Malatchi present a paper, "Talk" to President Stephens that named her "Queen and Head of their [Creek] Nation," and hinted that the colonists were present in Savannah at her pleasure.[116] Later that evening, she "rushed" in and "call[ed] herself King."[117]

The response of Georgia's administrators is telling. Their written proceedings deplore Bosomworth's influence in a way that resonates with similar concerns about the disruptive power of Whitefield's followers: "As those Indians came with different designs from any other Body of Indians that ever came here, and were highly *Spirited* up by the Bosomworths, that necessity would oblige them to treat them with all the civility and candour, that could be used (not withstanding the expences would be very large) in order to circumvent them, in their malicious and wicked designs."[118] The administrators also tried to catch her in what seemed to them a contradiction between her religion and race. They asked "'whether Mrs. Bosomworth had been baptized? Whether she had received the Sacrament? Whether she had not stood Godmother for children?' . . . Whether Mrs. Bosomworth was an Indian or a White Person?"[119] She insisted that baptism had not terminated her "natural right" to Creek authority and land. Instead, as her claims to both Christian conversion and Creek leadership made clear, she reasoned that her baptism had advanced rather than terminated her authority.[120]

As a last resort, Georgian officials briefly imprisoned Bosomworth in the local jail, thereby temporarily forestalling any more claims. By mid-August, they believed they had gained the upper hand: the Creeks had accepted generous gifts and left town peaceably, and Bosomworth had delayed her voyage to England. Yet she continued to claim interpretive authority by circulating her version of events back in the Creek Nation. Malatchi, on his return to Coweta, had sent runners to other Lower Creek talwas, spreading news of her disrespectful treatment in Savannah and warning that it signaled Georgia's untrustworthiness and that it hinted at a secret plot to capture all Creek land.[121] She traveled to Charleston and then down to her trading post at the forks of the Altamaha River to coordinate the dispersal of this interpretation of events, following a publication route that bypassed Savannah. Finally, during the next spring, she traveled to Coweta to gain various micos' marks on documents that supported her narrative and claims and granted her full authority to make treaties with England.

In making these personal and proxy journeys across the Lower Creek Nation, Coosaponakeesa commanded interpretive authority over her march on Savannah. With paper, movement, kinship, spectacle, and conversation, she engaged in a practice of relational publication that, through inscription and geographic movement, materially manifested her authorship and authority, much as the SPG missionaries had used texts as evidence and enactments of religious authority. Coosaponakeesa's march on Savannah was a vivid locus in a fluid practice, a moment within a larger embodied and textual performance that increasingly emphasized the circulation of bodies, objects, and words and thereby spoke to her diverse audience's varying conceptions of authority and influence. Proclaiming her essential presence, narrating her history, and obtaining the signatures and marks of her supporters, she crafted and circulated a vision of the Southeast's colonial neighborhood wherein transnational paths would lead through her.

Coosaponakeesa's personal fortunes, tied to a colonial neighborhood defined by a Georgian-Creek friendship that she had mediated, seemed to be even more vulnerable than those of her nation, which might turn to alternative Native and non-Native partners if Georgian relations were to sour. Her legal battle with the colony, waged through the creation of memorials, the gathering of documentation, moments of spectacle, and the circulation of bodies and texts along transnational paths, emerged from various communicatory and affiliatory practices, both Native and non-Native. Her relational publication practice suggests an ongoing and supple merger of material, geographic, and linguistic forms, one that was simultaneously embodied, textual, and spatial.

In the eighteenth-century Southeast, Coosaponakeesa's relational publication practice was a dynamic response to the neighborhood's shifting terrain. It underscored that colonial bonds were not stable but must be performed and adapted again and again. As in the cases of Pocahontas, Thanadelthur, and Ainse, her practice was not always fully legible to her audience, past and present, Native and European, but her remediation of a variety of performative, affiliatory, and circulatory strategies was clear. Her Creek witnesses could read her attestations of commitment to their interests, and English readers could witness her adoption of their legal, textual modes.

I begin with Coosaponakeesa as well as these other Native women authors—Pocahontas, Thanadelthur, Sally Ainse—in order to suggest that we as contemporary scholars are distracted by the familiar components of eighteenth-century women's writing. We observe women's textual practices through the lens of a European, elite, male scriptive repertoire and miss what is unexpected and what is repurposed and made new in early American women's publication. Thus, these Native women and their practices ask us to seek the strange in the familiar space of the neighborhood and attend to its intimacies when recovering histories of communal transformation.

2

Vexing Motherhood and Interracial Intimacy

On thursday, 3 December 1761, Phillis, an enslaved black resident of Newport, Rhode Island, received distressing news. That afternoon, with the approval of her master Timothy Allen, she had attended a meeting of the First Congregational Church's female society. As usual, the meeting took place in the humble home of Sarah Osborn, a devout white schoolmistress who owned Phillis's seventeen-year-old son, Bobey. During those meetings, Phillis likely welcomed the occasional reports she had of Bobey, who since the age of ten had worked and lived miles away in Berkley, Massachusetts, at the home of an Osborn relative.[1] Unfortunately, what she heard that day was unwelcome: Sarah Osborn wanted to sell Bobey. Unable to hold her tongue and join the society in offering supportive prayers, Phillis instead divulged her distress.

The following morning, when Osborn woke, she waited for her husband to rise while it was "yet dark" and drew the "curtains" around her bed, leaving "Just" enough space "to Let in the Light." Then, enclosed in her makeshift prayer closet, she turned onto her "knees" and "stomach." "Soported with Bolster and Pillows," she wrote in her diary while her home was yet quiet.[2] Recording the specificities of her spiritual life had been an integral part of her worship for twenty years, and as a conscientious evangelical woman, she treated her state of grace as a matter-of-fact and consuming consideration. On this particular day, however, with Phillis's disconcerting reaction still fresh, she deviated and registered mundane details: "A Pleasant afternoon with dear friends of the society[.] god assisted in Prayer and all was well till I askt the opinion of

Philliss about our selling of bobey which contrary to my expectation vext her."[3] Immediately shifting to a defense of her plans, she noted that Bobey was a burden on the household as they "Have not business for Him," a statement supported by her decision ten years earlier to loan him to her former brother-in-law in Berkley, whom he now "Loves." But now that Bobey was a young man, he was at "risque of being made unsteady or quite spoilt or of going to sea" unless he had the direct supervision and care that a "steady" master who both resided with and owned him would provide.[4] To Osborn, her decision to sell Bobey was benevolent and virtuous. When Phillis became "vext," Osborn censured her for being overcome by "fondness" and "anger"—"her reason seems at Present to be Laid aside"—a critique that hinted at Phillis's selfish emotional excess.[5] Comforted, Osborn closed the entry with prayers, her sole regret that the incident might "unfit" Phillis "for the Lords table."[6]

The next day, Osborn again awoke and awaited her husband's departure, drew the bed curtains, gathered her bolster and pillows, turned onto her stomach, and began to write. This morning, though, the seeming confidence with which she had concluded the preceding entry was shaken. No longer able to puzzle calmly over Phillis's lack of "reason" and resign the conflict to God, she instead felt the first pangs of an agonizing spiritual crisis. She confessed that she could not "Leave thinking of this affair."[7] She then lamented, "All this Morning is gone and I cant get nigh [to God] in any wise." She worried that she, not Phillis, was unprepared for taking communion the next day because she had "a roveing Heart cold affections worldly thots."[8] Her mind and spirit now captivated by the conflict, she strove to approach God but instead experienced a sense of distance that resembled the rift with which she had threatened Phillis and Bobey.

What follows in this chapter is a layered story with Phillis's and Osborn's intimacy at its center. Asymmetrical and at times uncomfortable, their intimacy arose within and alongside their quotidian interactions as neighbors. And it was that intimacy's ineluctable and pervasive nature which animated Osborn's crisis. As a young woman, she had experienced conversion as a marriage and felt a divine calling to nurture others, which imbued her maternal identity with a certain authority. Phillis's vexation questioned the fitness of Osborn's care for Bobey and thereby her execution of her calling.

To counter the spiritual crisis that Phillis's competing maternal claims had begotten, Osborn turned to her diary and addressed God, seeking a renewed closeness. As she textually interwove her mundane, maternal, and spiritual affiliations, her diary mapped a more capacious territory for motherhood, one that, like Phillis's, repudiated separation. Rather than forestalling transformation, her seemingly private correspondence with God entwined with the material circulation of bodies, affective exchange, and the performance of piety to become relational publication. Gathering a new neighborhood of spiritual progeny, her practice engendered a religious revival in Newport that crucially involved a number of black Christians. That revival linked back through Osborn's nurturing to Phillis's expression of vexation.

Osborn's practice of relational publication differed from Coosaponakeesa's in that she directed the written words of her spiritual diary primarily to God rather than to a diplomatic audience of Native and colonist interlocutors. When Osborn drew the curtains around her bed, she in effect cordoned off her relationship with God and the expressions of her diary. But that scriptive privacy was always dialogic, inhering only at the moment of writing. She emerged from her improvised closet to make public through pious performance and additional writing—letters, autobiography—the singular intensity of her spiritual relationship. Even the ritual of morning seclusion attested to the sincerity and rigor of that performance.[9] How she interacted with her neighbors articulated with written text to alter the relational dynamics of her community. Despite their temporal, geographic, and cultural separations, Osborn and Coosaponakeesa resemble each other in that their practices of relational publication built a partnership between text and embodied performance. Just as Coosaponakeesa's circulatory practice involved traversing the transnational neighborhood that she sought to adapt, Osborn's circulatory practice located the scene of writing in her bed—the place of intercourse and childbirth—and made her home the center of her neighborhood. Both used relational publication to remap the neighborhood, and at times those remappings proceeded in unexpected ways.

Osborn was not the only Newport woman making her sentiments public in this moment. In her diary entries, we find an archival glimmer of Phillis's oral and affective performance. Osborn's and Phillis's intimacy transpired within a set of neighborly relations that included the female society, their church, the provinciality of colonial Newport, and

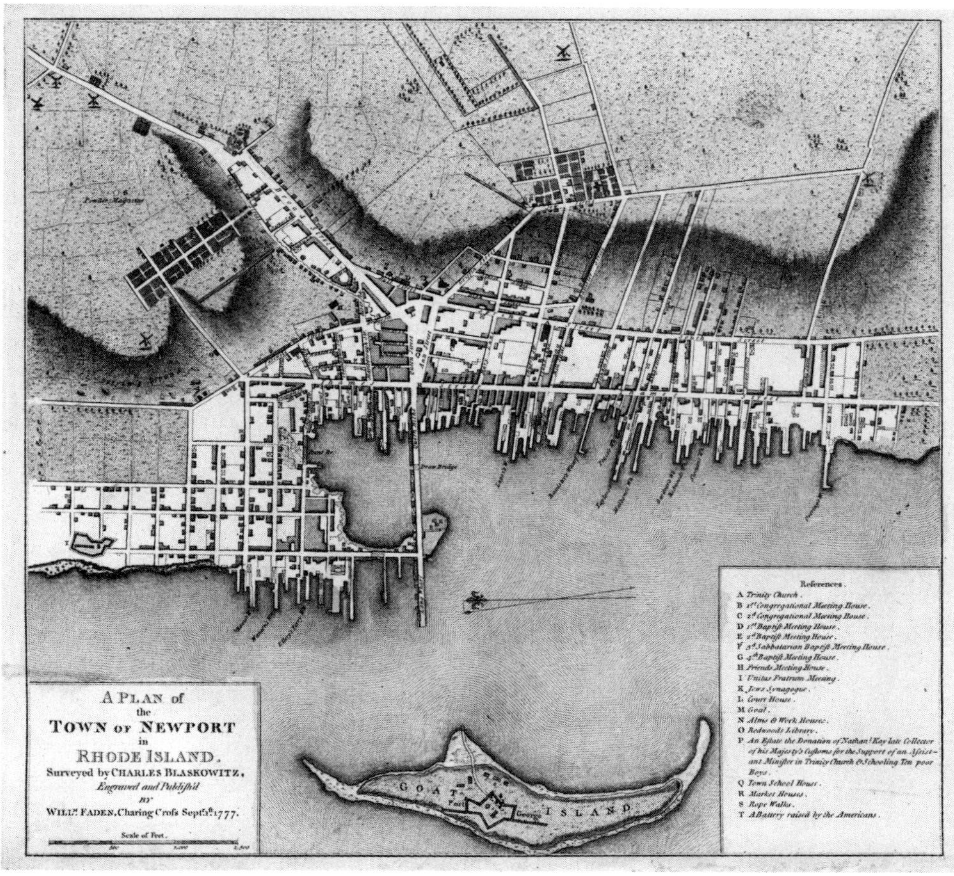

FIGURE 6. *A Plan of the Town of Newport in Rhode Island* (1777). The main thoroughfare is Thames Street. In a town of this size, it would be difficult to avoid one's neighbors. Image courtesy of the Library of Congress, Geography and Map Division (call no. G3774.N4 1777.B5).

their mutual bondedness to Bobey (see fig. 6). At the time of the crisis, the forty-seven-year-old Osborn was an established schoolmistress, a poor but well regarded member of Newport's First Congregational Church, and the pious leader of her church's female society.[10] Born in England in 1714, she had immigrated to New England and settled in Newport while still a girl. A wife, mother, and widow before the age of twenty, she had struggled to support herself and her son Samuel before remarrying in 1742. Samuel died only two years later, in 1744, while an apprentice in Rehoboth, Massachusetts, and soon after her friends presented her with an infant slave, Bobey.[11] Her second husband was Henry Osborn, a businessman and widower with three sons. When he became ill several months after their marriage, Osborn opened a school to support a household that now included herself, her son, her invalid husband, her stepchildren, and other dependents. Though it was not lucrative and her family remained financially insecure, often relying on charity, the school was nevertheless large and successful enough to continue. By the time of the crisis, she was operating it out of her home, with seventy students, male and female, black and white, rich and poor, locals and boarders, an unusual mix for a colonial-era school.[12]

In comparison, we known little about Phillis. She was born about ten years after Osborn was, circa 1724.[13] The identity of her master during her childhood and early womanhood is uncertain, nor do we know if she ever resided with the Osborns.[14] When she was about twenty years old, she gave birth to and was separated from Bobey.[15] This separation appears to have occurred during his infancy, for Osborn told a correspondent that Bobey was "brought up with us as our own from the cradle."[16] In 1754, Phillis and Bobey were further separated when Osborn sent the ten-year-old to live and work with her first husband's brother in Berkley (see fig. 7).[17] By 1757, Phillis was the slave of Timothy Allen.[18] That same year, she was baptized into the First Congregational Church of Newport, where Osborn was also a member and her steadfast advocate.[19] Phillis joined First Church's female society once it resumed in 1760 after an extended hiatus. Meeting weekly in Osborn's home, the society potentially offered Phillis regular opportunities to inquire for news of her son.

Despite the paucity of details about Phillis's life, she was a vital presence in Osborn's negotiation of the spiritual crisis that preceded her remarkable instigation of Newport's evangelical revival. Peaking in 1766–67, the revival involved a substantial swath of the city's residents, including white men and women of all ages and classes as well as the local black population. At Osborn's urging, Congregationalist minister Samuel Hopkins became involved with these black Christians, soon after cementing his conversion from slaveholder to public and influential abolitionist. Thus, the transformations in Newport's religious and racial affiliations connected to the "vext" exchange between Phillis and Osborn.

The story of Phillis and Osborn adds a new thread to the complex account of New England's eighteenth-century abolitionist movement.

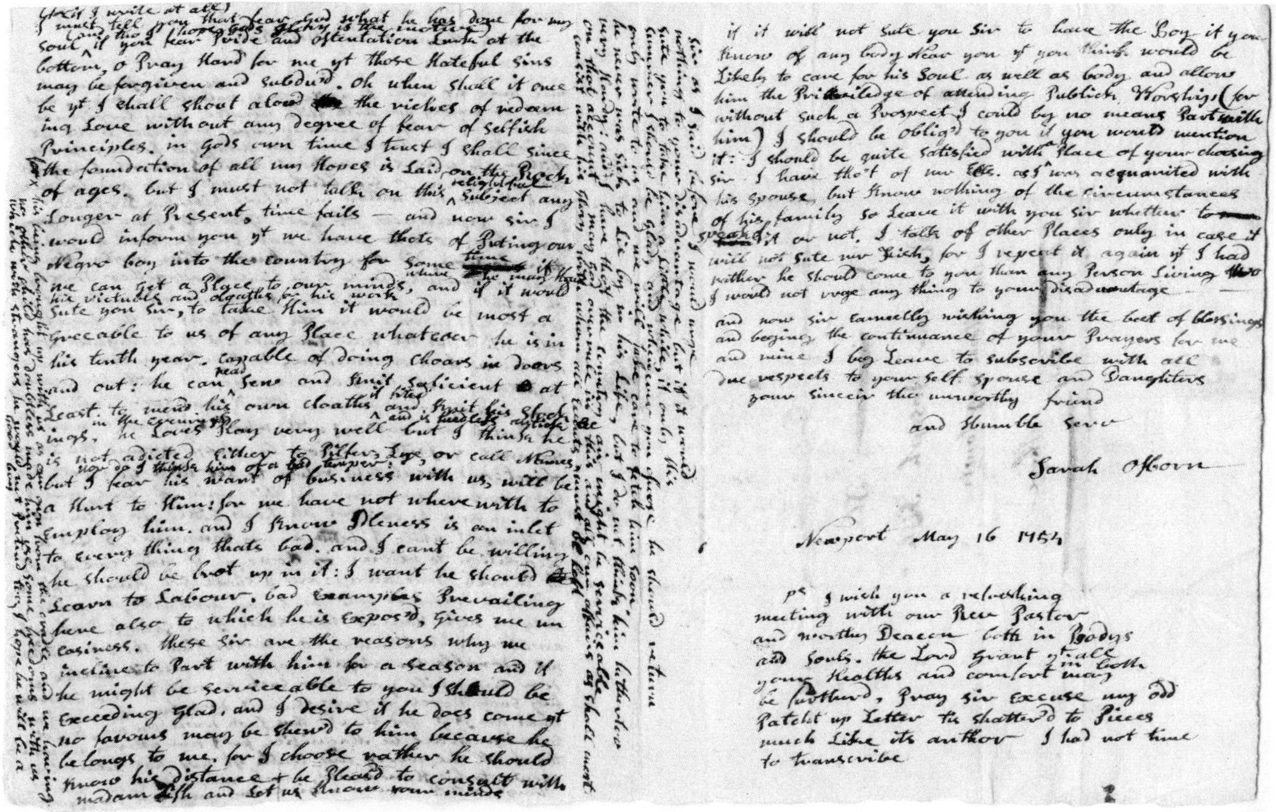

FIGURE 7. Sarah Osborn, letter to Joseph Fish, 16 May 1754, verso. This letter mentions Osborn's reasons for seeking a new household for Bobey, some of which are practical and some of which relate to her concerns about his "freedoms" with her and his lack of "Hard[iness]." It also suggests that she may have found the decision emotionally agonizing: the letter, with its margin notes and insertions, concludes with a postscript asking Fish to "excuse [her] odd Patcht up Letter tis shatter'd to Pieces much Like its author." Image courtesy of the American Antiquarian Society.

Most scholars accept that a combination of secular and religious factors contributed to its emergence. One, as Joanne Pope Melish notes, was a growing belief in "British oppression as evidence of divine judgment on colonial slavery."[20] Detailing what he calls the "contagion of liberty," Bernard Bailyn draws a link between abolitionism and the revolution's reliance on antislavery rhetoric.[21] In their study of evangelical advocates, Kenneth P. Minkema and Harry S. Stout argue that the climate of "social transformation and ideological crisis" compelled New Divinity theologians (including Samuel Hopkins) to put Jonathan Edwards's doctrine of disinterested benevolence into practice and thus preach against slavery from the pulpit and in print as a sign of their universal good will.[22] Still other scholars have focused on abolition in relation to capitalism or humanitarian sensibility.[23]

Yet rarely does this body of scholarship account for how enslaved persons themselves may have contributed to the emergence of the movement. Even those who study the period's abolition in a transatlantic context (the Mansfield Decision abolished slavery in England and Wales in 1772; Great Britain abolished the slave trade in 1807) vigorously debate the influence of vaunted black activists and authors such as Olaudah Equiano and Ignatius Sancho while rarely delving into the much less visible ways in which abolitionist sentiments may have arisen from quotidian interactions.[24] This alternative genealogy becomes apparent if we are attentive to intimacy within neighborhoods. There, it occurs across political, racial, class, and gender boundaries. It gives rise to awareness and knowledge of particular others. Intimacy may involve but does not necessitate shared feeling and desire. When situated within the amplifying practice of relational publication, it elucidates the unruliness of communal transformation.[25]

Osborn's and Phillis's intimacy appears to have included emotional and even affectionate bonds, but exchange might also have occurred at the level of maternal praxis. As I read Osborn's diaries, letters, and memoirs—an archive rarely analyzed by the literary eye—I seek to recover her practice of relational publication as well as the echoes and nature of the women's intimate exchanges.[26] Viewing this moment of Osborn's spiritual crisis as a heightened opportunity for such exchange, I trace how their differing yet mutually constituting identities as mothers catalyzed a series of transformations, beginning with Osborn and subsequently enfolding the neighborhood.

Crisis

On 7 December 1761, Osborn recorded the third diary entry of her spiritual crisis. She began with a lament: "O Lord forgive thou knowest the tempest in my breasts Lord shall I never get the world under my feet thou that knowest all things knowest my conflicts ever since Thursday Night."[27] She disclosed that she had been considering relenting out of "tenderness to Phillis and Bobey"; after all, her "Heart cling[s] to them." But acknowledging her anger at Phillis, she admitted that in fact "resentment" had prompted her plan to relent.[28] In the midst of her writing, she then reversed course and appeared to return to her original decision to sell Bobey. Asking God for the "grace to overcom[e] my anger and grief," she decided that her primary responsibility would be to her "god and conscience."[29]

In this vacillating entry, Osborn expressed a feeling of betrayal. She remarked that Phillis "cant believe that Either his Master or I Have Honesty enough to speak the truth, or at all to aim at His good."[30] Moreover, she declared that she had never been "unfaithful" to Phillis, whom she "always thot Had a better opinion of" her. These statements resound with hurt and arose from her intimacy with Phillis. One component of that intimacy was Osborn's ownership of Phillis's son, an unofficial yet still appreciable connection. Another was their participation in the same female society and membership in the same church. In addition to these verifiable forms of intimacy, we can conjecture about others. First, enslaved black persons often lived alongside their owners, sharing the same domestic space, including meals and family prayers. This integrated arrangement meant that enslaved persons also lived alongside the other members of their owner's household, such as relatives, dependents, apprentices, and other domestic servants—indentured and enslaved—as well as the black, white, and Native residents of the larger community.[31] In short, Osborn and Phillis would have shared the intimacy of a neighborhood. Perhaps this was why Osborn felt that Phillis's anger was a moment of disloyalty, just as Phillis may have seen Osborn's plan to sell Bobey as a betrayal.

For Phillis, Osborn's betrayal may have felt like an assault, though not because of their shared responsibility for Bobey. Phillis likely saw child rearing as diffuse. As Claire Robertson reasons in her comparative analysis of gender and labor in precolonial African and antebellum

African American lives, it was not women's "central activity most of the time."[32] Thus, Phillis, even during whatever brief time she lived with Bobey, depended on others to help her care for Bobey. The fact that she and Osborn were members of the same church may have even made Osborn's responsibility for her son more palatable as she may have considered Osborn a spiritual sister. Yet in the wake of enslavement, the mother-child bond was one of the few in which a black woman in the Americas could act with a modicum of "autonomy and creativity."[33] She could pass on her culture and memories, perform labor on her family's behalf, and initiate or extend kinship ties.[34] In Phillis's case, maternal autonomy had already been severely disrupted—first, when she and Bobey were separated and, second, when Bobey was sent to Berkley. Osborn's plan to sell Bobey thus foretold another blow in a sequence of violence experienced by Phillis.

For Osborn, Phillis's betrayal ruptured her maternal confidence as she may have viewed herself as a mother to both Bobey and Phillis.[35] And, as a mother, she was responsible for their spirituality. In her examination of mothering in colonial New England, Laurel Thatcher Ulrich describes it as extensive, including not only children but also servants, neighborhood children, and grandchildren.[36] Because of a colonial mother's numerous duties, as well as the fragility of life, it was imperative to instill piety in one's charges, a process that involved inculcating obedience to authority, divine and otherwise.[37] Osborn herself, rushing in 1744 to the deathbed of her beloved ten-year-old son, then an apprentice in Rehoboth, was most concerned with ensuring his salvation, not saying goodbye or comforting his final moments.[38] Moreover, many of New England's religious leaders, such as Cotton Mather, advocated Christian education for enslaved persons and identified it as the responsibility of slave owners.[39] They saw a linear correlation among God, a slave owner, and an enslaved individual that echoed the links among God, parents, and children. Therefore, Phillis's defiance—especially because Osborn had acted out of concern for Bobey's soul and because Phillis had become "vext" during a prayer meeting—exposed to Osborn and the neighborhood her inadequacy as a spiritual mother, simultaneously distancing her from her progeny and from God.

Phillis was able to reveal such rifts because she possessed a direct and recognizable maternal authority over Bobey that rivaled Osborn's less evident authority over him as spiritual mother. Phillis's emotional response was a reminder that Osborn was not, in fact, Bobey's biological mother. As the mother who gave birth to Bobey and as a neighbor, Phillis's anger could not simply be ignored. Significantly, Osborn remarked on her affection for Phillis and Bobey at precisely this point in the crisis. Though she had initially criticized Phillis for her "tenderness," now she admitted that she herself felt "tenderness" and revealed that her "Heart cling[ed] to them."[40] In mirroring Phillis's "tenderness," even as she continued to insist on her own duty, Osborn's words suggest that the path to her spiritual crisis's resolution lay not in disregarding, placating, or compromising with Phillis but in either negating or securing for herself Phillis's remaining affective authority. If Osborn could present herself as Bobey's only mother, sincerely attending to his spiritual *and* affective needs, then her decisions would be unequivocally the right ones, and she could reconcile with God.

To present herself as *the* mother instead of *a* mother, Osborn needed to perform a task that in some ways had seemed already complete. Ever since her conversion experience almost two decades earlier, soon after the death of her first husband, she had felt a divine call to nurture a spiritual family. In an anonymously printed version of a letter to a friend, *The Nature, Certainty, and Evidence of True Christianity,* she wrote of her conversion as a moment of spiritual and physical surrender: "I do know that God compell'd or *sweetly constrained me* to *throw down* the Weapons of my Rebellion and to *submit* to HIM as *Prince* and *Saviour.*"[41] She ecstatically articulated thankfulness for her surrender and compared it to a marital act: "Oh happy Choice! oh happy I, that I liv'd to see that Day wherein God betroth'd me to himself in loving Kindness and tender Mercy!"[42] Osborn recalled her conversion as a pleasurable and physical submission to God, a marriage in which she performed the conventionally subordinate feminine role.[43] The private moment of rapturous conversion was a "surrender" to God that demanded new quotidian practices of piety. She spoke of and performed her post-conversion transformation and described that moment in her writing, publishing her state of grace to her neighbors—who were likely aware of *Nature*'s true author—as well as insisting, through performative and textual repetitions, on its irrevocable consummation.

When Osborn cast her divine relationship as a marriage, she employed a metaphor recurrent in women's *and* men's colonial era spiritual writings. Inspired by biblical passages like Matthew 25:1–13 (the parable of the bridegroom and the virgins), New England ministers declared, "It is a marriage-covenant that we make with God . . . therefore we must do as the Spouse doth, resigne up our selves to be ruled and governed according to his will."[44] Scholars of American religion have long noticed this propensity, and Osborn was not unique in turning to this image.[45] Yet, perhaps because her conversion experience occurred soon after her husband's death and perhaps because so much of her prayer occurred through the act of writing, this metaphor recurs with particular potency in her writing.

Comforted by a sensual and marital experience of spirituality in her early widowhood, Osborn returned again to God as part of her grieving process in the face of additional family losses. In a letter written to her closest friend, Susanna Anthony, soon after the death of Osborn's son, she movingly explained how God had repeatedly consoled her:

> Sometimes [God] will visit me with affliction; he will take away the husband of my youth, and thereby cause me to fly to the Widow's God, and rejoice in him, as the best of husbands! At another time, he will take away a tender father, and enable me to acquiesce in his dispensation, and rejoice in him, as my father's God, as my God; and a father of the fatherless! Then he will remove an only brother, and thereby cause me more fully to know, what it is to be resigned to his will, and to adore his sovereignty!
>
> Again, lest my heart should be joined to idols, he will have an only son! and show me at the same time, that he is better to me, than ten sons! Ah, than ten thousand sons, or all earthly enjoyments![46]

God was Osborn's kinship network, one to which she actively "acquiesce[d]." Her joy in these relationships—God as husband, God as father, God as brother, God as son—arose from her experience of grace and from the solace they brought in the face of loss. Her supple affiliation with the divine resolved the fissures in her earthly family. Her connection to God overlay and refashioned her experience of familial relationality, placing the divine not only at the center of her spiritual world but also at the center of her mundane exchanges in a neighborhood.

Osborn's familial and frequently marital relationship to God also comforted her at other moments. For example, in 1754, during a time of spiritual doubt, she found solace in the knowledge that an "omnipoten[t]" God might reclaim her unfaithful soul. She imagined this moment as another wedding ceremony and even inscribed God's vows onto the page: "I will, she shall be cleansed, I will, she shall be Holy: . . . I will subdue her iniquities I will keep her by my mighty Power thro faith unto salvation, I will strengthen her, I will uphold her by the right Hand of my righteousness. I will . . . take Possession of her soul and body for my self."[47] Similarly, during a major earthquake that shook New England in 1755, she again depended on God to sustain her. Writing to Joseph Fish on 10 December, several weeks after the earthquake, she reported that, before it struck during the night, she "awak'd" and "lay delightfuly contemplating [God's] adorable Perfections." When the ground trembled, rather than fearing God's "fierce wrath," she reposed "becalm'd in His bosom sucking by faith the breast of the Promises given me by a faithful God" and sensed that he was giving her "a Pledge of his Love and faithfulness."[48] Lying in bed, enjoying the pleasure of her relationship with God and serenely welcoming the tremors that were terrifying others, she found reassurance of her grace through reconsummating her relationship to God and circulating that reassurance via letter.

It was in these moments of spiritual surrender and divine comfort that Osborn experienced a call to nurture others. In her 1755 earthquake letter to Fish, for example, submission to God's will motivated a vigorous spiritual empowerment. At times she simply lay in bed; at others she was "sucking" at God's "bosom" and "dart[ing]" to Him in "ejaculations." This active and erotic language of submission peaked with her euphoric plea: "O love him more my soul oh yt I could so speak of the glorious excellencies of my dear redeemer as to be made an instrument in his Hand of bringing thousands and ten thousands to bow to the sceptre of his grace." She wanted to be an "instrument" in God's "Hand," and she desired that "thousands and ten thousands" would "bow to the sceptre of his grace."[49] She pictured herself as a divine tool, subject to his will. While she included the requisite expression of worthlessness, she presented herself as something of a handmaiden, invested with God's agency, his "instrument" and "sceptre."[50] Unlike those who interpreted the earthquake as a sign of God's displeasure, Osborn experienced it as a moment when she, like a proper Christian wife, became an extension of her husband's will and authorized to bear and raise offspring according to his image.[51] The moment was an injunction to enact her relationship with God within her neighborhood.

Obedience to this divine call would have helped reassure Osborn of her spiritual espousal. As Jonathan Edwards lectured in his influential *A Treatise Concerning Religious Affections,* "practice is the most proper

Evidence of a true *Coming to Christ,* and *accepting* of, and *closing* with him."[52] While works could not confirm grace, spiritual defiance would be a grievous sin. Marriage to God required Osborn to voluntarily and wholly submit herself to Christ, just as a wife should submit herself to her husband. Such submission might seem to affirm women's disempowerment in a patriarchal system, yet Amanda Porterfield has shown that women in Puritan New England gained "indirect influence and authority" over adult men and "direct authority over others as mothers."[53] Moreover, Susan Juster, whose analysis complements Porterfield's by analyzing sexual politics and evangelicalism in the eighteenth century, finds that midcentury evangelical women developed a religious language of authority anchored in their "ecsta[tic]" conversion experiences. This idiom, "rooted in physical and emotional attachments," would have intersected with women's relationships with their dependents and other members of their households.[54] Thus, Osborn's orthodox faith positioned her to obtain a measure of authority—at least outside the pastoral setting—through spiritual surrender.[55]

Osborn's neighborhood offered her ample opportunity to pursue her calling and deploy her maternal authority. She was accountable for the spiritual education of her stepchildren and -grandchildren as well as her servants, slaves, and students.[56] She also folded non-dependents into her divine family through the female society. She articulated this sense of maternal responsibility at various moments in her writing. For example, while describing her conversion, she first declared that she felt "ravished with [Christ's] love" and then aligned "more intimate communion with God" with becoming "instrumental in advancing his kingdom and interest in the world."[57] Elsewhere in her memoirs, she relied on a rhetoric of parturition to describe her work, rapturously confessing, "Surely I longed that all the world, but especially those dear to me by the bonds of nature or friendship, might be convinced of sin, and come to a glorious Christ. I thought I could even spend and be spent for them. I thought I could travail in birth until Christ was formed in them."[58] While praying about her school in a 1760 diary entry, she created a capacious nurturing space when she pleaded for God to "take hold of the heart of every one thou committest to my charge, if it may be thy holy will. In the arms of faith I bring them every one to thee."[59] In her writings, she referred to the female society on multiple occasions as a "nursery for piety."[60] For Osborn, the neighborhood of society, home, and school was a fertile ground for spirituality, places to make public her obedience and intensify her marital relationship to God.

Time after time in her writing, Osborn appears to be simultaneously humble about her capabilities and assured of her duty. She surrendered to God and therefore readied herself to "bring them every one" in her "arms of faith." If it was God's will, she was prepared to be mother to all. Her words imply confident devotion to her purpose in God's family, even when she agonized over what she viewed as her unworthiness. Her pious performance manifested her written words, a relational publication that imagined her household and nurturing at the center of a revised neighborhood. Her home was indeed a nursery for piety, and her progeny were numerous and diverse. Out of spiritual obedience, she reared her offspring, instructing, rebuking, and, especially in the case of adults, guiding by example. After all, she was the mother, and they were the neighborhood's children to be properly raised.

Resolution

Phillis's resistance to Bobey's sale questioned Osborn's sincerity and status as mother. Thus, given her frequent expressions of her maternal calling, Osborn's spiritual crisis was no surprise. Her newfound doubts about the efficacy of her spiritual nurturing led to indecision and uncertainty, which to her indicated a fissure in her relationship and obedience to God. Moreover, Phillis's forceful communication of her tenderness for Bobey, something Osborn initially criticized and then mirrored, suggests that Phillis's resistance also caused Osborn to question how she mothered.

A sense of intensifying crisis pervades Osborn's diary entries. She prayed, "Lord I beseech thee deliver my Soul O Lord calm my spirits."[61] She painfully admitted, "I am weary of this unholy Heart." She grieved and pleaded, "I cant controwl the torrent of thots that whirl me down the stream from the fountain Head O Lord Pitty and forgive I Hate them and yet ere I am aware indulge them too oh How the world is eating out my duties Lord appear for me."[62] On 12 December, she darkly revealed, "I am Still at a distance from God dull dry barren wandring I am tuging at the oars continually I carry self Loathing."[63] At first her entries demonstrate that she was drowning in a "torrent" of doubt and that such a loss of control was overwhelming her. Then, finding herself "dull dry barren," she figured her soul as unproductive in terms of her personal spiritual fruits and suggested that her other spiritual fruits—her step-children and -grandchildren, her schoolchildren, her fellow members of the female society, even Phillis and Bobey—were either no longer hers or corrupted because this moment had disconnected her from God, the spousal foundation of her religious family and the source of her maternal authorization.[64] Her prayers to God for a rapprochement were repeatedly ineffectual, and she attempted again and again to use her spiritual diary as a lifeline to pull herself out of the vortex of her despair.

Finally, on Sunday, 13 December, a week after the crisis began, Osborn awoke, enclosed herself in her closet, and again attempted to write and pray her way back to God. On this morning, her normally clear and steady handwriting had deteriorated into an uncontrolled scrawl. As she prepared to go to church, she agonized over the situation and its effects on her relationship with God: "O Lord take my thots of[f] from this subject and turn them to thy Self oh that I could Leave off thinking and fall to Praying and Leave all with God to determin Just as He sees best I am wearied out and Heart Sick of thinking and weighing one thing with another and after all cant tell what is best Lord Help and Make the Path of duty Plain."[65]

Then, as her handwriting progressively cleared, she reiterated her two options. On the one hand, she could sell Bobey, an option justified by the family's shaky finances. On the other hand, she could keep him. After all, she was uncertain that a new master would guarantee his spiritual well-being. She began to explore this second option; and as she wrote, her words tumbling over themselves, she decided to cancel the sale:

> Then I turn and think and why should we Part with Him why cant I still trust Him in the Hands of that gracious god that at first gave Him to me and believe that He will take care of both Him and me believe He was given to me in Mercy when I was chierfuly giving up all at the call of divine Providence then god gave Him me and was it not in a covenant way was it not in Mercy and [is]nt it ungrateful in me to think it was for a Scourge Had I not better Hope in the Mercy of God and commit Him to Him to keep for me who Has Preferrd Him so Long and Preserv'd Him from falling in to gross sins too He is Honest and averse to drink and is as His Master says more and more faithful & He shall do us all the service god sees best for us He shant nor He cant go to sea Except god Pleases He can contrawl Him if we cant and His Life His Health His Living is in gods Hands the whole disposing is of the Lord and I think I Had rather commit Him to him to keep for me then to commit Him to the care of

> any Man this is my Present frame and now Lord Help me to Leave Him to thee Now Lord un viel thy glorious Perfections and attract my Heart this day for Jesus sake I beg it[.][66]

Phillis is nowhere present in this breathless passage. Instead, it continually refers to a triangular relationship between Osborn, Bobey, and God. The first several lines include three variations of the statement that God "gave" Bobey to "me."[67] It seems that Bobey was both a gift and a charge, and to sell him would have been a rejection of God's will. Osborn then twice wrote the phrase "keep for me." Although God "gave" her Bobey in the past, her use of the word *keep* characterized her and Bobey's relationship as ongoing and chosen. She had to choose to heed her calling and spiritual obedience. Textually, Osborn was Bobey's only remaining mother, and she was determined to surrender to her duty, even if that meant that the household's financial problems would continue.

The emotional torrent of previous entries has abated, replaced by an acquiescent maternal affection. Increasingly confident in her new role as Bobey's divine mother, Osborn wrote during the next several days about receiving forgiveness for her previous inability to "Leave all with God" and persuading him to complete his spiritual "adoption" of Bobey.[68] Osborn had reconciled with God. By displacing Phillis in an act of textual violence, she resolved the spiritual crisis. She repaired the rifts in her maternal authority, divine family, and relationship to God by realigning the neighborhood's bonds in her diary. She wrote herself as a new kind of mother, one who in some ways resembled Phillis because she concerned herself with spiritual *and* affective needs. Now, like Phillis, she could not abide a termination of her ties to Bobey.

This violent moment marks an altered trajectory in Osborn's spiritual life. Her early writings indicate a rather smooth progression from spiritual espousal to divinely called mother, ministering to her family, school, and female society. She could humbly but authoritatively minister to them because they had explicitly come under her household care or because they had asked, as the women of the female society did, for her guidance. In contrast, despite Phillis's inescapably subordinate position, her "vex[ation]" about the planned sale of Bobey had caused Osborn to falter. In her own household, another mother had denied Osborn's maternal authority and questioned the centrality of her home to the neighborhood. Inscribing prayer after prayer to God, seeking to resolve her crisis, she consumed Phillis's affectionate motherhood and altered her spiritual course. Her diary remapped the neighborhood's spiritual and mundane affiliations without a bond between Bobey and Phillis.

Reverberations

For Phillis, the aftereffects of Osborn's spiritual crisis were immediate and likely celebrated. Emotionally, the textual violence would have had little repercussion on Phillis's feelings for Bobey, and she would have continued to view herself as Bobey's mother. Materially, Bobey would not be sold, and mother and son would retain their ties, which were admittedly tenuous and mediated. In the case of Bobey, whose perspective is absent from the archive, it is impossible to know whether he welcomed or lamented Osborn's change of heart, just as his feelings for Phillis and Osborn are irrecoverable. While records do not show what happened to them in the wake of this spiritual crisis (though Osborn's diary implies she continued to loan Bobey to her former brother-in-law), we do know that Phillis died in 1779, still bearing the surname Allen, and that Osborn did not mention possessing slaves in her 1794 will. We also know that, in 1774, six black persons resided with Osborn.[69] Perhaps that number included Bobey, or perhaps it did not.

From Osborn's perspective, however, the aftereffects were unpredictable and wide-ranging, and the familial language with which she continued to describe her religious work suggests that events during the last three decades of her life had some of their roots in this crisis. During the first eight years of this period, she fomented and led the evangelical revival that involved much of Newport and began her long relationship with Samuel Hopkins, the Congregationalist minister and eventual public abolitionist. Her subsequent activities reveal that her decision to keep Bobey had been a significant moment in a transformed relationship to persons of color, one that emerged from her relational publication practice. By spanning scriptive text and embodied performance, she rewrote her spiritual motherhood and made that change public in the way in which she performed her piety in the neighborhood.

In 1764, some local black Christians, probably members of Osborn's church, approached her and asked her to lead them in an Ethiopian society similar to the already well established female society. Unlike her work with children and white women, the instruction of black people, especially those who were enslaved, was a contentious task. In accepting this role, she might undermine white authority and black submissiveness in both individual households and the city's general society.

Osborn saw herself as a mother to this group of black Christians, a view she made apparent in a letter to Joseph Fish justifying her decision to lead the Ethiopian society: "There is several Ethiopians thotful who Having their Liberty to go where they List on Lords day evenings have ask^ed Liberty to repair to our House for the benefit of family prayer read[in]g &c and I have thot it a duty to encourage them only charging them never to disobey their Masters &c." Her words appear almost defiant in their insistence on the "dut[ifulness]" of her actions. After all, the "Ethiopians" were joining in "family prayer," and she "charg[ed] them never to disobey their Masters."[70] She reinforced black persons' subordinate position and ascribed childlike qualities to them.[71] She carefully negotiated the limits of religious education for persons of color, implying that an autonomous spiritual life does not equate with insubordination. Nonetheless, she cast herself as a divine mother who must nurture their spirituality.

Apparently, Osborn's insistence on the propriety and even necessity of her actions was at least somewhat convincing. Rather than resulting in widespread ostracization, the founding of the Ethiopian society, though criticized, marked the onset of a religious revival in Newport that was centered in her home. Possibly, her actions indicated to others in her community, including white men, that she could mother them as well. An increasing number of people, including Baptists and others who were not members of Osborn's church, began joining preexisting meetings. As they did, she organized them into groups by race, gender, age, and other factors and designated certain times for each meeting. By 1767, many days ended or began with a religious meeting at her small house; according to her calculations, more than five hundred "souls" were attending each week.[72]

A 1767 letter to Fish provides most of the extant details about the meetings.[73] In it, Osborn continued to cast her work with the Ethiopian society as nurturing instead of radical. When working with "the poor Blacks on Lords day Evenings," she did not pray with them because she was not a minister.[74] Instead, "I read to them talk to them and sing a Psalm or Hymn with them, and then at Eight o clock dismiss them all by Name as upon List. They call it School and I Had rather it should be calld almost any thing that is good than Meeting. I reluct so much at being that Head of any thing that bears that Name." In some ways, then, her work resembled what she did as a schoolteacher. She instructed these black Christians in piety, just as she instructed the "little ones" who attended her school. At another point in the letter, she portrayed them as "cling[ing] and beg[ging] for the Priviledge" of coming to her home, a description that characterizes them as childlike and attests to a shared emotional relationship that appears maternal in its configuration.[75] She reasoned that she should sing with them, an activity she would generally reserve only for children, because they "appear to [her] no otherwise now then children tho for Stature men and women."[76] By repeatedly emphasizing continuity between children and the members of the Ethiopian society as well as her affection for them, she styled these meetings as a manifestation of family community over which she presided pedagogically and maternally.

Osborn's sense of her leadership as divine nurturing filtered more subtly into her descriptions of her work with white constituencies. Discussing Friday evenings, when white church "Brethren," including men, came to her home, she downplayed her role, just as she did in her writings about the female society where we know she was the acknowledged leader: "As to friday Evning friends, my dear Sir I by no means Set up for their instructor. They come indeed for Mutual Edification and Sometimes condescend to direct part of conversation to me and so far I bear a part as to answer etc. but no otherway."[77] She focused upon her home as a place to gather and minimized her presence. However, because this was *her* home, *her* domestic space, her words offset her humble intentions and reminded Fish that God had called her to nurture and support these meetings even if she was not the vocal leader. When she subsequently described "these Gatherings at our House" as tending to "a Sweet Sementing bond of union that Holds us together in this critical day," she figured her home as the binding glue of a new religious neighborhood; its position as a domestic space in which she was mother, teacher, and wife suggests that this neighborhood was a family.[78]

Osborn's spiritual care of white Christians, though markedly different from her work with the Ethiopian society, confirmed her calling to instruct black Christians. It placed all those who attended meetings—black and white—in relationship with each other through their relationship to her. Her home was a nursery for piety where she had brought forth a multiracial spiritual family composed of adults and children, rich and poor, men and women, free and enslaved. As the de facto matriarch of God's family in Newport, her work with each portion of the population iteratively augmented the necessity and propriety of her work with the others, including black Christians.

Yet the Ethiopian society was the centerpiece of the revival as black Christians' vulnerable class offered Osborn a unique and powerful opportunity to fulfill her calling as a spiritual mother. In the case of enslaved persons, their condition as property branded them outsiders whose connections to each other were vulnerable (as the case of Phillis and Bobey amply emphasizes). In the case of free black persons, the color of their skin marked a history of natal alienation that, since gaining freedom, they may have begun to offset but that still isolated them from the white population.[79] Thus, the local black community in Newport was in some ways a motherless population.[80] Through her informal ministry, Osborn repeated her adoption of Bobey over and over again. Her repetitious maternal performance may have been especially urgent in light of Phillis's continued presence in the geographic neighborhood. Osborn provided willing black Christians with a spiritual education, thereby imperfectly recognizing their humanity, yet insisted on their childish nature. Through this process, she extended her divine family and maternal authority and spread her understanding of religious worship to others outside her home. By repeatedly making public the maternal affection she had textually culled from Phillis, she transformed her transgressive education of black Christians into a divine mother's proper behavior that, in turn, allowed her to extend her spiritual nurturing to many, many others.

The Newport revival waned along with the decade, but both the female and the Ethiopian societies remained vibrant. When, in 1769, Osborn's church began to search for a new minister, she and the female society were instrumental in calling their next minister, Samuel Hopkins, an older man who had studied under Edwards.[81] Even as a guest preacher, he met with the female society, something his predecessor and other Congregationalist leaders had rarely done, despite Osborn's efforts. He also began helping in Osborn's school and with her religious education of the local black population, at her request.[82] Impressed by her piety and "theology," he "took tea at her house" on Saturday afternoons after spending the day preparing for the Sabbath.[83] According to Sheryl A. Kujawa, "Hopkins credited Osborn for her helpful input into his Sunday sermons."[84]

In 1771, Hopkins, a slave owner until shortly before his arrival in Newport, began preaching against slavery, and in 1776, he published his abolitionist pamphlet, *A Dialogue, Concerning the Slavery of the Africans.*[85] Though it is unclear if Osborn also became an abolitionist, others have argued for the instrumental role she played in Hopkins's newfound fame as a "champion of antislavery."[86] David Grimsted calls her enlistment of Hopkins her "triumph" because he extended her informal ministry in ways she could not.[87] Nonetheless, even if she had become an abolitionist, it seems apparent that she was most concerned with saving black peoples' souls.

What has gone unremarked is how enslaved black individuals themselves helped originate the abolitionist movement that grew out of Osborn's and Hopkins's relationship. It is unlikely that Hopkins would have so quickly or vigorously turned against slavery without his involvement with the black Christians of Newport.[88] The intimacy of Osborn's new neighborhood allowed both the Ethiopian society and others of African descent (such as Phillis Wheatley, who shared her poems with Osborn through either Susanna Wheatley or her enslaved Newport friend Obour Tanner) to breach the boundaries placed around their spirituality and humanity.[89] The "promiscu[ity]" of their religious circle, as Osborn termed it, had helped to shift the region's relationship to slavery.[90]

Even as we recognize the role of black Christians in Newport's antislavery movement, we should not lose sight of Bobey's mother, Phillis. The evidence suggests that Phillis's vexation so harrowed Osborn that she shifted her imagination of her affiliatory relations; she reacted by textually adopting Bobey and incorporating Phillis's affectionate maternity into her own. As a result, her divine motherhood opened to, possibly even demanded, the spiritual adoption of more progeny. It is telling that the Ethiopian society formed after Osborn's spiritual crisis, not in the 1740s during the Great Awakening revivals, as the female society did. Perhaps these black Christians had already sensed Osborn's newly affectionate demeanor toward them even as they recognized the limitations of her sympathy. In short, it is possible to trace this series of events—Osborn's spiritual crisis, her adoption of Bobey and eventually other black Christians, the Newport revivals, Hopkins's introduction to the Ethiopian society, and his abolitionist proselytization—to Phillis's circulation of her maternal vexation.

This alternative genealogy becomes visible if we attend to relational publication and the reciprocal and recursive exchanges between neighbors. In her diaries, Osborn sought to obviate one disruption to her understanding of her neighborhood, yet as she negotiated certain associations—with God, with Bobey, with Phillis—the neighborhood's intimate fabric demanded that she reimagine a greater affiliatory terrain. Her relational publication was coextensive with Phillis's words and the material neighborhood, written text and pious performance.

By delineating the relationality of women's publication practices and its articulation with neighborly bonds, we see how an enslaved class of people, living in forced and uneven intimacy with their oppressors, could have altered public life. We can detect possible echoes of one enslaved woman—a woman who left behind no writing of her own—in a region's social transformations. Without doing so, we risk re-silencing Phillis and missing other such echoes. This is not to say, however, that intimate exchange had no limits. After all, Phillis's anger did not lead to her manumission or, it seems, even to an apology from Osborn. In fact, Osborn sought a new way to contain the affective expression of her black "children" even as she gained a more capacious and powerful understanding of her spiritual calling.[91] Osborn's infantilization of the Ethiopian society's members implied their filial affection. Their filial affection then confirmed her divine calling to mother God's children, even as their childish status assured their continued subordination.

Yet it is also important to observe that, as a series of exchanges, intimacy is unruly, fluid, and reciprocal. By accounting for relational publication and the neighborhood, I am suggesting that social change evolves from interpersonal conflict and crisis as much as it does from institutions and charismatic leaders. New England's abolitionist turn may not have originated only in the pandemic of revolutionary rhetoric, or the region's discomfort with the prospect of a slaveholding republic, or the increasing moral power of the Society of Friends' antislavery stance, or the pragmatics of capitalism. It may also have originated in the vexed words of an enslaved woman who opposed the sale of her son.

3

The Consolation of Phillis Wheatley's Elegies

The perusal of Phillis Wheatley's book proposals is a bittersweet endeavor. Along with this enslaved Boston poet's breakout elegy, "On the Death of the Rev. *George Whitefield,*" and the now frequently anthologized poems "To the University of Cambridge" and "Thoughts on Being Brought from Africa to America," the proposals mention a host of unknown poems, thereby inspiring both gratitude for the bounty of her extant writings and regret for what is missing.[1] One of the most tantalizing titles is "On the Affray in King-Street, on the Evening of the 5th of March." Lost, published anonymously, or never written, this poem about the Boston Massacre of 1770 would have been her only known elegy, however oblique, for a fellow African.[2]

Wheatley, who lived on King Street, may herself have witnessed portions of the massacre.[3] She and other Boston residents would have been aware that the first casualty of the night, Crispus Attucks, was of mixed African and Native ancestry. His identity was so well known that it was noted in newspaper accounts and became fodder for the perpetrators' defense.[4] Several months later, in his summation at the British soldiers' trial, John Adams placed Attucks, a "stout Mollato fellow," at the head of a "motley rabble of saucy boys, negroes and molattoes, Irish teagues and outlandish jack tars."[5] He blamed Attucks's "mad behaviour" for the "dreadful carnage of that night."

But even before Adams spoke those words, Boston was transforming Attucks from racial scofflaw to patriotic martyr (see fig. 8). On 8 March, the men who had died in the massacre—Crispus Attucks and three others—were buried together. A joint funeral procession of "Ten or Twelve thousand," according to extravagant diarist John Rowe, wound through the city streets to the Old Granary Burying Ground (see fig. 9).[6] There, the men were interred in the still-fresh grave of another recent young martyr, Christopher Seider.[7] Eighteenth-century historian David Ramsay explains that the joint burial "express[ed] the indigna-

FIGURE 8. Paul Revere, *The BLOODY MASSACRE perpetuated in King-Street BOSTON on March* 5th *1770 by a party of the* 29th *REG*^{T} (Boston, 1770). In this image, the most lasting of the Boston Massacre, Revere omitted any indication of Attucks's (or any other participant's) black or Native identity, with the possible exception of one wounded figure's darker hair (see lower left corner). Image courtesy of the American Antiquarian Society.

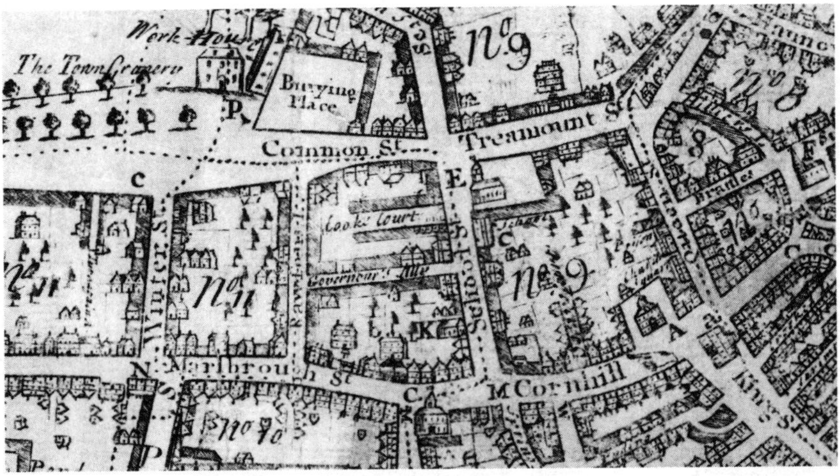

FIGURE 9. Detail from William Price, *A New Plan Of Ye Great Town Of Boston In New England In America With The Many Additionall Buildings & New Streets, To The Year, 1769* (Boston, 1769). The map notes the location of the Granary Burying Ground (top), where Crispus Attucks was buried, and King Street (lower right), site of the Boston Massacre and Wheatley's residence. Image courtesy of the Library of Congress, Geography and Map Division (call no. G3764.B6 1769.P7).

tion of the inhabitants at the slaughter of their brethren, by soldiers quartered among them, in violation of their civil liberties."[8] He further pronounces that the "events of this tragical night, s[a]nk deep into the minds of the people, and were made subservient to important purposes," and that anniversary orations between 1771 and 1783 helped keep "fresh" the "blessings of liberty" and the "horrors of slavery."[9] The deaths of Attucks and the others gave rise to a feeling of affiliation among Bostonians, who experienced collective "indignation" about the "events of [that] tragical night." They maintained that affiliation through public commemoration and restricted that affiliation by erasing Attucks's race from public memory.

For colonial Bostonians, the relationship between public mourning and affiliation was well established. The flexible performance of public rituals delineated paths of affiliation and thus reconstituted neighborhoods in the aftermath of death.[10] Bells tolled to announce the funeral, aurally creating a zone of mourning. After women washed and dressed a body, it was carried through the streets in a procession that involved friends and family and linked private residences to the graveside. Processions for notable communal figures might begin at a more public venue and be especially circuitous and long. At the graveside, mourners sang and prayed, and loved ones tossed handfuls of dirt over the coffin or shrouded corpse. Family members sometimes gave out gloves as invitations to join the procession, and the chief mourners, clergy, and pallbearers might receive rings as mementos (see plate 3). An elegy inscribing the deceased's piety and conjecturing his or her salvation might also circulate with the corpse and among the bereaved. After the funeral, an inscribed headstone and footstone would be placed at the grave. Thus, communal reconstitution involved the public circulation of corpse, mourners, sound, word, and mementos that traversed a locality. Death cleaved the neighborhood, and survivors mended the rift by following paths of affiliation among the deceased's family, friends, and neighbors.

These circulations, however, were circumscribed when performed in response to a black Bostonian's death. Since the early eighteenth century, the city's selectmen had been enacting statutes to constrain and segregate nonwhite burial practices, believing them to be of "ill Tendancy."[11] In 1721, they ordered that only "one Tolling of a Bell" would be allowed for "Indian, Negro or Molatto" funerals (as opposed to the two permitted for white funerals) and determined that persons of color should be "Carried the nearest way to their Graues."[12] In 1723, they mandated that such burials could occur only near sunset, at the "nearest burying place," and never on Sundays; they reiterated that processions should travel via the most "direct" route.[13] In 1735, they instructed the city's sextons to warn "Inhabitants" that they would be "Preventing and Reforming Disorders at the Funerals of Negroes," in accordance with the law.[14] And in 1744, the city's gravediggers, concerned that the South Burying Ground was becoming so "full that they cannot Bury the Dead without Disturbing them, pray[ed] the Town . . . will provide some place to Bury Strangers & Negroes."[15] While these men could not excise black persons and funerals from Boston's geography, they could make them akin to "Strangers" by seeking to minimize their presence, deny their grief, and remove them to the margins. There was little room in the neighborhood for individual black mourners, much less a black collective united through their public performance of grief.

In proposing an occasional poem on the Boston Massacre two years later, Wheatley would have been facilitating the affiliatory memorialization that had occurred in its aftermath while also marking the erasure of Crispus Attucks's race within it. She demarcated a distinctive neighborhood for persons of color in Boston's territories of affiliation and mourning, one that was simultaneously visible and unseen. This reorientation of neighborhoods and its inflection with black particularity recur in her many elegies, especially those for a son or daughter. Through elegiac verse, she surveyed the circulatory practices of mourning and mapped neighborhoods in the interests of self-consolation and self-determination. In her poetry, her enslavement placed her between a neighborhood of living mourners, confined by grief, and another neighborhood of the deceased, liberated by their experience of the forced migration to heaven wrought by death.

The relations of Boston's white mourners initially directed Wheatley's publication practice. She was an accomplished elegist, made famous by her poem on the death of George Whitefield; in its wake, she was tasked with producing funeral elegies for her dead neighbors, many of them children.[16] The daily exchanges in and between households, in church and in the parlor, wove a relational fabric for her elegies, which were occasioned by specific incidents of loss. Distributed among a neighborhood of white mourners, they helped perform the public repair of particular relational ruptures. As Joanna Brooks reasons in her provocatively titled essay "Our Phillis, Ourselves," Wheatley's elegies operated within a "transactional, sentimental culture of mourning" in which she "mobilized" her symbolic association with "grief" to build a "network of . . . [white women] supporters" who used her "to perform the emotional labor of condolence and sympathy."[17] But Wheatley was more than a savvy amanuensis for her enslavers' mourning: her elegies were acts of relational publication that reimagined the neighborhood she had been commissioned to restore. As they appraised death's transformation of lines of exchange and positioned the enslaved as the only conduit between the living and the dead, they distinguished two separate but adjacent communities, at last mapping a space where her black neighbors could gather to grieve. The circulation of her poetry by hand and mouth invited an isolated and mourning black audience to join her procession and refigure their experience of coerced dislocation as a passport to a new transcendent neighborhood. As her elegies circulated beyond Boston and its environs, they proffered the same invitation to other bound and enslaved communities: consolatory neighborhoods proliferating with elegiac circulation and consumption.

My discussion builds on what has been a productive conversation about death, grief, and enslavement in colonial and postcolonial America. Paul Gilroy, Joseph Roach, Sharon Holland, Karla F. C. Holloway, Anissa Janine Wardi, and Dana Luciano, among others, have all addressed this topic.[18] They see enslaved Africans' loss of home and kinship ties as both an irrecoverable trauma and a shared experience that gave them and their descendants an affective bond through which to reconstitute community, especially when participating in the formal and informal rituals surrounding death. For example, in examining the African American mortuary culture of nineteenth-century New Orleans, Roach determines that the "occasion created by death offered this community an opportunity to affirm its semiautonomous but discreetly submerged existence within or against the obligatory rituals of . . . the dominant culture."[19] Like Roach, all of these scholars view texts and performances relating to bereavement as sites through which to describe some of the beginnings and unique forms of African Americans' communal reconstitutions and artistic production. Erik Seeman's *Death in the New World* adamantly places studies of colonial mortuary practices in a multicultural context: "Putting death at the center of the history of the New World reveals the critical role of real and perceived cultural parallels in cross-cultural encounters."[20] These practices acted as a locus for delineating differences and commonalities that could then be "exploit[ed]" in the interest of oppression or rebellion.[21]

In addition to tracing and locating some of the roots of this fruitful scholarship in colonial Boston, I am interested in blurring the distinction between material practices and literary publication, a distinction that often leads to the perception of Wheatley's writing as an isolated exception, the fruits of a genius rather than an emblem (albeit a striking one) of the evolving and vibrant cultural production of the eighteenth-century black diaspora.[22] By analyzing the intersection between funeral practices, textual circulation, and neighborhoods, I am working to identify how the intimacy-producing potential of relational publication transformed the controlled and coercive affiliation in a physically restricted and delimited geography.

Wheatley's Elegies for Children

In Puritan New England, death made poets of the living. Desiring to memorialize the deceased but constrained by the austere solemnity of their funerals, mourners "conspired" and "labored" to write "tributes of grief and respect," which they attached to biers and interred with corpses.[23] They then distributed printed copies "decorated gruesomely with skull and crossbones, scythes, coffins, and hour-glasses, all-seeing eyes with rakish squints, bow-legged skeletons, and miserable little rosetted winding-sheets."[24] An anonymous author in the *New-England Courant* sniped that by 1722 there was not "one Country House in Fifty which ha[d] not its Walls garnished with half a Score of these Sort of Poems, (if they may be so call'd)."[25] Like other aspects of colonial New England's cultures of death, the circulation of elegies helped a neighborhood recover from loss.

Phillis Wheatley was much in demand as an elegist. In addition to her lost covert elegy for Attucks, she wrote at least twenty-seven elegies, of which nineteen are extant.[26] Though some were produced without direct prompting, many were not: a network of mostly white women "commissioned from her original poems on subjects close to heart."[27] Thus, a set of relations among deceased, mourners, and enslaved poet motivated the composition of these poems, and Wheatley's craft was a servant to the affective demands of her neighborhood. Yet part of her appeal as an elegist lay in her own particular experiences of bereavement; and the elegies, when considered collectively, disclose another subject for analysis: her silence on the matter of her own grief even as she publicly contemplated the loss of others. Several scholars, including Julie Ellison, have observed an "evasion of the victim's position" in "Wheatley's self-protectiveness."[28] Yet her elegies, specifically those for children, also rely on her affinity for the dead. The difference between her experiences and that of her patrons—she *was* the lost child—allowed her to survey the postmortem relations that the mourners could not. Through her elegies, she collated location with the emotions and experiences that followed the death of a son or a daughter, thereby mapping separate neighborhoods.

Though they were offered as consolation for grieving parents, Wheatley's elegies for children placed the living and the dead at an unbridgeable vertical distance from one another, thereby insisting that consolation was impossible. For example, in "To a LADY and her Children, on the Death of her Son and their Brother," the poet describes the difference between the mother's and the dead son's experience of death:

> Th' unhappy mother sees the sanguine rill
> Forget to flow, and nature's wheels stand still,

But see from earth his spirit far remov'd,
And know no grief recals your best-belov'd:
He, upon pinions swifter than the wind,
Has left mortality's sad scenes behind
For joys to this terrestrial state unknown,
And glories richer than the monarch's crown.
Of virtue's steady course the prize behold!
What blissful wonders to his mind unfold![29]

The lines depict death as an upward flight on "pinions," or feathered wings, from mortal earth into "joy[ful]" skies. We can imagine the "sad scenes" of life becoming small and insignificant and "virtue's" "prize" growing ever more apparent as the deceased ascends. Wheatley's exultant declaration—"What blissful wonders to his mind unfold!"—likens the first sight of a virtuous life's reward to the "wond[rous]" expansion of the "mind." In contrast, the mother's world narrows while her son dies. Caught up in her unhappiness, she remains earthbound as she watches the blood cease to "flow" in the "sanguine rill" of his veins and as his body's "wheels stand still."

Seeking to console the mother, Wheatley directs her to look up and see her son's "spirit far remov'd" from earth. She reminds the mother that her son now "recal[ls]" "no grief" and that "no grief" will "recal[l]" him back to life. But after extending this message of solace, Wheatley changes course in the next and final stanza, which abandons airy images of death and directs the bereaved to stop mourning:

No more in briny show'rs, ye friends around,
Or bathe his clay, or waste them on the ground:
Still do you weep, still wish for his return?
How cruel thus to wish, and thus to mourn?[30]

Moving beyond the period's customary calls for resignation, the words scornfully classify tearful expressions as impractical longings for the return of the dead. Weeping mourners do not heed the evangelical Christian message of grace and heavenly bliss because the they are incapable of perceiving, affectively or sensorially, what the dead can teach them about life, the afterlife, and, by extension, the poem's message of consolation. Instead, they are trapped by grief. Thus, the elegy vertically maps two separate communities: one spiritually transcendent, blissful, and dead; the other earthbound, dejected, and alive.

In "On the Death of a young Lady of Five Years of Age," Wheatley reinscribed this vertical line. The poem opens by narrating the journey of the dead girl, Nancy, to heaven:

> FROM dark abodes to fair ethereal light
> Th' enraptur'd innocent has wing'd her flight;
> On the kind bosom of eternal love
> She finds unknown beatitude above.[31]

In heaven Nancy "feels the iron hand of pain no more," and Wheatley even imagines the words by which she requests to learn a new "language":

> "Thou, Lord, whom I behold with glory crown'd,
> By what sweet name, and in what tuneful sound
> Wilt thou be prais'd? Seraphic pow'rs are faint
> Infinite love and majesty to paint.
> To thee let all their grateful voices raise,
> And saints and angels join their songs of praise."[32]

Nancy's arrival in heaven inspires her to sing hymns to God, and she speaks with humility and gratitude. Meanwhile, Nancy's parents engage in "fruitless groans," "tears," and "plaintive moans" and feel a "rising tumult of the soul."[33] Questioning their selfish grief, the poem advises them to think about Nancy's "bliss" and "restrain [their] tears." It closes by reminding them that God "gives and takes away" and that they can join their daughter in heaven through a Christian life:

> Eye him in all, his holy name revere,
> Upright your actions, and your hearts sincere,
> Till having sail'd through life's tempestuous sea,
> And from its rocks, and boist'rous billows free,
> Yourselves, safe landed on the blissful shore,
> Shall join your happy babe to part no more.

In this elegy, death is a journey through which the deceased child understands God and joins a heavenly neighborhood of similar discernment. Nancy "behold[s]" God's "glory"; death gives her a divine view and, by extension, divine comprehension. She learns God's "sweet name" and the "tuneful sound" with which one should praise God. She joins with others' "grateful voices" in singing to God's glory. Wheatley's elegy calls on the parents "to imitate [Nancy's] language" and thereby transform their loss into an acquisition of spiritual knowledge and community before their own deaths. Yet the word *imitate* suggests the fruitlessness of such a call; their utterances will be mere imitations of Nancy's truer strains. Thus, their sounds of lamentation continue, and Wheatley adds the alternative consolation that at least they can live a Christian life and ascend to their daughter in heaven, thereby not only reuniting with her but also learning for themselves what Nancy now knows.

Wheatley's "A Funeral POEM on the Death of C. E. an Infant of Twelve Months" follows a similar structure, describing first the infant's experience of the joy of death and then the parents' selfish grief, finally closing with a consolatory exhortation. Like Nancy, Charles Eliot acquires new knowledge when he dies:

> THROUGH airy roads he wings his instant flight
> To purer regions of celestial light;
> Enlarg'd he sees unnumber'd systems roll,
> Beneath him sees the universal whole,
> Planets on planets run their destin'd round,
> And circling wonders fill the vast profound.
> Th' ethereal now, and now th' empyreal skies
> With growing splendors strike his wond'ring eyes[.][34]

His new knowledge is expansive and grows as he gets ever more distant from earth and gains ever more perspective. As a result of his shift in understanding, he receives an angelic welcome. Like Nancy's parents, his engage in "unavailing moan[s]," and their "pensive bosoms" "heave" with "groan[s]."[35] The poem reasons that, even if he could return, he would not.[36] His death has endowed him with a "superior air" and immunity to the temptation of earthly glories, including "thrones and dominions."

By depicting a wordless and helpless infant as a self-assured being after death, Wheatley casts death as an irrevocably transfigurative journey that remains spiritually unintelligible to those who have not yet traversed the same route. In her poem, death severs parents and children, but the pain of that separation weighs only on the living. Although the poem on Charles's death was ostensibly intended to console the parents, it portrays such efforts as futile—for instance, when it describes a nightly ritual in which the parents fancy their child's return:

> ["]Delightful infant, nightly visions give
> Thee to our arms, and we with joy receive,
> We fain would clasp the *Phantom* to our breast,
> The *Phantom* flies, and leaves the soul unblest."[37]

Even in their dreams, the parents cannot "clasp" their "phantom" child. Replicating their loss each night, they remain bound by sorrow. In describing their state as "unblest," the poem marks their grief as an impediment to their relationship with God. To parents who lack knowledge and the ability to gain it, the only alternative consolation the elegy can provide is the expectation that someday they too will die and their cycle of daily bereavement will end. Only then will they be blessed.

Elsewhere, the poem chastises Charles's parents who, through "thoughtless wishes, and prepost'rous love," seek to "tear him from the realms above."[38] The parents are simultaneously cruel in their desires and ridiculous in their emotions. Recall that the elegy for Nancy characterizes her parents similarly. Caught up by their bereavement, they express "fruitless groans," "tears," and "plaintive moans" and feel a "rising tumult of the soul."[39] In both instances, mourners are impotent at communication and exchange.

It was in that unbridgeable distance *between* mourners and the dead that Wheatley, properly neither, located herself.[40] The territory she mapped for her persona was a space of discernment and authority from which she could relay the otherwise incomprehensible experiences of the dead and rebuke and instruct their mourners. Her claim to discernment and authority arose from the resonance between death's vertical journey and enslavement's horizontal journey. She herself had undergone a transfiguring dislocation, crossing the Atlantic in "pinions," though hers took the form of iron fetters rather than the feathered wings of Mrs. Boylston's son.[41] Like Nancy, Wheatley had felt "the iron hand of pain"; she had arrived at a new home and asked "by what . . . name" she should call her master; and she had learned a new "language."[42] Wheatley had "sail'd through . . . [a] tempestuous sea," escaped "rocks" and winds, and arrived safely. Here, the elegy evinces a slippage between the transspheric vertical and the transoceanic horizontal, one that recurs when the poet compares heaven to a "blissful shore" in the elegy for Nancy and elsewhere, as in "On the Death of J. C. an Infant," terms it "the port of happiness."[43]

Wheatley invites a sustained comparison between herself and Charles Eliot when she speaks for him. A "raptur'd" Charles Eliot declares on his arrival in heaven:

> "Thanks to my God, who snatch'd me to the skies,
> E'er vice triumphant had possess'd my heart,
> E'er yet the tempter had beguil'd my heart,
> E'er yet on sin's base actions I was bent,

E'er yet I knew temptation's dire intent;
E'er yet the lash for horrid crimes I felt,
E'er vanity had led my way to guilt[."][44]

By placing the word *snatch* in Charles's mouth and using it to describe his death, Wheatley indicated that he and she were alike in their experience of being snatched from their parents' homes.[45] The anaphora in the next several lines—"E'er vice," "E'er yet," "E'er vanity"—suggests their prominence and importance, as does their enclosure in quotation marks. By means of the phrases "vice triumphant," "the tempter," "beguil[ment]," "sin," and "temptation's dire intent," the first four anaphoric lines imply that childhood was a time of prelapsarian innocence. However, Charles and, by extension, Wheatley were not like Adam and Eve. They did not willfully disobey God, and they did not fall, which *snatch* underscores by shifting agency away from them. They acquired knowledge of salvation instead of sin. Wheatley marked the end of the fourth anaphoric line with a semicolon and then concluded the anaphora with two more lines. In the fifth—"E'er yet the lash for horrid crimes I felt"—she both augmented the sense of relief she believed that Charles's parents should feel about their son's escape from a sinful life and suggested her own difference. She had feared and perhaps felt the lash despite having committed no crime, an experience that the end placement of commas and a semicolon visually accentuates.

Wheatley's "On being brought from AFRICA to AMERICA" offers a parallel to Charles's speech. Whereas he praises his death as a merciful pardon from a life of sin and pain, she reports:

'TWAS mercy brought me from my *Pagan* land,
Taught my benighted soul to understand
That there's a God, that there's a *Saviour* too:
Once I redemption neither sought nor knew.[46]

She suggests that coerced transportation delivered her from a spiritually ignorant life with no promise of salvation. Like Charles, she spoke to the inhabitants of her new home, but unlike him, she had no intermediary who could perceive her words and transmit her message back to her mourning family. Her parents did not have the partial solace of knowing that her abduction had resulted in spiritual salvation and would have been aware only of her absence and captivity. To them, she was all but dead.

Wheatley's implied social death recalls historian Orlando Patterson's field-transforming contention that natal alienation is a constituent element of slavery.[47] Explaining the social death of natal alienation, he notes, "Not only was the slave denied all claims on, and obligations to, his parents and living blood relations but, by extension, all such claims and obligations on his more remote ancestors and on his descendants."[48] Slave communities did retain and develop revised cultural practices and kinship structures in the Americas, especially in plantation economies, so it is oversimplification to say that enslaved persons' understood themselves as "truly . . . genealogical isolate[s]."[49] Yet Patterson's schema still speaks to Wheatley's situation. When she was about seven years old, she was forcibly brought to Boston, a city whose population was 95 percent white.[50] There is no indication that any member of her family arrived with her. Though an indentured servant also resided in the Wheatley household as late as 1766, the Massachusetts tax valuation list of 1771 notes only one "servant for life" in the Wheatley household.[51]

As her poems collectively suggest, Wheatley was able to write these elegies and proffer fruitless consolation to the parents because her enslavement had given her an affinity to their dead children. She rerouted the parent-child bond through herself, mapping the living and the dead as distinct neighborhoods. In turning to her, white Bostonians called on one of their most abject neighbors—an enslaved African girl—to mediate their performance of mourning, even as they foreclosed the consolatory practices of the city's black residents. In the elegies, however, they become the abject neighbors, she the voice that withholds consolation by noting their affective immobility. Earthly funerary rites—bells, groans, procession, burial—are mere shadows of the joyous songs, "airy roads," and ecstatic unions shared by the neighborhood of the dead. Wheatley's elegies participate in the communal reconstitution required in death's aftermath, but the neighborhood they imagine for their white audience retains grief and loss. Only by virtue of her own forced migration could Wheatley witness that other neighborhood where consolation and transcendence were possible.

Wheatley's Consolatory Message to Her Black Neighbors

Early American elegies spanned the performative and the material. In addition to adorning biers and being read aloud at gravesides, they were read aloud in homes and at churches. Mourners kept printed copies as mementos, and they appeared as broadsides and in periodicals.[52] While other components of mourning rituals—the sound of the bells, the sight of the procession—might passively involve strangers or even briefly enfold them, the performative and material circulation of an elegy could traverse and extend the temporal and geographic network of participation.

Perhaps the democratic and familiar nature of the elegy explains its appeal to a range of early black authors, not just to Wheatley.[53] Through the elegy, they were able to serve a community from which they were otherwise barred. David Shields explains, "To enroll the community in its act of memory [on behalf of the deceased], the elegy amplified the community's self-regard, identifying it as the place whence great persons emerged and for whose benefit they labored."[54] An elegy offered a black poet an entrée into a desirable community, and its circulation might initiate a parallel community. As Max Cavitch writes in *American Elegy,* "an occasional form, commonly devoted to detailing its subjects' lives and connections, elegy sometimes helped to restore a sense of the severed affiliations from which blacks suffered disproportionately."[55] Due to the performative nature of elegies' circulation, both literate and nonliterate black persons encountered black-authored elegies and could imagine themselves to be members of a black elegiac community. Unwittingly, white subjects, patrons, and agents of circulation facilitated and witnessed the performance of elegiac surrogacy, thus enhancing the process. "The key to understanding how performance worked *within* a culture," Joseph Roach avers, "is to illuminate the process of surrogation as it operated *between* the participating cultures. The key, in other words, is to understand how circum-Atlantic societies, confronted with revolutionary circumstances for which few precedents existed, have invented themselves by performing their pasts in the presence of others."[56] Black-authored elegies could initiate, repair, or affirm a black community, one made more substantial because it was being "perform[ed] in the presence" of a white audience.

Enslaved people were excluded from circumatlantic communication networks, an exclusion made more palpable by the way in which Wheatley's circumstances resonated with the communication gap between the children and parents that she limned in her elegies. As Stephanie Smallwood reminds us, the Middle Passage was disorienting, not only because of the strangeness of open water but also because of the "general impossibility of . . . informational feedback."[57] For most newly enslaved Africans, the Middle Passage was a voyage into the unknown; they did not have preestablished knowledge of their destination from letters, friendly mariners, or returning emigrants, as their free white counterparts did when they left Europe. For slaves, there was no way to send word home.

But death might offer them a chance to send a message back. Evidence suggests that enslaved Africans throughout the New World shared a "belief in the transmigration of the soul back to Africa" after death.[58] Funerals were often "merr[y]" occasions, something white Bostonians and other Euro-Americans frequently found shocking.[59] This shared belief echoes a common African perception of permeability in the boundary between life and death. Vincent Brown describes "supernatural inquests" among circumatlantic black communities in which the corpse was questioned about death during the funeral procession.[60] Anthropologists and historians of African cultures offer another example of the soul's liminality: certain African cultures in West Africa held two burials for the dead, one primary and one secondary. Between the two rituals, according to historian Thomas McCaskie, the deceased were "detached from the social" but capable of intervening, often maliciously, in human affairs.[61] For a black diasporic population, communicating and moving across the barriers between America and Africa might become briefly possible at a funeral.[62] Death was an opportunity to restore the ancestral connections disrupted by the social death of enslavement.

In vocalizing the grief of her white audience, Wheatley gave voice to her black neighbors; she proffered a new territory for their imaginative inhabitation, offsetting the dislocation of enslavement. Her elegies invited the diasporic black audience of Boston and its environs to sort their relations into two neighborhoods and reside in the conduit between the living and the dead. The conduit's permeability mirrors the permeability between life and death that many Africans identified between and during funerals. Her dead subjects' blissful and transcendent discernment might have furnished solace to her black neighbors, a consoling and uplifting message about their own status.

The consolatory invitation is most clearly borne out in "To the Honourable T. H. Esq; on the Death of his Daughter." Written to slave trader Thomas Hubbard on the death of his adult daughter, Thankfull

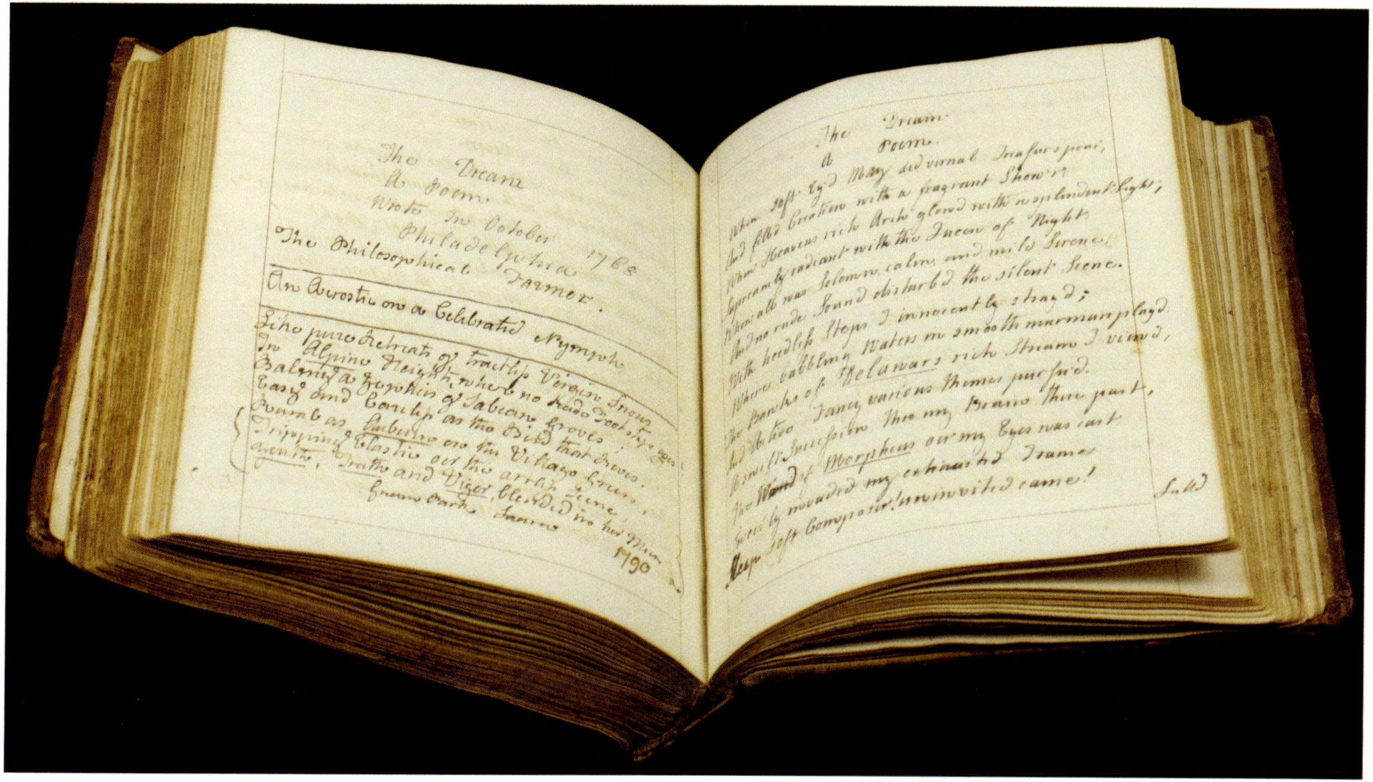

PLATE 1. The first page of Elizabeth Graeme Fergusson's "The Dream." Not one to waste space, she appears to have later transcribed another poem, "An Acrostic on a Celebrated Nymph," onto the blank page below the title. The nymph's name is "LIBERTY." Image courtesy of the Library Company of Philadelphia.

Nations Amies et Ennemies des Tchicachas.

Ces Figures ont étées Tirées, D'aprés l'original qui etoient Sur une Peau, que Mingo-ouma Grand chef de Guerre de la Nation Tchikachas a donné au Capitaine de Pakama, pour apporter a Sa Nation, et aux François afin qu'ils Vissent le Nombre de leurs amis et aussy leurs Ennemis, les premiers Sont Marquez en Noir et les Seconds en Rouge. 12

Les Ronds marques des Villages et Nations Entieres.

A. Les Anglois, B. Les Kaoüitas, C. Les Kachétas, D. Les Vtchiré, E. Les Toucoulou charakis, F. Les Charakis, ceux cy parlent une langue Differente des E. G. Les Affasquez Abékas, H. Les Alybamonts, I. La Mobille ou les François, K. Les Tchakts,

L. Toute la Nation Tchikachas qui est Blanche en dedans mais d'on les Environs ne Sont que Sang: Elle est blanche parcequ'ils pretendent qu'il ne Sort que de bonnes parolles de leur Villages, mais que ceux des environs perdent l'Esprit en ne l'écoutant point, ce qui rend ses Terres Teinte de Sang. M. Les Villages et Nations Heuronne Irquoise, et ceux qu'ils Appelent Nantouague. N. Les Villages et Nation des Tamarois Peanquichias &c. O. Les Arkansas, ou Okappa. P. Les Chakchouma Sur lesquels ils doivent Aller Frapper incessament Q. Ce Sont des chemins de Guerre qui ne Se rendent pas, jusque au Villages, par ce qu'ils esperent qu'ils deviendrons blancs, en faisant la paix avec ceux vers ou ils tendent R. Riviere des Alybamonts et chemin de cette Nation à la Mobille il n'arrive pas jusqua la Mobille, par ce qu'ils disent qu'ils noseroient y Aller, mais que Malgrez cela est blanc pour nous, S. Chemin blancs qui vont chez leurs Amis, T. Chemins de Guerre, V. Chemins de chasse des Alybamons. blancs: 7bre 1737.

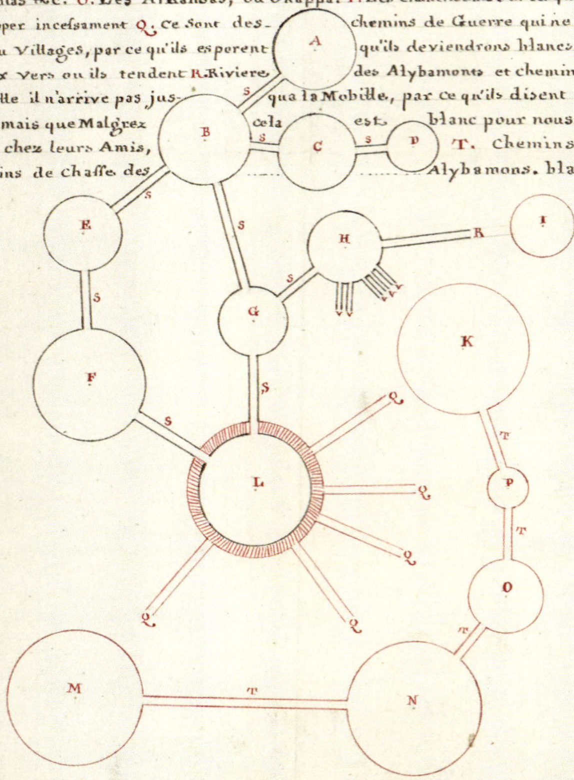

Plate 3. Mourning ring for John Gray, the infant son of John and Mary Otis Gray of Boston. He died in 1763, six days after his birth. The ring is made from gold, enamel, crystal, gold foil, and hair, and its inscription reads, "J:GRAY OB.17.SEP.1763. AE 6D." Image courtesy of the Massachusetts Historical Society.

Plate 2 (*opposite*). The 1737 map "Nations amies et ennemies des Tchikachas." The map represents an Alabama war leader's understanding of Chickasaw military topography and was redrawn and transcribed by Alexandre de Batz, a French colonist. It is worth noting that de Batz enclosed the circle "A"—"Les Anglois" or "The English"—with text. A possible translation of the key for "L" is "The entire Chickasaw nation are a people who are white inside, but the surrounding areas are nothing but blood; their nation is white, because they claim, that only good words come out of their village(s), but that those of surrounding areas lose their wits by not listening to them, and this makes the land dyed with blood." Image courtesy of the French Archives Nationales d'Outre-Mer. FR ANOM. Aix-en-Provence (FR CAOM F3/290/12). All rights reserved.

Plate 4. Theodor De Bry, *XVIII. Repraesentatio Ceremoniarum, Quibus in Sepeliendis Defunctis Utuntur,* an engraving from part 6, *India Orientalis,* of De Bry's multipart *America.* The image offers a "representation of ceremonies, which are used in the burial of the deceased" in West Africa. It first appeared in Pieter de Marees's *Description and Historical Account of the Gold Kingdom of Guinea,* originally published in Dutch in 1602. De Bry used Marees's book as the textual and visual basis for this part of *America* (with some fascinating changes; see, for example, Groesen, *Representations,* 191). In English, the Latin caption reads, "We wanted to show with this image with what rituals they accompany their dead and in what manner they are accustomed to commit them to the earth. A. is the tomb, set up, as they themselves report, with every furnishing for the deceased. B. shows the procession of women, leading and accompanying the funeral; those who precede the funeral, playing wash basins and other instruments, sing and dance; the others follow the funeral with much weeping, producing grief and sorrow. C. shows how the women crawl in and out through the tomb, and, when the deceased has been put into it, how it is a covering in some way for the earth. D. shows how, when the burial has been completed, they then enter the sea and, once their bodies have been properly purified, they then go home and refresh themselves with food and drink." Image courtesy of the Huntington Library.

PLATE 5. Mohegan covered basket, plain-woven ash and oak, 11" by 18⅛" by 12¾", ca. 1815. Note the pathway that leads up and then turns back down to the opposite corner. The small dots alongside signal the presence and movement of Mohegan persons. Image courtesy of the Connecticut Historical Society.

PLATE 6. Prudence Punderson, *The First, Second, and Last Scene of Mortality,* ca. 1776–83. Image courtesy of the Connecticut Historical Society.

Plate 7. Image from *Kiki Smith: Sojourn,* an installation at the Brooklyn Museum (2010). Gallery 1A featured *Annunciation* (2008, cast aluminum sculpture and wooden chair), *Messenger II* (2008, cast aluminum, white and yellow gold leaf), *Visitation III* (2007, ink, graphite, colored pencil, mica, and collage on Nepal paper), and *Visitation of the Bird I* (2007, ink, graphite, colored pencil, mica, glitter, and collage on Nepal paper). Before entering gallery 1A, the first of the exhibit, visitors pass Prudence Punderson's *The First, Second, and Last Scene of Mortality* (plate 7) as well as an introduction to the exhibit, which includes this reference to Punderson's piece: "Smith's imagination was fired by a chance encounter with a reproduction of . . . *The First, Second, and Last Scene of Mortality*. . . . In this remarkable piece, Punderson outlines the course of a woman's life, with scenes of birth and death flanking a remarkable rendering of a young woman independently engaged in creative pursuits." Image courtesy of Brooklyn Museum Archives. Records of the Department of Painting and Sculpture: Exhibitions. *Kiki Smith: Sojourn.* [02/12/2010–09/12/2010]. Installation view.

PLATE 8. Kiki Smith, *Her Bouquet* (2007–8; ink on Nepal paper with glass glitter, lithographic crayon, and silk tissue; oil paint on mouth-blown clear antique glass with white and yellow gold leaf; two works on Nepal paper). Note the three botanical images as well as the bouquets held by the two figures. This botanical proliferation recalls Punderson's needlework and suggests possibilities for the incomplete sketch at the center of her work. What would the completed sketch have looked like? © Kiki Smith, courtesy Pace Gallery.

PLATE 9. Image from of *Kiki Smith: Sojourn,* an installation at the Brooklyn Museum (2010). Gallery 7 featured *Closed Coffin (on table)* (2008, ink on Nepal paper with graphite and lithographic crayon), *Open Coffin (on table)* (2008, ink, graphite, and lithographic crayon on Nepal paper), *Heute (Now)* (2008, wood, lamp glass, coffin, drop-leaf table, ten dandelion puffs made of glass), and *Mortal* (2007, suite of woodblock prints on Tanbo paper). The tops of the glass dandelions are just visible inside the wooden coffin. Image courtesy of Brooklyn Museum Archives. Records of the Department of Painting and Sculpture: Exhibitions. *Kiki Smith: Sojourn.* [02/12/2010–09/12/2010]. Installation view.

Leonard, it portrays her transfiguration from bereavement to transcendence. Previously, Wheatley had written Leonard an elegy on the death of her husband. Now it is her father's "bosom" that is "rack[ed]" with "incessant woe" while Leonard's persistent grief over the loss of her husband has finally ended:

> She unreluctant flies to see no more
> Her dear-lov'd parents on earth's dusky shore:
> Impatient heav'n's resplendent goal to gain,
> She with swift progress cuts the azure plain,
> Where grief subsides, where changes are no more,
> And life's tumultuous billows cease to roar;
> She leaves her earthly mansion for the skies,
> Where new creations feast her wond'ring eyes.[63]

As it continues, the elegy alludes even more directly to Leonard's pre- and post-death affective state: "She, who late wish'd that [her husband] might return, / Has ceas'd to languish, and forgot to mourn."[64] The experience of forced dislocation can be so massive and powerful that one "forg[ets]" to grieve.

All around the Atlantic, diasporic black communities were turning to death to envision a vibrant post-enslavement, post-transportation future. Even before arriving in the New World, these communities were no strangers to the use of funeral processions (see plate 4). These communities, especially in the South, decorated burial sites with objects that often symbolized water, such as shells and jugs, thereby interpreting the Middle Passage's watery graves not as individual and racial inconsequentiality but as the first instances of a collective practice that honored the beginnings available in endings.[65] In colonial New York City, black residents built a cemetery on the outskirts of town that has commemorated their dead for centuries and that, since its rediscovery almost two decades ago, has generated a new community from the descendants of those interred.[66] In Newport, Philadelphia, and Boston, the desire to properly bury black bodies was "a motivating force behind the organization of [African American] mutual aid societies."[67] Likewise, Wheatley's poems demarcated a communal presence for her region's otherwise dislocated black mourners. They invited her black neighbors to read their particularity as a transfiguring experience and transcendent discernment. The elegies rearranged affiliation in the geographic neighborhood and asked black Christians to reside in a virtual neighborhood with Wheatley. As her black neighbors heard the poems read and shared what they had heard with others, the elegies became part of the technology of communal reconstitution, a funeral process in verse to substitute for the lost and prohibited funeral processions of Africa and urban America.

To speak of Wheatley's contemporaneous black neighbors is to speak of something verifiable and substantial. There were several black persons who possessed and read Wheatley's works. She corresponded with and sent book copies to Obour Tanner, a black Christian woman in Newport, Rhode Island.[68] While living with his master in Hartford, Connecticut, Jupiter Hammon read her writings and published verse in response. In a poem addressed to Wheatley, he mirrored her transoceanic and transspheric juxtaposition of enslavement and death.[69] She wrote a poem to Scipio Moorhead, a black artist living in Boston, who probably made the portrait of her that continues to be circulated.[70] Black servants who lived in the homes of her elegiac subjects' families and friends likely heard Wheatley's poems read aloud as part of the informal mourning rituals. Their masters may have hung memorial copies on their walls. A number of her elegies, including her poems to and about Thankfull Leonard, appeared as broadsides and were printed in newspapers in Boston, Newport, Philadelphia, and London.[71] Some print shops had black workers who may have assisted with typesetting and engraving.[72] In other words, even black persons from households without a direct interest in Wheatley's elegies may have heard her poems read aloud, and some may have been involved in the production of her work.

New England's black population was tightly clustered: during the latter half of the eighteenth century, at least 900 lived in Boston; at least 1,000 lived in Hartford County, Connecticut; and at least 1,200 lived in Newport.[73] Thus, it seems probable that her poems were read during black gatherings. Tanner most likely shared Wheatley's poems at the evangelical prayer meetings that she and several hundred black residents attended weekly in Newport.[74] This large black audience was capable of experiencing her poems as performative and material acts and envisioning themselves as part of another, transcendent neighborhood. Distributed as manuscripts and printed texts as well as by hand and word of mouth, they were part of a relational publication practice, their exchange coterminous with neighborhood intimacies, signaling particularity through form and circulation.

Comprehending Visions of the Black Atlantic

In presenting enslavement as deathlike in that it resulted in divine knowledge and transcendence over earthly concerns, did Wheatley undermine the emancipatory message expressed elsewhere in her writings?[75] If she cast herself as superior and authoritative through her affinity with the dead, was she celebrating her enslavement? In offering a consolatory message that encouraged her black neighbors to transfigure their experience of forced dislocation into spiritual transcendence, did she bifurcate those neighbors into those with memories of transportation and those without, those who had converted to Christianity and those who had not? While these questions are complex and discomfiting, we should remember that Wheatley and her poetic persona are distinct from one another. Moreover, her poetry is firm about the immorality of those who enslave.[76] Its emancipatory message often rests on the view that infringing on another's freedom, either for political or economic reasons, is an act of tyranny and cruelty. As Wheatley wrote in "To the Right Honourable WILLIAM, Earl of DARTMOUTH," when she imagined her father's loss upon her enslavement, what else could she do "but pray / Others may never feel tyrannic sway"?[77]

Notably, Wheatley's revised geography of mourning and affiliation articulated with a circumatlantic evangelical network of patrons and print. She made her name with an opportune elegy on Whitefield's death and furthered her reputation through her purposeful acquisition of the patronage of Selina Hastings, Countess of Huntingdon. She publicized that patronage by dedicating her book to Huntingdon.[78] As Vincent Carretta contends, "Whitefield and Huntingdon linked Phillis Wheatley to the larger transatlantic network of evangelical Christians."[79] Although one might read these connections as a way of enfolding Wheatley into the evangelical network, one might also note the evangelical sanction that such associations afforded to her communal map.

Wheatley capitalized on this sanction to support a prophetic vision of violent redemption in her scriptural interpretation, "Isaiah LXIII. 1–8." The poem, like its biblical source, uses the metaphor of a winepress to envision the approach of a figure adorned in clothing stained "purple" by a bloody trampling of God's enemies.[80] The figure claims the victory as entirely his own —"Mine was the act"—and announces that his actions "aton[e]" for others' "vices."[81] Adding details not present in scripture, Wheatley describes the battle scene and recounts how "beneath his feet the prostrate troops were spread, /And round him lay the dying, and the dead." She concludes by reassuring her reader that God's people have nothing to fear from this violent avenger:

> Against thy [God's] Zion though her foes may rage,
> And all their cunning, all their strength engage,
> Yet she serenely on thy bosom lies,
> Smiles at their arts, and all their force defies.

Like a child or a lover, the bloodthirsty Zion lies safely and peacefully in God's arms. She does not fear the antipathy and plots of her enemies and seems to anticipate their brutal destruction.

Wheatley's choice of this passage may seem odd. In the King James version, the meaning of the original is somewhat opaque, a jarring juxtaposition of carnage and "lovingkindnesses." Yet in his widely read eighteenth-century biblical commentary, Matthew Henry explains that Isaiah's vision is but a "Specimen" of other "Victories," foremost being one "obtain'd by the Grace of God in Christ, over our spiritual Enemies."[82] Thus, the passage may have attracted Wheatley precisely because it imagines God's vengeance against those who would deny God and offers a site, as William Scheick argues, for the "displacement of her anger toward those who have enslaved her race."[83] Moreover, she was not the first evangelical author to select this passage. In 1687, British clergyman John Norris poetically interpreted it, Henry wove Norris's poem into his exposition, and John and Charles Wesley revised and expanded on it for their collection *Hymns and Sacred Poems.*[84] In interpreting and extending this source, Wheatley was engaging in a spiritual conversation about Christian deliverance and offering an alternative vision of violent consolation and redemption. She invested Isaiah's prophecy with immediacy for a dislocated community of black Christians, suggesting that they shared a redeemed future.

Such moments of exclusive redemption clarify the nature of the new neighborhood mapped by Wheatley's elegies for children. Black particularity and consolation in that territory was predicated on both a conversion to Christianity and forced migration. Only those who had shed their "Pagan land" and "benighted souls" during their coerced dislocation could reside between a blissful Christian heaven and a community of bereaved mourners; only they might be redeemed with the blood of Christ. In arranging her territory through a markedly black

Christian vision, Wheatley channeled the revolutionary potential of a distinct black community. Anticipating violent redemption, she moved away from a slave uprising toward a burgeoning black theology movement that resonated with the work of other evangelicals.

Joanna Brooks aligns such theology with a Lazarus motif of resurrection and regeneration. In *American Lazarus,* she identifies the "separatist impulses" that infused the work of evangelical black preachers such as John Marrant, Richard Allen, and Absalom Jones.[85] Like Wheatley, "their pioneering contributions to American literature came about in connection with this broader regeneration, and they reveal[ed] how religious formulas such as conversation, revival, and resurrection answered the alienating and mortifying effects of slavery, colonialism, and racial oppression." Wheatley's vision of neighborhoods delineated distinct but interconnected communities that redeemed an inescapable history of coercion by suggesting that black persons' forced dislocation might mark them as spiritually favored.[86] She presaged the separatist parishes that arose later in the century and read themselves as "special witnesses to and emblems of [God's] overruling power" by locating distinct and favored neighborhoods of black Christians in an extensive evangelical Christian geography.[87] The fact that her elegies named only white mourners and their dead suggests that they were the type to the antitype of black Christians, who could redeem their history of enslavement in a new neighborhood.

Predicated as it was on *un*freedom of movement, the redemptive promise of Wheatley's vision was available to other bound individuals. White apprentices and indentured servants, Native persons living in Euro-American territories: they, too, might have read her acts of textual and circulatory publication. Her work encouraged a conceptual reversal of bondedness. It was a mark of spiritual authority in the present moment rather than a sign of inferiority, deferred promise, or uncertainty. Having reimagined spiritual favor, her practice of relational publication initiated a potentially fluid proliferation of virtual neighborhoods at the nexus of white, black, and Native Christians.

John Marrant's work shares Wheatley's vast view, and his comprehensive vision exemplifies a redemptive theology for the bound. Before arriving in Birchtown, Nova Scotia, in 1785, he had experienced a number of circumatlantic circulations, both chosen and coerced. Born free in New York in 1755, Marrant lived in several southern colonies as a child.

His memoir reports that, during his youth in South Carolina, he was captured by the Cherokees and that he was impressed by the British navy during the American Revolution.[88] After the war, he immigrated to London, where he was ordained by the Countess of Huntingdon's evangelical circle, known as the Huntingdon Connexion. In sailing to Birchtown, an all-black settlement of Loyalist refugees, he joined a community that, like him, had faced serial and often coerced unmoorings.

Once in Birchtown, Marrant established a Huntingdonian church. His message of regeneration depended on a visionary rhetoric of circulation such as the one in his 1786 funeral sermon for parishioner John Lock, which begins with the biblical verse Philippians 1:21: "For me to live, is Christ; and to die, is gain." To instruct Lock's mourners about living a deliberately Christian life, Marrant explained that the verse was delivered by the apostle Paul, who "labour[ed] to shew the Philippians the grand design of the Christian living in Christ, and what shall be the gain of them that live a holy life."[89] Marrant glorified Paul for being "willing to leave this body, and [see] in the clearest light what he should gain in so doing. Yet, seem[ing] to have a sympathising feeling for those of his fellow-creatures who has their face Zion forward." Marrant painted Paul as a figure who comprehended simultaneously mortal and eternal life. Yet even as he located Paul between the two, he described the "fellow-creatures" that Paul left as "fac[ing] . . . forward," a view he could have seen only by facing *backward.* Marrant continued to convey the perplexities of the divine through similar linguistic reversals. Elsewhere in the sermon, for example, he related Lock's dying message about his children: "he said I leave them in the hands of that God whom I hope to see soon, and before the sun goes down to day. So he bid us all farewell, and saying, Lord Jesus Christ into thy hands I commit my spirit; and so gave up his soul into the hands of that God who gave it."[90] As Marrant explained, Lock left his children *behind* with God in order to go *to* God. He *has given* his "soul" to the one who "*gave*" it.

Marrant's theological wordplay presents redemption as a time when journeys continue but the confusion and pain of the coerced circulation experienced in life resolves itself through the transcendent comprehension acquired through death. He tells his audience: "The divine harmony and connection of the whole be out of sight [now]; but when believers come to 'walk through the valley of the shadow of death,' all darkness will be scattered before the meridian sun, and the beauty and harmony of the divine perfections, will be seen in the clearest light. This is reserved for heaven, where [believers] shall see unclouded glory, have dark scriptures made plain, seeming contradictions cleared up, and reconciled."[91] The word *reconciled* suggests that the expansive view and clarity achieved in ascending to heaven is communally and individually restorative, as believers become reconciled with those that have preceded them and to their "shadow[ed]" histories.

In the interim, Marrant was delivering to a living congregation his sermon about the clarity that awaits believers after death. Moreover, his sermon was arguing that ministerial clarity must precede publication: "what reproach soever [true Ministers] may suffer, for espousing and publishing [God's gospel and interest], yet they are so sensible of the grand design, carried on for the discovery of the glory of the divine character, in the salvation of sinners, that they account it their highest honour, to own and profess, preach and defend it."[92] Publication—written, oral, performative—facilitates the establishment of a redeemed community that will achieve its own clarity after death. And Marrant certainly did publicize: as John Saillant and Joanna Brooks remind us in their anthology of eighteenth-century black writings, he was "one of the early black Atlantic's most prolific authors."[93] This particular sermon was self-published in London, along with his *Journal.* Unlike the coerced circumatlantic circulation of black bodies, this self-directed circulation acted as a "reversion," to use Marrant's own term.[94] The past was translated into a new edition, and the ownership of that history reverted to its original owners. Thus, Marrant presented and disseminated a comprehensive vision of redemption that enfolded the past and the future, offering consolation and retribution for black Christians as well as others who sought to convert their bondedness into transcendence.

Wheatley's comprehensive vision was bloodier than the one in Marrant's sermon, perhaps because, unlike him, she did not see a return to Africa as viable. Whereas Marrant, to quote Saillant and Brooks, viewed a "migration to Africa as a transfiguration accomplished by dying to the racist and slaveholding New World and being reborn in Africa," Wheatley refused to return, seeing such a journey as isolating, "hazardous," and humiliating.[95] The matrix of neighborhoods that she mapped through her elegies was to some extent fictive and hidden, and that tension between a consoling self-identification as transcendentally discerning and the ongoing effects of enslavement darkened her vision. To sustain consolation and perform relational publication, she wrote and rewrote her elegiac verse, which was then circulated and recirculated, read and reread.

Nevertheless, her ability to make public her vision of such a community may have facilitated its later manifestation in the physical geography of the Americas. Like Coosaponakeesa's repurposing of missionary circulatory practices alongside Native kinship and colonial trade networks, Wheatley's relational publication practice combined elegies, mourning rituals, material exchange, and evangelical print. Her practice retained and reimagined the particularities of her region's neighborly affiliations. The circulation of her work beyond her geographic neighborhoods itself became a medium that black Christians comprehended and read in a way that insisted on the distinctiveness of themselves and their experiences.[96] Wheatley's poems, most tangibly in print, manifest a vision of multiplicitous and multiplying neighborhoods wherein particularized black spiritual authority held sway. They circulated her articulation of prophecies that redeem oppression through violent deliverance. They offered a model for affiliation that other bound communities could claim for themselves. Beyond the writing itself, the circumatlantic journeys of her elegies emblematized a circulatory network that was altered and appropriated to enact a reversion of the traumatic history of coerced circulation.

Wheatley in Mourning

In March 1774, Phillis Wheatley wrote to her friend and reader Obour Tanner about the recent death of her former mistress, Susanna Wheatley:

> I have lately met with a great trial in the death of my mistress; let us imagine the loss of a Parent, Sister or Brother the tenderness of all these were united in her.—I was a poor little outcast & a stranger when she took me in: not only into her house but I presently became a sharer in her most tender affections. I was treated by her more like her child than her servant; no opportunity was left unimprov'd, of giving me the best of advice, but in terms how tender! how engaging! This I hope ever to keep in remembrance. Her exemplary life was a greater monitor than all her precepts and Instruction, thus we may observe of how much greater force example is than instruction. To alleviate our sorrows we had the satisfaction to se[e] her depart for the *upper* Courts of the Lord. Do, my dear friend, remember me & this family in your Closet, that this afflicting dispensation may be sanctify'd unto us.[97]

In this letter, Wheatley perhaps came closest to writing an elegy about someone whom she herself deeply mourned. In doing so, she abandoned her elegiac style and expressed something of her own grief, demonstrating her vulnerability and the limits of a poetic persona that claimed otherwise. Wheatley was not dead, and neither were her emotions. Thus, her vision of a transcendent neighborhood and its invitation to her black audience reflected the inevitable "inexact" "fit" of surrogates, to use Roach's terms.[98] Even as her work refigured the traumatic events of enslavement, it was a reminder of what had been irrevocably lost.

The death of Wheatley's beloved former mistress was only the first in a series of losses. John Wheatley, Susanna's husband, and Mary Wheatley Lathrop, their daughter, both died in 1778. Though the family had emancipated Phillis in October 1773, they had continued to support her; she lived with Lathrop in Providence after John Wheatley, a Loyalist, fled revolutionary Boston. With their deaths, she lost not only her adoptive family but also her literary patrons. Even though she continued to write and to publish in newspapers and broadsides, she could not find a publisher for a subsequent volume, and most of her writings from this period remain missing. Wheatley married John Peters in 1778, and the young couple, like most free black persons, soon found themselves in financial difficulties. She died six years later, in 1784, while her husband was probably "in prison for debt."[99] Her funeral took place near her home, and a procession may have traversed the neighborhood to the nearby Granary Burial Ground, the same cemetery that held the remains of Crispus Attucks and John and Susanna Wheatley.[100] I wonder if her mourners took the direct route and if the bells tolled.

In his introduction to Wheatley's writings, Vincent Carretta imagines an alternate biography: "Had she remained in London in 1773, Wheatley very probably would have found a publisher for her second volume. Interest in her work and her status as a woman writer of color certainly continued after her departure."[101] We can imagine the life she could have led, the role she could have played in Britain's abolition movement, the financial security and artistic virtuosity she could have attained, and the even richer archive she could have left. There is much to mourn. Yet as Wheatley's letter to Tanner intimates, imagining loss can be a generative act. Tanner was, like Wheatley, an enslaved African. When Wheatley wrote, "Let us imagine the loss of a Parent, Sister or Brother," she was referring to the correspondents' shared experience of bereavement and enslavement. Both could imagine such a loss all too well because they had already experienced it. In inviting Tanner to imagine her newest loss, Wheatley enfolded her former mistress into their history. Similarly, as her black audience read or heard her elegies, they received the same invitation: "let us imagine the loss." They transformed the isolation of loss into a collective act and perhaps, for a moment, forgot to mourn.

4
Unions of the Soul

"A MORE PERFECT UNION." These words from the first line of the U.S. Constitution collapse distinct political states into one, presenting the national future not as a break with the colonial past but as a refinement of affinities. The process, however, involved disunion as much as it did purification, on the grand scale of nations and the more intimate one of neighbors. When paired with the Constitution's elder brother, the Declaration of Independence, the concurrence of separation and clarification manifests textually. Indeed, the Declaration terminated other affiliatory documents—the colonial charters—and the war's conclusion and the Constitution's ratification guaranteed there would be no restoration.

In Pennsylvania, the stronghold of American Quakerism, the colonial charter was the same one granted to the religious visionary William Penn.[1] An oblique authorization for his "Holy Experiment," its forced nullification represented failure for the region's Friends, a loss of their promised land. For them, national union required excising fidelity to sectarian affiliation. Philadelphia revolutionaries, responding to Quaker pacifism, vilified Friends as Loyalist traitors: too loyal to England, too loyal to Quakerism.[2] Through exile, imprisonment, and fines, the revolution forcefully ended the Friends' gradual and at times willful relinquishment of regional authority.

A sisterhood of texts parallels the Declaration-Constitution fraternity. Using relational publication as refinement, it offsets the enervation of Quaker Pennsylvania and engenders a new neighborhood. Here, *refinement* refers to a process of incremental improvement, one of distillation and clarification. Recall that the Society of Friends depended organizationally on epistles.[3] Through the ritualized composition and exchange of texts, Meetings administered affiliation. While male Friends responded to the revolution by increasing the volume of their writing and situating their political stance in and beyond the religious community, certain women Friends refined a more insular and rigorous communal charter through poetic exchange, one that pertained to the particularized relations of a neighborhood. Foregrounding the material craft of composition, selection, and arrangement, they transposed the trauma of expulsion into a manuscript performance of proper affiliation. Such a neighborhood did not offer a more effective or egalitarian vision of an impersonal nation. Rather, it attested to the war's impious politics and banished enemies from a union reconstituted through the practice of transcription. These women replaced politics with intimate governance and with a vision of community bound by reciprocity, familiarity, and, above all, piety.

The locus of that parallel textual sisterhood is Milcah Martha Moore's commonplace book, a collection of 126 entries by others—often Friends—and selected, arranged, and transcribed by herself. Moore, a Delaware Valley Friend disowned for her ill-timed consanguineous marriage, remained unofficially active in the Society through her family connections, her husband's medical practice, and her continued Meeting attendance.[4] Long before the revolution, she prefigured the Society's abjured presence because she was simultaneously indispensable and excluded. In this commonplace book, kept during a period that roughly corresponds to the early revolution, we can trace the arrangement and circulation of her communal vision and its relation to her interlocutors.[5]

Commonplace books are compilations of texts that a single person has transcribed but typically not authored.[6] Transcribers include those textual moments that they find interesting, meaningful, amusing, or otherwise worth saving. For centuries, keeping a commonplace book, or commonplacing, was a component of education; many students were required to maintain a book, design its arrangement, or include specific texts. The goal was to demonstrate moral content and teach students organizational and handwriting skills. Such books also had a manifestly social goal, for compilers frequently circulated their manuscripts among friends and acquaintances. For Quakers, who valued a personal experience of God, the transcription of spiritual and instructional texts into a commonplace book was an appropriate activity, especially on the Sabbath. In a literary circle, the activity was a way to generate conversation, share ideas, and preserve the manuscript productions (some of them improvisational) of a salon or other belletristic gathering.

Most of the entries in Moore's commonplace book are poems that contemplate politics, community, religion, and friendship. Quakers Susanna Wright (1697–1785) and Hannah Griffitts (1727–1817), both unmarried and renowned for their unrelenting piety and prolific authorship, contributed roughly ninety entries. Elizabeth Graeme Fergusson, a non-Quaker salonnière who lived on the outskirts of Philadelphia, contributed a small but important subset.[7] The remainder are the compositions of relatives, other Friends, transatlantic luminaries, and anonymous poets. Thus, Moore's transcriptions drew on previous acts of textual exchange, by turns shaping and refining unions and excising unfriendliness and impiety.

A study of *Moore's Book*'s constitution of friendship illuminates how her cohort leveraged relational publication to counter the divisive turmoil of the American Revolution. The book was a product of interpersonal exchange and relied on relationality: relatives and friends were the authors and subjects of most entries. They and other relations serially circulated the original texts in person and in letters, at times making handwritten copies for simultaneous distribution, at times even publishing the works in print. Although a stranger or a newspaper reader might have been mystified by their pseudonymity, a neighborhood would have recognized that "Fidelia" was Griffitts, "Laura" was Fergusson. But the book relied on relationality in other, less visible ways. Moore assembled her chosen entries, juxtaposing and layering them into a vision of interpersonal dynamics in which pious exiles and outcasts become citizens and friends. Even as the revolution was violently dispersing neighbors, the book was gathering them anew. Like the Declaration-Constitution dyad, it was a material performance of a new community, materialized in residents' circulation and reading of the text. In this way, *Moore's Book* contrasts with Wheatley's elegies. The neighborhood of *Moore's Book* was mundane and singular, its territory held by presence and participation. Its consolation lay in its particularity and insularity rather than its transcendence.

A study of Moore's commonplace book and her literary circle reveals much about women's publication during the revolutionary period.[8] In explicating the causes of the revolution, scholars have exhaustively focused on the rise and power of print but rarely on women's manuscript culture. Like the belletristic productions of elite literary circles discussed in David Shields's groundbreaking *Civil Tongues and Polite Letters in British America, Moore's Book* exposes the aesthetics and "modes of communication" that "instructed politics in private society."[9] Yet because few scholars have examined the dynamics of political commentary and manuscript publication in religious communities, especially heterosocial ones foregrounding women's voices, *Moore's Book* tells us something new.[10] It attests to the persistence of sectarianism and an abiding concern with the retention and arrangement of particularity—a conversation anchored in relational publication and invigorated by a surge in republican print.

Words of Comfort

In meeting the hazards of isolation with relational publication, *Moore's Book* capitalized on a religious, regional, familial, and personal history. Indeed, Quakerism wielded textual composition and circulation as extensions of proximity, especially in times of crisis and geographic exigency. Its foundational genre, the epistle, transformed its followers' powerful but potentially divisive solitary spirituality into the fabric of religious affiliation. Generated as official reports between Meetings or composed by eminent Quakers, including a cohort of itinerant male and female transatlantic preachers, epistles were circulated widely; archived in the minutes of Meetings; and copied, excerpted, and forwarded. As the practice and archive of Friendship, they tangibly linked Meetings.

A faith with an essentially "positive view of mankind," Quakerism contends that all have the opportunity to experience salvation personally through the inward light of Christ.[11] Eighteenth-century Friends sought to remove any impediments to this direct, individual experience. As the noted seventeenth-century Friend Robert Barclay declared in his influential and frequently reprinted *Apology for the True Christian Divinity,* "every true Christian is a *Child,* a Friend, a *Disciple* of Christ."[12] For members of the Society, God, the ultimate friend, persists at the center; and the self-appellation *Friend* (unlike the epithet *Quaker*) insists on relationality through Christ.[13] It denies the fractional prospects of the Society's own theology.

Epistles were the medium of that denial, balancing singular experiences of Christ and the self-authentication of the inward light with the demands of corporation. It mediated separate and potentially isolating spiritual experiences through textual exchange. As Matthew Horn contends,

> Around the Quakers' sacred centre of the individual Quaker and the living voice of God, the Quakers constructed a ring of public texts that they could mine when they needed to find a binding, non-subjective yet collaborative authority to superimpose on deviant members. This authority of the peripheral text, being a coded authority, invited individuals to approach, interpret, and form the message and in doing so to fashion a canon that they would be obliged to submit to, seeing that they themselves were the co-makers of the canon.[14]

This ring, composed of official Meeting epistles as well as the words of eminent Friends that had been elevated to the status of epistles, gained weight through iterative transcription, circulation, and oral repetition. The Quaker press actively performed that elevation when it selected texts for printing, frequently inserting the word *epistle* into the title of the printed work. Other epistles entered the ring as they were read aloud in Meetings, copied into minutes and then into official Meeting epistles, and recirculated and retranscribed in whole or in part by other Meetings and individual Friends.

Here, print and manuscript circulation were complementary, as epistles appeared in both forms. In seventeenth-century England, the Society frenetically leveraged the press to print and distribute its writings, including epistles. Rather than replacing manuscript exchange, such a strategy appears to have invigorated it. One critic complained of not only the Society's "printed Libels" but also the "Manuscripts that flye as thick as Moths up and down the Country."[15] Through the eighteenth century, British and American Friends compiled libraries, exchanged texts, transcribed excerpts, and read them aloud at Meetings as evidence of past moments of immanent divinity that might prompt more.[16] They conceived of publication as spanning print, manuscript, and oral media; as personal and communal. The revolution disrupted their transatlantic correspondence yet intensified its value. With fewer local ties outside the Society, American Friends found encouragement to remain steadfast to their faith in the ritual of epistolary reportage as well as the revisiting of past epistles, made fresh through individuals' encounters with persecution and uncertainty.

In Pennsylvania, Friends were not the only participants in a vibrant manuscript culture. As Shields amply testifies, literate eighteenth-century colonists relied on belletristic practices to define a range of "distinct" and "novel" private associations.[17] For the educated elite, the creation of manuscript ephemera functioned as an aesthetics of bondedness. Through texts, they might test their intimates' taste and judge which differences to bridge and which to reinforce.[18] Textual and sociable circulation combined to trace lines of affiliation and engender a repertoire of familiarity. For the region's well-to-do Friends, distinguished by religion and class, belles lettres extended rounds of polite visiting, mostly among women, that promulgated a culture of elite sensibility in Friendly Philadelphia and its environs.[19]

In both belletristic and Quaker conceptions, friendship was useful for erecting we-them divisions.[20] It functioned as a shorthand for communal belonging while signaling a shared agreement on its constitution—affective but also intellectual, linguistic, religious, experiential, and so on.[21] Yet, as with letters and the neighborhood, particularity persisted. The ordering and ranking of friends is a common practice—good friend, old friend, former friend—and early American Quaker women were no exception—"Dear Friend," "beloved Frd.," "solid Friend."[22] Their Meeting minutes detail the surveillance and reportage that the Society required, revealing that women Friends not only visited the disobedient and demanded letters renouncing misbehavior but also testified orally and in writing to other members' remarkable and exemplary "conduct."[23] Quakerism, with its groupings and regroupings through Meetings and its emphasis on inward light and testimony, allowed for the implicit evaluation of friends within a friendship.[24] Thus, friendship contained likeness and difference, and its protocols sought to govern both.[25] In this way, friendship resembled Christian neighborliness. The biblical injunction to love thy neighbor as thyself located reciprocal obligation within the neighborhood, while admitting that difference could breed reluctance. Without that difference, acquiescence was too easy, no longer a sign of submission to Christian duty and love.

The word *Friendship* entwines the religious relationship with the more familiar affective relationship, and for eighteenth-century Friends the commonplace book bridged both conceptualizations. For individuals, the book was an ideal place to transcribe epistles and belletristic compositions. In its pages, they were able to arrange spiritual and communal knowledge to mirror their sense of geographic and affective affiliation. By selecting entries and creating juxtapositions, they refined the particularities of friendship and the borders and intricacies of likeness and difference. During the Renaissance, when the commonplace book gained prominence, Erasmus's *De Copia* advised students of rhetoric to list useful *topoi,* or places, such as virtues or vices, and then to compile examples under each *topos.* Thus, one could textually and mentally arrange knowledge for easier study and recall during argument. Not only did the transcriber comprehend the arrangement of entries as spatial, but the strategy "guarded against future losses of information."[26]

For Milcah Martha Moore, the commonplace book was the ideal cornerstone of a relational publication practice with which to respond to the isolation of revolutionary politics. She, too, experienced affiliation as spatial, though that experience often occurred through geographic removal. Her first removal occurred in 1752, when she was eleven years old and residing on the Portuguese island of Madeira with her parents, the American-born Friends Richard Hill and Deborah Moore Hill.[27] As they had done with several of their other children, they sent her to Philadelphia to live with her married sister Hannah, where she joined not only her siblings but also a prominent and interrelated network of Friends. Through her brother-in-law Samuel Preston Moore, Moore met her future husband, Charles Moore, who was Samuel's brother and her own cousin twice over. (They had sibling parents and maternal grandparents.) Yet unlike equally related Hannah and Samuel, Charles and Milcah Moore were disowned rather than reprimanded for their disobedience to Society strictures.[28]

As Jack Marietta explains, disownment is the public "explusion [*sic*] of irregular members."[29] It indicates that an individual is out of union with the Society. In eighteenth-century Philadelphia, disownment did not mark a "fall from grace or damnation," nor was it permanent, though disowned individuals could not participate in the business Meetings in which unified Friends reached consensus about communal governance.[30] If Friends could convincingly and publicly testify to their contrite reformation, they might be readmitted.

Moore's second removal, her 1767 disownment, reflected the Society's increasing concern with spiritual clarity.[31] This internal focus had not always been the case. Friends had founded the colony of Pennsylvania and had historically dominated its assembly; it had long been a place where Quaker theology had secular applications.[32] For many decades, Quaker leaders had been relatively successful in applying their sectarian tenets to their colonial dominion. However, by the mid-eighteenth century, Pennsylvania Friends began to withdraw from statecraft as a result of internal cleavages over politics, wealth, and indifference to discipline, areas that reform-minded Friends argued distracted the Society's members from the inward light. This movement reinvigorated a lax disciplinary process, and disownments of Friends escalated. It produced "a purified Society of Friends—much more strict, much more divorced from the world, much more consistent."[33]

Another reason for secular withdrawal was the conflict between the colony's military needs and the Society's pacifist credo. Although the colony's Friend politicians historically had avoided directly supporting a militia, frontier violence and early losses during the French and Indian War pushed Friends in the assembly to authorize its first defense fund and militia.[34] The Philadelphia Yearly Meeting, the highest decision-making body for North American Friends, urged its members to resign from the assembly, while non-Friends, who now constituted a majority of the colony's population, saw this as a chance to support internal candidates. Rather than characterizing voluntary and involuntary secular withdrawal as a punishment, the Society's reform-minded leadership praised it; they believed that "God would favor a people who conformed to his ordinances and in effect would raise a wall around to protect them."[35] More than encouraging their followers to be emblems of a strict standard of practical piety, they envisioned a barrier that would insulate the Society from a polluting world.

As a consequence of the Society's gradual recession from Pennsylvania politics and its insistence on peace, Moore experienced her third removal. The revolution cemented the Society's disengagement and bred internal schisms as disobedient Friends were expelled for supporting military efforts. They were out of unity with their neighbors, Quaker and non-Quaker alike. Fractured and embattled, the community dispersed before the British occupation of Philadelphia.[36] Now a disowned refugee of a despised and riven sect, Moore retreated with her husband and her faith to rural Montgomery County.

How different was this moment from past removals. Arriving in Philadelphia, she had substituted her parents and several siblings for a foster sister-mother and a new neighborhood of relatives and friends. After disownment, she had continued to reside in that neighborhood, her sectarian status but not her residence affected. Thus, for Moore, who could no longer turn to her neighbors for consolation, the revolution coincided with crises of geographic, familial, and spiritual isolation. She wrote to her sister Hannah, "Does thee remember when I was last in Town I told thee how I had been terrified one Night in my Sleep, at find.[g] I was left all alone, & being told that I was forsaken of my God as well as Man? I wak'd myself screaming." Her removals suggest that her "terr[or]" was neither abstract nor irrational and expose her fear of another separation. In the letter, she offered an "Interpretation": "I've long been an Outcast as to the Society, but oh! My beloved Sister, judge of my Distress when I tell that I have experienc'd in Reality the other Part of my Dream which so frighted me, in my Sleep. The Lord shew'd me my dreadful & sinful State, then left me to myself. Oh the anguish of my Soul at that Time, is not to be express'd."[37] She identified God as her asylum and last companion.[38] Abandonment, not departure, terrified her. Imagining her spiritual crisis as geographic isolation, she lamented her "widely different" "Situation," thereby locating herself in an unbearably peculiar space.[39] She had been "left" to "[her]self," disconnected from all, and immobilized.

Now letters and visitors offered respite; reunion occurred through circulation. "Thy Letters," Moore confided to Hannah, "are a great Comfort to me, & [I] seldom receive one from any Body else." A 1778 letter from another sister, Margaret Hill Morris, suggests that Moore was not alone in finding consolation through letters.[40] Calling Moore by her family nickname, Morris explained, "I can't send thee, my precious Patty, such an acceptable letter as thine was to me. My good brother[-in-law George Dillwyn] has called me an idolator, because I sometimes kiss the letters before I open them; but I assure thee it is not my own name on the back I kiss."[41] The women bridged separation through correspondence; Morris embraced in proxy her sister-as-letter. Such opportunities, however, were uncertain and rare, so Morris also maintained a chronicle of her experiences for Moore. Widowed and now head of her household, she explained that, despite the journal's partly "waggish moor [mood?]," she wrote "most of it after the family were abed, and I sat up to keep guard over my fences, &c., while the soldiers were next door, for fear they should pull them down to burn."[42] Morris concluded her journal by collecting and arranging "the scraps of her late diary into one piece" and requested that Moore share it only with uncritical "family" and "partial friends." Via her journal, Morris responded to war's isolating effects through relational publication, gathering and refining a surrogate neighborhood of affectionate, pious sympathizers.

With its texts and subjects culled from the same circles, *Moore's Book* is a sustained example of such practices. It assembled and distilled the affiliatory impulses of other women Friends' wartime relational publication practices. For Moore, commonplacing during the revolution was a robust counterpart to letter writing and visiting.[43] Her book arranged a new neighborhood that replaced the now distant and dismantled geographic neighborhood that had cushioned her removals before the occupation.[44] Through deliberate craftsmanship and juxtaposition, she surpassed replication and created an alternative structure of friendship that responded to the period's alienating politics.[45] She used a clear and regular script, included catchwords at the bottom of pages, added flourishes between entries, and provided marginal brackets for triple rhymes. Her transcriptions were clean and generally accurate.[46] Furthermore, almost every entry identified the selection's title and author.[47]

These markers of careful transcription indicate that arrangement and circulation were central concerns; *Moore's Book* was a new kind of epistle for her friends. As with Horn's "ring of public texts," it accretively assembled a fluid canon for communal governance and protected against loss, textual and personal.[48] Her initial transcription strategy (she began with a substantial section of Wright's poetry framed with some verse by Griffitts) evolved to serially query those themes and their proper practice. Each time she moved from one entry to another, a neighbor-reader might encounter a juxtapositional dialogue and participate in communal refinement. For these women, the more perfect union of post-revolutionary America was not the anonymous fraternity of democratic citizenship but the neighborhood, in which familiarity produced friendship and reciprocity and pious residents guided each other.

Rehearsing Friendship

The commonplace book demands a distinct reading strategy. As with the Bible and devotionals, one can read sequentially (from cover to cover) or circuitously (circling around an entry and experiencing a constellation of textual juxtapositions). In other words, one can approach *Moore's Book* through what Matthew Brown refers to as pilgrimage and rumination. His study of early modern reading practices in New

England directs us to recall both linear and nonlinear encounters with books. Devotional texts, commonplace books, and miscellanies particularly encourage nonlinear, ruminative reading in which readers select a textual moment and "peruse."[49] Yet readers also understand themselves as journeying across a book.

A pilgrimage through the opening sequence of *Moore's Book* provides a guide through which to peruse later entries: it accumulates friendship and then refines its meaning and practice through iterative encounters. The sequence collects a textual conversation, wherein the friendship is materially delineated through arrangement and transcription; the meaning of friendship itself is the subject of that conversation. It both structurally and substantively considers friendship.

When Moore opened her blank commonplace book to write, she chose "An Essay on Friendship" as her first selection. Written by her unmarried cousin Hannah Griffitts, who remained in Philadelphia during the British occupation, the poem begins:

> The Friend requires, & friendship does demand,
> At least th' attempt from my inferior Hand.
> The Heart shall dictate & the Pen rehearse
> And keep the Subject flowing with the Verse[.][50]

In the poem, both "Friend" and "friendship" insist on writing, with the "Pen" channeling the expressions of the "Heart" and form and content "flowing" in concert. Authorship is the technology of union, and the verb *rehearse* reveals much about the dynamic nature of that technology: the pen might report, recollect, catalogue, or practice. It is no mere mimicking servant but the instrument of communal refinement. It incrementally examines friendship's "demand[s]," "attempt[ing]" and weighing its performance. Lines of verse make known friendship itself, with iterative inscriptions gradually clarifying its "require[ments]," distilling impediments, smoothing its flow.

By selecting this poem, Moore disclosed that the affective and spiritual bond of friendship was a theme of her book and offered an initial axiom for understanding its tenets and applications. Characterizing friendship as a "Union of the Soul," the poem instructs the reader to keep "a noble unaffected Piety" at its "Centre."[51] It then defines piety's corollaries and directs the practice of friendship:

> The other Virtues, here may claim a Place
> [Piety] is the chief & this alone the Base,

The Bond to strengthen, it requires we find,
Similitude of Passions & of Mind,
Alike in Tempers, as alike in Love,
Mutual their Faith & Confidence to improve
By simpathetic Tenderness are known
And feel each others Sorrows like their own,
Kind to their Failings, to their Virtues Just
With watchful Care they guard the sacred trust,
A feeling Heart, a sympathizing Soul
Can with a friend in all their Griefs condole
Joy when they Joy, & when they sorrow, mourn
Sighs to their Sighs, & Tears to theirs return,
In Silence weep, & bear the tender Part,
That wounds the Soul & melts the bleeding Heart,
For oh! in every Grief their Friend has known,
It strikes as deep & pains them as their own,
"In those dear Bonds of mutual Union ty'd,
"No time can break nor distant Lands divide."[52]

According to this rubric, similarity of temperament and opinion as well as reciprocity of feeling supplement and "strengthen" friendship. Such similarities are pleasurable because they allow friends to know each other more precisely as well as witness and "guard" mutual piety. The poem furthers this characterization when it repeats that friendship is a "Union of the Soul":

True friends we find in Union of the Soul
Are like the constant Needle to the Pole
And ever fixing there, whose guiding Ray
Directs the Trav'ler in the dubious Way[.][53]

Grounded in piety, friendship exacts morality.

In Griffitts's poem, the reciprocal and moral demands of friendship require proximity. To regard one's friends with "watchful Care" in order to "Joy when they joy," to "return" their "Tears" with one's own, one must live close. Thus, friendship is the province of neighborhoods, wherein daily exchange makes possible such precise observation and permits friends to monitor each others' affective and moral conditions.

The quandary, of course, was that the revolution had scattered neighbors and friends. How could distant friends maintain their bond? As the tangible existence of this commonplace book makes clear, relational publication offered a way forward. The poem's opening couplet offers a first-person image of "my inferior Hand," which suggests that acceding to the demands of "friendship" through the act of writing blurs the distinction between author and transcriber. Like Griffitts, Moore had picked up the pen as an act of affective service. Much as a true friend "Sighs to [her friend's] Sighs," Moore wrote as her friend wrote. Though geographically and temporally distant, their hands converged by tracing the same words across the page. Transcription itself emerged as an act of reciprocity, and the iterative circulation and copying of writing—poems, letters, journals, commonplace books—mapped lines of exchange, performatively and materially refining a new neighborhood.

After transcribing this poem on friendship, Moore turned to its rehearsal through documentation. Nearly all of the next twenty-five poems were by Susanna Wright; only two near the section's end were by Griffitts, the result of a correspondence between the two poets. Wright was an esteemed Friend who resided on the Pennsylvania frontier in Chester County, about eighty-five miles from Philadelphia. Never married, she wrote poetry, experimented with silkworms and other areas of horticulture, engaged in political campaigning, acted as a secretary for the local magistrate, and corresponded with Philadelphia friends such as Benjamin Franklin and members of the prominent Norris and Logan families.[54] For both Moore and Griffitts, Wright appears to have been "a kind of elder stateswoman."[55] The section documents the productions of a person who might have been a friend and a poetic exchange that might have established friendship.[56]

"Where," asks the speaker of Wright's first poem, the undated "A Meditation," "shall I this unfathom'd Secret find / Of what thou art?"[57] The pronoun ambiguities of "this" and "thou" in these opening lines link the poem back to Griffitts's "An Essay on Friendship," thus extending friendship's rehearsal into this documentary section.[58] In other words, in arranging her book, Moore proposed a question: where can I find the "unfathom'd Secret" of friendship? Because the remainder of "A Meditation" focuses on the biblical story of Jonah, who finds God in the belly of a great fish, as a way to contemplate personal suffering, sin, and Christian salvation, the commonplace book's most immediate answer may be that the source of friendship lies in solitary religious contemplation. Thus, Moore's organizational strategy pointed the reader back to Griffitts's core principle of friendship: "A noble unaffected Piety."

I am not arguing that the subject of Wright's poem alone is anything other than an explicit consideration of original sin and Christian salvation. Rather, Moore's introductory juxtaposition of "An Essay on Friendship" and "A Meditation" presents piety as a precursor to friendship. Together, the pair advances that friendship, properly defined, emerges from and confirms, perhaps even deepens, one's piety. In this formulation, participation in friendship manifests one's individual spirituality, and a particular friendship's authenticity and virtue lie in the piety of its members. By framing the Wright section with the work of Griffitts, Moore transformed what might have been a lifeless archive into an ongoing rehearsal of friendship, a continuing query into its nature, practice, and evolutions. She brought together the artistic productions of two distant Friends and placed them in conversation. The book was starting to collect a new neighborhood.

Moore turned to an individual attribute—piety—to understand a relationship, a move that mirrored the book's opening arrangement, which, rather unusually, focuses on the work of Wright, a poet renowned for her crisp spirituality. Including her sequence of twenty-four poems added authority to *Moore's Book* and its formulation of friendship.[59] Much as piety operates as a precursor to friendship, Wright's pious productions launched the book, suggesting that the book itself matched the criteria for friendship's establishment. It sustained a performance of the friendship protocols that the first poems advocated.

Like "A Meditation," the rest of Wright's sequence explores friendship alongside piety.[60] In an untitled poem, she laments "a false World" in which "Friendship's basely made a Trade—an Art, / That holds but while 'tis on the gaining Part."[61] In "To a Friend.—On some Misunderstanding," she appears to be exasperated at her inability to "Cure" a friend's "strange unkindness."[62] She chastises her friend for such intractability and reminds the friend that "human Nature" obliges "A Constant, long & solitary Train" of imperfect "Passions" and "Folly."[63] In "On Friendship," she riffs on the biblical precept *God is love* and reasons that divinity arouses "that pleasing fire" of friendship between sexless "Souls."[64] In the next poem, "To the Memory of Charles Norris," she mourns the loss of the "best of Men & best of Friends," picking up the predominant subject of her poetry, mortality.[65] Able to bid Norris and other elegiac subjects safe journey, she uncertainly meditates on her own death.[66] "How shall I plunge amidst the numerous Dead?" she asks. "What, shall I be unbodied?—how & where?"[67] Elsewhere, she envisions death as a more intense "Flame" than friendship's pleasing fire, as, through decomposition, "Corruption" yields to "New Charms," "refin[ing]" the soul by degrees.[68]

By rehearsing friendship within Wright's scrutiny of theology and mortality, this section and its frame refine the "unfathom'd secret" of friendship's "source" and practice. Piety and affection emerge as rigorous, temporal, and intertwined; in their purest forms, they are types to the antitype of divine communion in the afterlife. Mundane friendship is potent but suspect and requires periodic evaluation. Wright effuses that a friend "colours all our Days with Happiness" and then confesses,

> But if my Friends too dang'rous Blessings prove,
> And I grow giddy with excess of Love,
> Or if they change,—which too, too much I fear,
> For Frailty is to human Nature, near,
> How shall I stand a Tryal so severe?
> When of my Friends, or of their Love, depriv'd,
> I'll all resign—for long enough I've liv'd.[69]

Friendship changes as friends do, subject to the same degenerations and distractions as its practitioners are.[70] The maintenance and monitoring of friendship requires ongoing acts of intimate exchange.

This section's rehearsal of friendship culminates with a three-poem conversation between Wright and Griffitts (writing under her pseudonym "Fidelia"). The first is Wright's reflection on her sixty-fourth birthday in 1761, the second is Griffitts's response, and the third is Wright's response to Griffitts. While the first poem is not explicitly about friendship, the poems that follow model friendship and hint at its uses, instructively inserting a past exchange between the women into the book. Wright's "My own Birth Day.— August 4th 1761" steps backward to the "Patriarchs Days" of the Old Testament to reflect on the long sweep of time, the veiled brevity of the poet's unusually long lifespan, and mortality's unceasing succession of "swift Decays" and "transient Blast[s]."[71] She testifies to loss and bereavement and reassures herself that, through her soul's immortality, "the mortal shall surpass the natal Day."[72]

Griffitts's response does not deny Wright's claims but offers poetic composition as a consolatory surrogate:

> Amidst these Cares that crow'd the human Throng,
>   Serenely glows Venera's evening Ray,
> She wakes her Lyre to Harmony of Song,
>   And smooths the awful Passage of Decay.[73]

Venera's song eases the prolonged transition from painful life and old age into death.[74] Griffitts proposes that sensitivity to Venus's inspiration increases with age, especially in Wright's case:

> Distinguish'd view in this superior Mind,
> The Fire of Wit matur'd by ripening Age,
> And striking Sense with soft Submission join'd.
> Inspires Venera's animated Page.[75]

Wright's response, "S.W. to Fidelia. In answer to the foregoing," rejects this proffer of temporary consolation. It declares that her "ebbing Spirits languid flow" and describes "Fancy's drooping Wing" as "Unplum'd by Time" and unable to "rise / To seek a second Spring."[76] Instead, "Faiths" and "gentle Hope" "sustain" the "immortal Mind," which, "Unconscious of Decay, / Feels all her Powers of Action Strong."[77] Wright's poem insists that it is Griffitts herself who has the "Spark of Fire divine" and whose poetry "glow[s]." The text designates a poetic heir and distinguishes between Wright's cohort of the past and Griffitts's of the present. The closing lines make this division more stark:

> Thy Mothers social Hour was mine,
> As kindred Minds allied.
> Such wou'd thou be, cou'd youth to Age,
> The engaging Hand extend;
> Such wou'd I prize the tender Tye,
> And fondly call thee Friend.[78]

Wright identifies herself generationally and "social[ly]" with Griffitts' mother and regrets the impossibility of true friendship with the younger poet.[79]

This poetic exchange, in which friendship is proffered and rejected, further refines the source and practice of affiliation. Griffitts's verse performs friendship through its sympathy and praise, yet Wright's verse, in adhering to "Thy Mothers social Hour," holds to the past. Ratifying the divinely ordained mortality of friendship while claiming "Faith" "softens [her] Pain," her poem returns to piety, first the source and now the respite of friends. Withholding friendship from Griffitts, it nevertheless instructs, designating Griffitts as the heir to Wright's poetry and affection. Through composition, transcription, arrangement, and circulation, poetry operates as the vehicle of friendship's performance and education. Friendship emerges as bounded and mortal, dependent on but also productive of piety and affinity, each instance a new rehearsal and a potential legacy, an offering of a more perfect union.

By gathering and arranging this poetic correspondence, Moore indefinitely delayed the end of Griffitts's and Wright's correspondence, locating them instead within an ongoing conversation about friendship. In her book, their poems are closer than physical geography allowed—closer to each other and closer to Moore, whose hand and page were the technology of their ongoing union. As a relational publication, then, *Moore's Book* materially delineated a neighborhood of friends who were otherwise at an unbridgeable distance from each other. Moore was not in exile or even on the margins of this neighborhood but resided at its center and directed its exchanges.

After the Wright section, Griffitts becomes the book's predominant author: her writing comprises about 60 percent of the remaining entries, although Moore did intersperse pieces and sequences by other writers. The arrangement is mostly chronological and reflects the progression of the war, with verse that explicitly addresses revolutionary topics woven among other, mostly poetic, compositions.[80] As it alternates between political commentary and moral contemplation and between the voice of Griffitts and the expressions of others, the book takes the form of a protracted and evolving conversation. The accumulating ephemera of manuscript exchange produces an act of relational publication that arranges and queries the bonds and protocols of its underlying relations. The opening section's presentation of friendship functions as a reading strategy with which to take up the book, encounter an entry, and then migrate among others, collecting and refining friendship's practice.

How does a perusal of one entry and its poetic neighbors thicken friendship? Brown cites personal miscellany as a place where both composition and reading can be ruminatory: that is, where the author and reader (or author as reader) can engage in discontinuous transcription, study, and cross-referencing.[81] *Moore's Book*'s initial rehearsal of friendship's tenets—piety, reciprocity, temporality—articulates with its subsequent exploration of communal schisms and bondedness. Through juxtaposition, the entries shed the impious unfriendliness of revolutionaries, locating governance and affinity among those bound by shared piety, respect, and affection. The neighborhood rather than the nation holds sway.

Let us consider the eighty-sixth entry, Griffitts's scathing "upon reading a Book entituled Common Sense. Jany. 1776," which examines Thomas Paine's rousing tract through the critical lens of friendship.[82] The poem functions as a node to begin a further rumination on friendship, its refinement not definitive but ongoing and provisional (see fig. 10; I've included entry numbers from this point forward to correspond with the figure's chart). The poem addresses Sylvania and warns that *Common Sense* is a "fallacious tale" whose message is a "Snake beneath the Grass."[83] It then reproaches Paine for undermining freedom under the guise of patriotism and accuses him and his cohort of tyranny:

> Orders confounded,—Dignities thrown down,
> Charters degraded equal with the Crown,
> The impartial Press, most partially maintain'd
> Freedom infring'd, & Conscience is restrain'd,
> The moderate Man is held to publick View,
> "The Friend of Tyranny & Foe to you,"
> Deny'd the common Right to represent
> Forbid to give his Reasons for Dissent,
> Whilst base Informers—(Own'd a public Pest)
> Are round the Land encourag'd & caress'd
> Our Representatives,—the Peoples Choice
> Are held contemptuous by this daring Voice
> Persons are seiz'd & Posts monopoliz'd
> And all our Form of Government despis'd,—
> —Then from this "Specimen of Rule" beware
> Behold the Serpent & avoid his Snare.
> 'Tis not in Names, our present Danger lyes
> Sixty as well as one can tyrannize[.][84]

In the poem, Griffitts enumerates what she sees as the hypocrisy in Paine's tract, presenting a list of crimes that prefigures the Declaration of Independence's catalogue of "injuries and usurpations."[85] Revolutionaries have "thrown down" "Dignities." They have "confounded" "Orders." They are "contemptuous" of the "Peoples Choice." "Conscience is restrain'd" within the new political climate. Their behavior contrasts sharply with the reciprocal bondedness of friendship, their defilement of social principles marking their unfriendly impiety.[86] Most egregious may be their "caress[ing]" of "Informers," people who live alongside their neighbors but betray the intimacy of daily proximity when they assent to the beguiling touch of the revolutionary "Serpent," choosing the bonds of fractional politics over local ties.

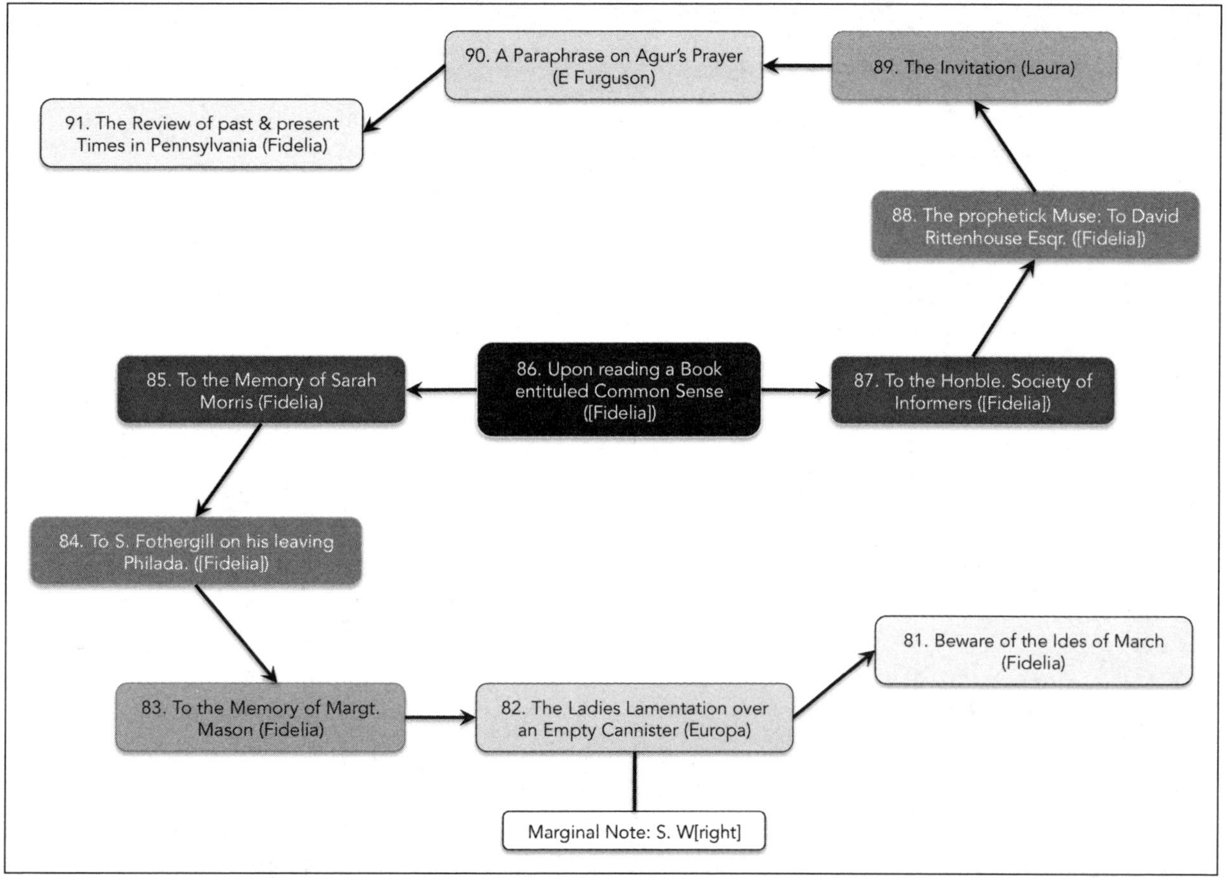

FIGURE 10. A conceptual chart of the circular route traced through this section of chapter 4. The analysis begins with entry no. 86 and then considers how it nests within the surrounding entries, developing meaning through arrangement. In the chapter text, the first mention of each of these poems is followed by its entry/chart number in parentheses.

Shifting from critique to instruction, the poem concludes by advocating caution:

> Ah! then awake Sylvania & beware,
> The fatal Danger of this subtle Snare
> Hold fast yr. own, yr. charter'd Rights maintain
> Nor let them weave the Snare into the Chain,
> And whilst firm Union stands the British Foes,
> Let not the native Hand yr. Date of Freedom close.[87]

The discerning speaker extends the mentoring hand of friendship to Sylvania, woman to woman. "Beware," she counsels, "Hold fast yr. own, yr. charter'd Rights maintain." Unlike the duly authorized text, the avid words of rebelling men are not to be trusted. Paine and the other revolutionaries seem to be artful seducers seeking to "snare" Sylvania and violate her virtuous "Freedom." The poem beckons Sylvania back to the page, back to friendship, reciprocity, and union. Like the works in the Wright section, it interacts with the entries that come before and after, part of an arranged iterative querying of friendship's tenets in a discordant political environment.

The next entry, Griffitts's February 1776 "To the Honble. Society of Informers" (no. 87) reverses course and addresses informers rather than Sylvania. Informing, according to the poem, is now a "Trade" that has been made a "noble employ" by "the Flame of Dissention."[88] Griffitts reproves the past's "old fashion'd Virtue . . . / (When Love warm'd the sociable Breast)." She encourages aspiring informers to "Search keenly for Foibles thy Neighbour may wear / Then nobly, expose them to sight."[89] The informer will accrue a "sure" "Reward": "In this Life full Honour attend on thy Trade / And the Balance be clos'd in the other." In return for mundane laurels, the informer abdicates God's favor. His actions are impious, contrary to the commandment of neighborly love. Informers have no place among friends, and the poem's commonplace publication serially exiles them from the union, the opposite of Sylvania's invitation.

If we continue to circle around "upon reading . . . Common Sense," we come to its predecessor, "To the Memory of Sarah Morris who died at Philada. Octobr. 24th. 1775" (no. 85), an elegy to a transatlantic Quaker preacher who traveled extensively.[90] Like other Griffitts poems about speaking Friends, this elegy emphasizes the appropriateness and virtue of publicly proclaiming one's religious principles. Thanks to Moore's arrangement, sympathetic readers have already been primed to associate friendship with instruction. Now, in this poem, we learn that Morris "point[ed] the Path" to others and that, by paying attention to the individual's "State," she always "Directed" the "Proper Portion" to each person she met.[91] She appears to have been a model of friendly reciprocity, both spiritual and affective: her "generous Mind" was "Where christian Virtues did with Social blend, / And form'd th' Instructor in the chearful Friend."[92] Juxtaposed with the verses about divisive revolutionaries, the poem encourages the reader to dutifully receive the book's instruction in proper friendship.

Other proximal selections nest Griffitts's critique of Paine within a lively discussion about the forms and spheres of political conversation and behavior. The revolutionary public is too blunt and tumultuous; the friendly neighborhood counteracts upheaval by facilitating nuance and reciprocity. The arc traverses two of Griffitts's elegies for admirable Friends (nos. 83 and 84) and loops to a lyric address to David Rittenhouse (no. 88), advising him to keep to "Science" and "Labour not" in politics. Other selections concerning the tea boycott herald the elegies. "Beware the Ides of March" (no. 81) casts Britain's Lord North as Marcus Brutus and predicts that the 1775 breakdown in British-American diplomacy will "raise a Storm that will not suit us [Ladies]," who must "defeat" the British through a calm and "firm Resolve" against tea consumption.[93] "The Ladies Lamentation over an empty Cannister" (no. 82), written under the pseudonym "Europa," eschews an absolute boycott, expressing "Resentment" over the "Malice shewn to Tea" and vowing to find "fresh Recruits of Tea" despite the "noise & Bluster" of "King, . . . Parliament, . . . [and] North."[94] A marginal note in Wright's hand also blames the Continental Congress, arguing that a blanket ban "partake[s] of that Sp[iri]t of D[e]spotism, so loudly complain'd of in America."[95] "I have public sp[iri]t. enough," the note continues, "never to taste one drop of what has p[ai]d. the Duty, but for such as has not, I must venture to use it as the Mahometans do Wine, not openly but in a manner to elude scandal & not to give Offence."[96] Blind obedience to "public spirit" is a performance, but sites such as the tea table, the scientific society, and—as evidenced by Wright's insertion—the commonplace book allow for truer expression and honest exchange.

Wright's marginal note permits a moment of speculation. Moore directed much of the book's relationality by drawing on manuscript exchange with friends and family members and mapping and adapting those bonds through the arrangement of her book. Yet the book is also a material object with a presence that extended beyond Moore's composition. This moment is evidence of the book's circulation among those same bonds. What does it mean to touch a page that has one's own verse written in another's hand? To feel the heft of an object that arranges one's own creations alongside those of another? To relinquish that book so that it can journey to another friend? The book's relationality, then, lies also in its material circulation and the performance of its reading, annotation, and retransmission. The neighborhood dwells within its covers and along its routes, a product of a relational publication practice that enfolds transcription, arrangement, and circulation.

In the midst of such divisive politics, is retreat the answer? The book shifts to just this question, transitioning from the work of Griffitts to that of the non-Quaker salonnière Elizabeth Graeme Fergusson.[97] The first Fergusson entry, "The Invitation" (no. 89), written under the pseudonym "Laura," presents a seductive vision of complete female withdrawal:

> Come dear Amanda, prythee come,
> And share yr. Time with me
> The smiling Hours shall sweetly glide,
> From Noise & Scandal free.
> Thro' lonely Walks, & shady Bowers,
> We may delighted rove,
> Where no Intruders can invade,
> To ruffle gentle Love.
> Cupid shall guard us from all harm,[98]
> And shew his faithful Care,
> As we sit by some murmuring Rill
> And female Friendship share.
> The Town with all its sprightly Charms,
> Was not ordain'd for me,
> More lasting Happiness is found,
> Beneath a spreading Tree.
> Here sweet Simplicity presides
> And glads the virtuous Heart.
> And rural Elegance around
> Does Nature's Joy's impart.
> Instruction glides in every Brook,
> To sentimental Minds,
> Each Shrub conveys some virtuous Truth
> And earthly Bliss refines.[99]

Laura invites Amanda to "prythee come / And share yr. Time with me." She extols the pleasures of female friendship through sensual language that evokes languorous repose under "spreading Tree[s]" and beside flowing "Brook[s]."[100] This idyllic portrayal of female friendship as refuge contrasts with the rigorous reciprocity and piety demanded in the Wright section and advanced by later entries such as "Primitive Friendship described" (no. 96) and "Steady Friendship" (no. 108).[101] Fergusson's version of friendship instead foregrounds social detachment and pleasure.

Setting aside discussion of politics and dead luminaries, the poem enacts its theme of retreat. Through its transcription, Moore briefly relinquished a consuming disorder in favor of the sweet "glide" and "Simplicity" of Fergusson's version of friendship. According to Susan Scott Parrish, the poem's configuration of nature transforms a "naturally extreme colonial climate into a pastoral topos." While Parrish is referring to flora and fauna, this transformation can also be viewed as social, wherein the climate moves from political fragmentation to harmonious intimacy.[102] The poem's tactile embodiment of retreat resides as well at the level of verb tense: it moves from future speculation in the first twelve lines—"We may delighted rove"—to the immediacy of the present in the final eight—"Here sweet Simplicity presides." The reader is swept away.

Elsewhere, the book insistently situates friendship within a neighborhood, wherein friends practice piety and reciprocity. Here, Moore's arrangement guides readers into considering and then rejecting the invitation to absolute retreat, something it also does earlier around an untitled entry by Hester Griffitts (no. 44, "Come sweetly pleasing Solitude").[103] Yes, we learn, retreat promises a pleasurable release, yet it abstracts women from the neighborhood and their duties.[104] Moreover, Fergusson's blissful retreat resists temporality, slowing time and immersing friends in pastoral delight. In Wright's "A Meditation," withdrawal reverses isolation because it provides for prayer, a contemplation of worldly and sinful concerns. Jonah, the poem's biblical subject, sought to evade his duty to share a divine message, but prayer and isolation led to acceptance and a return to serving his neighbor. In contrast, "The Invitation" seeks to remove Amanda.

Moore seems to have experienced retreat as isolation that must be endured, at its best a moment to deepen piety and prepare to return to the neighborhood and apply the tenets of friendship. Her book's ebb and flow rehearses the layered themes of friendship, piety, and politics. Each entry exists as a node with which to begin a query. Friendly and unfriendly activities are serially sorted, approaching a refined neighborhood of friends, a more perfect union of souls. Wright's marginal note underscores that *Moore's Book* truly arose from a practice of relational publication, one constituted by particular exchanges among friends. It invited response; its circulations among transcribers, composers, and readers inscribed the evolving presence of the neighborhood on the landscape and in the margins and pages of other books and letters. Its local, particularized, relational publication sphere mirrored the process of selecting texts and friends.

I might have begun this rumination not with Griffitts's caustic critique of *Common Sense* but with the poem "Social Love" (no. 74), which tells of the search for

> that Love, benevolent & kind
> Which warms the Breast, expands the Mind
> And gladdens in the Welfare of the whole.[105]

Social love is what distinguishes humanity from "Beasts of Prey" and "meer Clods of Earth."[106] Through rumination, this poem leads the reader to "A moral sonnet" (no. 75), which mourns the death of a "young Songster in Wing," whose incautious delight in his freedom betrays him to the hunter's "murdering Eye."[107] Or the reader might look back at the poem's precursor, "The Query" (no. 73), which proposes that life is best enjoyed by the aged, whose knowledge of their mortality increases their "enjoy[ment]" of "Nature & Grace, & Life & Death."[108] These poems offer care, reciprocity, virtue, and temporality as antidotes to disorder, pain, and violence. More sympathetic to the young songster than to Paine, they suggest that impending revolutionary violence might have been tempered by friendship, especially in a neighborhood with virtuous elders such as Wright.

In *Moore's Book,* the selection and arrangement of entries exemplify how the definition of pious friendship authorized and structured political commentary. Staging the tenets of friendship and offering friendly and unfriendly examples, these poems collectively advance a political vision in which citizens are neighbors bound in mutual obligation. Yet the vision is not inclusive. Unfriendly persons—those who lack sufficient piety and disregard communal reciprocity—abdicate neighborly belonging. Following the principles of pious friendship, the book responds to revolution and social division by proposing politics as friendship, a protocol for affiliation based on the witnessing and monitoring of each other's piety and reciprocity. Ultimately, the relational publication performed by and through *Moore's Book* constitutes a political community that is circumscribed but engaged with others, steeped in feminine authority yet heterosocial, spiritually pious and contemplative yet active in earthly concerns, seeking stability yet as temporary as its mortal members. In presenting these contradictions, Moore may have sought to offset the violence and instability of the larger community and to produce a structure—communal and scriptive—within which to balance these competing drives.

Afterword

To CHART the unfamiliar landscape of revolution's aftermath, let us to turn to the letter. In North America, diverse women had long mediated the insistent challenges of pre-national eighteenth-century proximity through relational publication, reimagining neighborhoods of bondedness through text, performance, materiality, and circulation. Like letters, those acts affirmed and reordered particularity. They sought not to define partitions of similarity but to reimagine the uneven and at times violent arrangements of public life. Such work was no less urgent in the early republic, and the end of the eighteenth century saw a "sea-change" from mere letter writing to the art of correspondence, wherein a sustained epistolary exchange might "outline the proper course and conduct of an entire situation."[1]

Antebellum letters challenged, or perhaps restrained, the idea of the nation as a territory of likeness. They mediated between the extremes of detachment and amalgamation. Through real and fictional letters, women authors could counterpose a likeness that was too alike with an isolating difference wherein, ideologically at least, they were confined to the domestic—forever pre-citizens. They imagined a national geography that was not a single union and had no fixed borders, one that spanned multitudes of communities, a network of neighborhoods that continued to foreground particularity within and between. Even transnational affiliation was, on closer inspection, transneighborhood. Letters in a national framework helped to consolidate the work of pre-national relational publication. It persisted, participating in a broad conversation about American public affiliation that was now directed toward negotiating and retaining particularity in the nation. As a reading practice, relational publication attends not to when and how women have attested to egalitarian bona fides but where they have conceived particularized presence for themselves and their neighbors.

Consider Katteuha, a Cherokee Beloved Woman of Chota, who in 1787 wrote to Benjamin Franklin. Her letter responded to an unsolicited communication from him, motivated by his unexpected encounter with Cornstalk and other disappointed Cherokee diplomats as they returned from New York, where they had been unable to deliver a diplomatic letter to an out-of-session Congress. Suspending efforts to establish an epistolary conversation with Congress, Katteuha instead replied to the eighty-one-year-old governor of Pennsylvania, enlisting his help in "Keep[ing] the path clear & straight" between her nation and his.[2] Franklin was her counterpart in experience and prudence, a mature father and lover who should have comprehended the indispensability of women's fertility.[3] She mocked his aging virility with her reminder that "woman Does not pull Children out of Trees or Stumps nor out of old Logs, but out of their Bodies."[4] It was women's progeny, white and Cherokee, who were the recipients of diplomatic messages. After signing her letter, she marshaled other Cherokee women to endorse it and interpreters to witness its authenticity.[5] Katteuha relied on Franklin as a sage founding father to disseminate her wisdom and assemble his own collaborators so that their alliance could bear fruit and allay the costly unrest, even as she confirmed that she had relayed to her own nation his "Talk" calling for patience in the face of encroachment and violence.[6] She envisioned a transnational geography of openness and exchange wherein she and her "Brother" Franklin, no longer children themselves, would be each other's interpreters and agents, aunt and uncle matchmakers of a peaceful union.[7] In advocating a partnership model, she associated her letter with a long Cherokee history wherein complementary pairings balance competing forces.[8] Her letter suggests that letters—with their addressees, signatories, endorsements, witnesses, bearers, and routes—might have eased impersonal and inscrutable nation-to-nation diplomacy by remapping a neighborhood of balanced, particularized, and navigable relations.[9]

Consider as well Deborah Norris Logan, who in 1814 took up a new domestic project, the annotated transcription of a colonial archive moldering at the family estate. This archive was a trove of letters between her husband's grandfather, James Logan, Pennsylvania's provincial secretary, and William Penn, the colony's founder.[10] A preservationist desire inspired her years of labor, as did a belief that the Penn-Logan correspondence was rightly public property that should not be "secret . . . fugitives" from the "Annals" of history.[11] Equating Pennsylvania's statehood with a "majestic river," she "flatter[ed] [herself] that [she was] performing an acceptable service to [her] fellow-citizens in discovering to their view some of the remote rills and fountains which are [its] sources."[12] She admitted that chronology had motivated her initial arrangement, but more discoveries unsettled her method, enticing her to extend her project by creating an appendix and inserting subsequent findings.[13] Now bound uniformly into two-volume sets, her four manuscript books seem orderly, yet their oblong marbled covers open to expose irregularly sized paper, organizational mutations, transcriptions in other hands, and at one point a tipped-in letter and a scrap of footnote pinned to the page with a nail. Logan dilated her survey of Pennsylvania's "sources," mapping for our "view" an irreconcilably shifting genealogy of affiliations. Pennsylvania as "majestic river" no longer flowed implacably but seemed volatile, a confluence of irregularity.[14] Statehood did not wash over and erode particularity. Her epistolary arrangement functions as a history of and guide to the persistent unevenness of neighborly bondedness.

Or what about Annis Boudinot Stockton, who in 1793 sent her daughter late-night musings on Mary Wollstonecraft's *A Vindication of the Rights of Woman,* a book then in the "neighbourhood"?[15] Stockton dismissed Wollstonecraft's observation of "Slavish obedience" in women.[16] "The state of society may be different in Europe from what it is in America," she conceded, but "this country, the Empire of reason, is not monopolized by men." Pragmatically advocating "moderation and forbearance" with "every . . . person, that we are obliged to be in the habits of strict intimacy," Stockton suggested that, by virtue of God and politics, America's citizens had declared their interdependency, not their independence. The opening invocation of "neighbourhood" discussion thickened the possibilities for her audience and concatenated her "critique" to a preexisting conversation that spanned a public-private geography. Indeed, her daughter, Julia Stockton Rush, probably extended the conversational territory by sharing the letter with her husband Benjamin Rush, a public figure who respected his mother-in-law's wit, patriotism, and learning. Stockton's rational meditation on women's education and national affiliation documents how elite women could and did leverage neighborly relationships to engage in social and political commentary.[17]

And then there is Hannah Webster Foster's *The Coquette* (1797), an epistolary novel in which the spectacular failure of Eliza Wharton and Peter Sanford's liaison should not surprise even the most ardent proponents of reformed rakes' connubial superiority. Titular expectations to the contrary, the seducer Sanford is the tease, loath to send Wharton a letter. Recounting a propensity for intellectual rapport, she hints, "I have been accustomed . . . and am therefore attached to men of letters," but he still withholds intercourse. He arouses her with ephemeral notes that lure her to face-to-face encounters yet spurns the consummation of correspondence.[18] When Sanford does begrudge more than a few lines, he writes to Charles Deighton, a character otherwise absent from the narrative. Revealing his intent for perpetual elusiveness, Sanford crows, "I am a mere Proteus, and can assume any shape that will best answer my purpose."[19] His coquettishness makes him a foil for Wharton's other suitor, the too-willing Reverend Boyer, a man who is loose with his pen. He refuses to be a "sober lover" like Boyer is, dismissing him with a quotation from Pope: "Fix'd like a plant, to one peculiar spot, / To draw nutrition, propagate, and rot."[20] Frustrated by Sanford's refusal to correspond, Wharton allows him to draw near. She reconciles herself to closeness and gradually stops writing to her friends and relatives—"it is not so agreeable to me as it used to be"—but cannot determine how to "fix" attachment in the absence of epistolary exchange.[21] Instead, she herself has become fixed, propagating out of wedlock. Anticipating the completion of her epistolary confessions, she predicts, "I shall be composed," becoming a dead letter rather than of letters, rooted and rotting rather than an exchanging friend, daughter, and neighbor.[22] When juxtaposed with the rich manuscript culture to which it refers, Foster's epistolary novel reads as an anxious meditation on relational publication's possible supercession by republican print and the concomitant ruptures in women's neighborhood particularity and bonds.

All of these antebellum letters conjure a slippage between epistolary and physical attachment and tell us much about intimacy in the new republic. Ideally, democratic citizenship would subsume other more local attachments, public and private, such as those within and between neighborhoods. Constitutional ratification would function as a redemptive moment, fulfilling the typological promise of archaic and broken nationalisms associated with race, clan, and sect.[23] Democratic cohesion and contagion would enable world harmony across like-minded and -feeling nations. An illustration from the February 1789 issue of Philadelphia's *Columbia Magazine* diagrams these concentric rings of associations. Titled "Circle of the Social and Benevolent Affections," it places self and heart at the center, serially encompassed by family, township, country, sympathetic nations, and a world of "CHRISTIAN CHARITY, OR PERFECT PHILANTHROPY, CONSTITUTING THE DUTY, INTEREST & SUPREME HAPPINESS OF MEN" (see fig. 11).[24] There seems to be little room for neighborly affections—such as those among individuals, households, and towns—that are unmediated by "PATRIOTISM," and affective progress encompasses difference and discomfort. In another example, a 1794 celebration in Philadelphia of the French Revolution toasted the "great family of Mankind—May the distinction of nation and of language be lost in the association of freedom and of friendship, till the inhabitants of the various sections of the Globe shall be distinguished only by their virtues and talents."[25] "Distinction[s]" such as those of the neighborhood lose their potency after a successful revolution, becoming feeble vestiges of suspicious factionalism.

In light of such evidence, scholars of antebellum nationalism have made much of intimacy's urgency and transience. The new democratic fraternity ideologically required an anxious pursuit of intimacy, a pervasive (and evasive) feeling of kinship among anonymous citizens. Lauren Berlant, for example, broadly considers public intimacy as a kind of utopia that is constantly disrupted and denied by the messiness and isolation of reality.[26] Dana D. Nelson claims that "national manhood," or white men's fraternal civic identity, "entails a series of affective foreclosures that block those men's more heterogeneous democratic identifications and energies."[27] Similarly, Peter Coviello's study of antebellum literature figures intimacy as "proper[ly]" affective and connects its pursuit, primarily in the form of friendship and sympathy, with narratives of American nationalism.[28] Ivy Schweitzer "offer[s] an eccentric history of the dominant discourses of friendship as 'a masculine political invention' that non-elites, people of color, and women in early America could and did appropriate. Through their adaptations, marginalized groups claimed admission to an exclusive discourse of affiliation, perpetuating but also substantially and radically altering it."[29] Like Coviello, Schweitzer sees early American intimacy in the form of friendship as

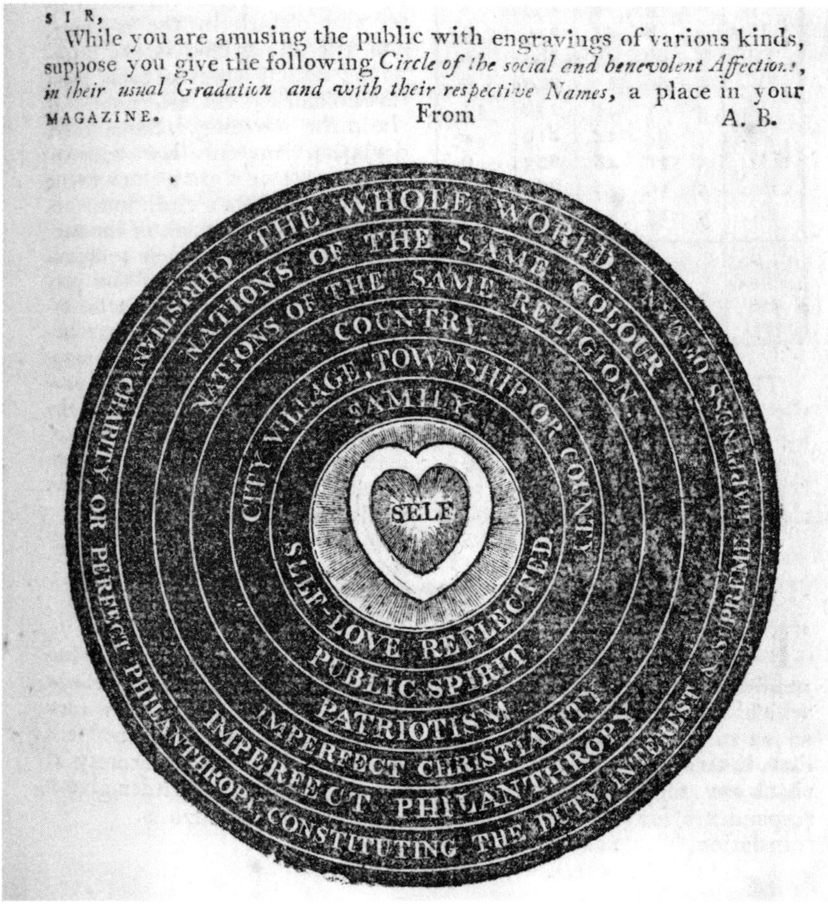

FIGURE 11. "Circle of the Social and Benevolent Affections," from *Columbia Magazine; or, Monthly Miscellany* (February 1789), 109. In the caption, the anonymous creator reassured readers that the affections were arranged in their "usual Gradation." Image courtesy of the Library Company of Philadelphia.

productive of equality through its "insistence on likeness."[30] Richard Godbeer identifies "parental affection, marital friendship, and loving brotherhood" as the "enlightened trinity" of the "new national family," with this last bond being "essential."[31] Such arguments persuade us that post-revolutionary citizenship and influence, especially in the antebellum period, was a function of a sense of intimate likeness.

Yet that intimacy, subject to an affective fantasy, was fleeting and even hollow.[32] Attachment, as *The Coquette*'s Sanford makes clear, evades fixation in "one peculiar spot." His close shaves with intimacy lead us to speculate that pursuit, not attainment, constitutes nationhood. He is aware of pursuit's addictive pleasures and the discontent of success, admitting to Deighton that, were he to marry Wharton, he "cannot be positive that even Eliza would retain my love."[33] But in the end Sanford is bankrupted by his lavish expenditures and abandoned by the heiress he married for money, a conclusion that warns as well against perpetual dodging. As the novel details Sanford's and Wharton's disastrous ends, it counsels against both excessive attachment and disconnection, both ceaseless motion and paralysis.

The Coquette tacks between these poles by and through letters. Read in the context of relational publication, their circulation and exchange counterbalance ruinous extremes and locate women's continued and distinct presence in the new nation, from which they are neither excluded nor subsumed due to their gender or desires. Evoking both connection and separation, the novel's form squares affiliation—not too close, not too far—as it shifts among voices. The neighborhood still holds sway. Likewise, the letters of Katteuha, Logan, and Stockton evince a concern for affiliation's topography, for witnessing and arranging the contours of particularity and bondedness. Katteuha staved off territorial encroachment by blazing a trail of communication that mediated between the Cherokee Nation and the new United States and thereby kept them separate. Logan successively discovered sources and added tributaries to her genealogy of Pennsylvania statehood, unable to resolve the rough banks and erratic ebbs and flows of political constitution. Stockton, on political margins by virtue of her gender, nonetheless observed an interdependent network of differentiated yet receptive fellow citizens, an intimately knowable public through which to spread civic views. Her letter, in its composition and exchange, materialized her grand American dream of an "empire of reason." For each of these women, letters-cum-relational-publication negotiated their particular anxieties and desires about nationhood and shifting neighborhoods.

But relational publication does not only involve letters, real or fictional. Where else do we find post-revolutionary continuity with relational publication? There are the early nineteenth-century baskets woven by Mohegan women in their Connecticut homeland and in Brotherton, an intertribal Christian nation in New York (see plate 5). Emigration to that community as well as land controversies in Connecticut made

Brotherton a contentious issue among Mohegans, and the pink, green, blue, and black motifs on their baskets had communicatory import.[34] As the remarkable Mohegan scholar and elder Gladys Tantaquidgeon explains, artisans would combine design elements such as trails, four-lobed medallions, leaves, and dots to signal "spiritual force" and "represent . . . their own primary considerations," including "paths traveled."[35] During a time of communal reordering, the baskets' arching trails, sometimes enclosing, sometimes separating, invoked the routes of life, sun, and migration. The Mohegan origin story, which tells of an eastward migration, was replicated in a westward return, a textured message of parallel migrations and nations, legible simultaneously as hope, loss, separation, betrayal, invitation, and continuity.[36] Like Coosaponakeesa's diplomatic circulation of self and text (discussed in chapter 1), Native women's relational publication confronted shifting territories of bondedness.

Such examples proliferate, making plain that many different kinds of forms are invested in the careful arrangement of multitudinous neighborhoods. There are Emily Dickinson's fascicles, including the twenty-fourth and its oft-discussed lines, "This is my letter to the World / That never wrote to me."[37] Dickinson's poetic craftsmanship seems to stitch together words, pages, poems, and booklets so that the contingency of union itself becomes the message, an oblique response to Osborn's experience of unruly intimacy (see chapter 2) and Moore's communal arrangements (see chapter 4). There is the 1841 book *Essays,* written by the mixed-race Native and African American educator Ann Plato. Between her prose essays and concluding poems, she nested elegiac biographies for lost friends that carefully quote their deathbed admonishments. There is Frances E. W. Harper's *Iola Leroy* (1892), a tragic mulatta novel refashioned to skip the tragedy.[38] For Iola and her brother, false telegrams and smuggled letters allow them to discover their maternal roots in blackness and slavery.[39] Elsewhere in the novel, remembered songs summon lost relatives to renewed intimacy. Plato's prose elegies and Harper's lyrical and epistolary insertions function as scaffolds of bondedness on which to reconstruct neighborhoods fragmented by death and commodification, much as Wheatley's elegies offered consolation to a disoriented black diaspora (see chapter 3).[40] Here, a reading practice that turns to relational publication asks us to unmoor women's publication history from print and books and observe technological, sensorial, temporal, and philosophic continuities.

In this light, I close with a final relational publication reading, one that folds the past against the present. Prudence Punderson began her embroidered picture *The First, Second, and Last Scene of Mortality* in 1776 at the start of the American Revolution (see plate 6). Having decamped from Connecticut to Long Island because of wartime violence and troop movements, she was unable to complete the project until 1783. Her masterpiece spans the revolution and connects colonial and national frameworks. As such, it is primarily concerned with arranging temporal affiliation, and she rendered herself at different points in her life. In the center is her present self as artist seated before the beginnings of a botanical sketch, of which only the stem is complete, and an inkwell, a straightedge, and a compass. To the left, she is enclosed in a black coffin on a table, marked "P. P."; the backdrop is a mirror shrouded in mourning. On the right, she is an infant in a cradle, rocked by a black servant girl, probably a likeness of the family's domestic slave, Jenny. Behind the servant is a portrait of a young woman who is turned away from a soldier. Her headpiece resembles that of the middle figure. Like Eliza Wharton, Punderson composed herself, but she did so in silk thread and careful stitches. Juxtaposing multiple "scenes," her mortality seems less absolute than Wharton's, as disparate selves are synchronous and as intimate attachments—to nursemaid, to suitor, to craft, to mourner—evolve or remain illusory.[41] Her needlework renderings interrupt the fantasy of orderly association as diagrammed in "Circle of the Social and Benevolent Affections." Self and affiliations are not nested but crisscross space and time. The "Circle's" "NATIONS OF THE SAME COLOUR" are not distant but reside within the home, and household walls are not inviolable to the penetration of neighborly intimacies, even when one turns away.

Punderson's needlework functions as an act of relational publication that makes public an invitation to a transtemporal neighborhood. Inspired by its depiction of artistic creation within the mortal span, the contemporary sculptor and mixed-media painter Kiki Smith accepted the invitation and composed her responses. Her 2010 exhibition *Sojourn* at the Brooklyn Museum in New York explicitly elaborated on Punderson, segmenting empty museum space into a progression of galleries that paralleled without replicating Punderson's arc (see plates 7–9).[42] Smith positioned *The Annunciation* (2008) in the center of the first room. The seated figure faced a painting of a tall, many-paned window and lifted its hand equivocally, perhaps welcoming, perhaps forestalling an approach. On the wall hung *Visitation I* and *III,* each a painting of a seated figure showered by dark shafts in the midst of which fly a bird. Here and in other galleries a series of modest bird sculptures were suspended, three-dimensional manifestations of the painted birds, at times casting shadows on the walls and paintings. Some of these sculptures share the name *Messenger,* associating them with the scene of annunciation, in which God sends the angel Gabriel to announce immaculate conception.[43] The installation wound past more paintings depicting more figures. Some were standing, others sitting. Some were solitary, some arrayed in a line, some cradled in another's arms. Many gazed out from the paper canvas, while others turned to avian messengers. Interspersed were framed mixed-media botanical pieces. The exhibition concluded with a portrayal of death. An unfinished wooden coffin on a drop-leaf table—empty except for glass dandelions—anchored the final gallery. Unoccupied chairs lined the wall under large paintings of more coffins, including one opened, with the corpse barely contained.

Throughout, Smith referred to Punderson's tableau, also on display as part of the exhibit. Both Smith's sculpted *Annunciation* and Punderson's embroidered nursemaid were seated, smooth-pated and androgynous, their gazes alien and expectant. Painted and molded avian curves evoked those of Punderson's center scene and the tentative loops of the tabletop botanical sketch, made with a feather quill. The sculpted and collaged slashes materially mirrored the texture of silk embroidery, an accumulation of linear stitches most visible on paned window, checkered floor, and the brick wall against which the girl presses her body. Smith's open coffin tantalized visitors, inviting them to relieve our suspense and peer inside Punderson's closed casket, only to find the corpse absent, having been replaced with the floral subject of her incomplete drawing or maybe reinterred in the paintings on the walls. The elapse between the second and last scene of mortality remains unknown.

Thus, Smith read a message in Punderson's needlework. Her reply adheres past to present without collapsing distinctions. Their works collectively gesture to spatial and temporal bondedness, framed enclosures that propose revised neighborhoods accommodating juxtaposition but not merger. Boundaries, difference, change: all are arranged and rearranged. In such works, the nation emerges as a fluid assemblage of neighborhoods, one that co-evolves with, instead of foreclosing, alternative forms of public community. We are challenged by neighborliness to see the persistence of relational publication. It disrupts a publication history for women that privileges print and is bound by writing, thereby eliding the material and performative and spatial valances of their work. It responds to the challenges of co-mingling and seeks to compensate for the hollowness and evanescence of fraternal civic bonds (and histories of exclusion and restriction) by turning to quotidian intimacies, the pleasures and pains and possibilities of particularity.

NOTES

Introduction

1. Dimock's "Scales of Aggregation," though dealing with mostly contemporary concerns, offers a provocative reason to juxtapose different levels of aggregation: "*scalar variety* exerts [pressure] on more conventional forms, such as the nation" (219). Thinking about "prenational" aggregation, along with other scalar varieties, "anchors" the transnational to "everyday life" (226). In my argument, neighborhood puts pressure on nation.

2. Here I refer to Anderson's *Imagined Communities*, a foundational study in scholarship on the relationship between print and American democratic origins. For two other key studies, see Habermas, *Structural Transformation*, and Warner, *Letters of the Republic*, which I discuss in depth later in the book. See also Ziff, *Writing in the New Nation;* Larkin, *Thomas Paine;* and Dillon, *Gender of Freedom.* Habermas especially has inspired a host of responses. For a broad sample, see the essays in Calhoun, *Habermas;* like the work of Anderson and Habermas, they do not exclusively address an American context. For other important challenges and complements to the concept of the eighteenth-century public sphere, see Cowan, "What Was Masculine about the Public Sphere?" and *Social Life of Coffee;* and Keen, *Crisis of Literature.* In *Creation of the Media,* Starr places these early years in the context of a longer history of American media. While I am concerned with reconsidering communal revolution and publication, others have questioned the dominance of republican print by turning to orality; for example, Looby's *Voicing America* contrasts "the silence of print" with "the grain of the voice" (3). See also Fliegelman, *Declaring Independence,* and Gustafson, *Eloquence Is Power.* The work of Anderson and those who followed his lead has also invigorated print culture historiography. For an excellent and thorough overview of colonial American book history, see Amory and Hall, *Colonial Book.* On the relationship between the early republic and the explosive proliferation of print, see Remer, *Printers and Men of Capital;* Loughran, *Republic in Print;* and Round, *Removable Type;* as well as the essays in Cohen and Stein, *Early African American Print Culture.* Loughran, in particular, challenges the Anderson-Habermas-Warner model. Also see Gross and Kelley, *Extensive Republic.*

3. The French-Algonquin Isabelle Montour, often referred to as Madame Montour, is fascinating and complicated. See Vincens, *Madame Montour,* esp. chap. 8; and Hirsch, "'Celebrated Madame Montour.'"

4. Hazard, *Minutes,* 3:296. Jacobs provides a concise description of diplomatic wampum: "A string consisted of a group of leather strips (called strands) which were about

three feet in length and tied together at one end. These were strung with grains of various colors. The colors were superimposed upon white and purple grains to signify war, peace, friendship, or whatever the occasion demanded. Red was most popular, being painted over grains in both strings and belts. The strings were used for minor occasions; the belts for major. In the construction of belts, the design was based upon the pattern of leather strips which ran horizontally and vertically. Particular events warranted the construction of large belts, some six feet in length. The greater the size of the belt or string the more valuable it was and the more emphatic it made any speech that the wampum accompanied. In each case, the string and the belt served as a 'word' or even a complete statement" ("Wampum," 598).

5. The black or purple "grains" were "worth twice to three times as much as the white" (ibid., 597).

6. Native communities used wampum in a range of ways: communicatory, archival, diplomatic, and monetary. Scholars have studied Haudenosaunee (Iroquois) wampum most extensively. See ibid.; Snyderman, "Functions of Wampum"; Michelson, "Iroquoian Terms"; Clarke, *Thacher Wampum Belts;* and Foster, "Another Look." Haas, "Wampum As Hypertext," and Warkentin, "In Search of the Word" interpret wampum within a media studies and a book history frame, respectively. Lenape wampum is discussed in Newman, *On Record,* and Fur, *Nation of Women,* both of which offer longer analyses of Lenape culture, communication, and diplomacy.

7. Hazard, *Minutes,* 3:296.

8. For a fuller narrative of this event and its repercussions, see Merrell, *Into the American Woods,* 158–67.

9. See Fergusson, *Poemata Juvenalia.* This poem occurs in an unpaginated section of the volume and is marked as entry 82. The poem itself runs to almost fifty pages and is approximately seven hundred lines long. Although the poem was inscribed in 1790, it was written in 1768 at Graeme Park, according to Fergusson's note, which adds: "How little did I think when I was writting this Rural Peice that I should have my Husband and Nephew exild in Consequence of the Independancy." For more on this fascinating poem, see Wigginton, "Letters from a Woman."

10. Fergusson's footnote reads: "Mr John **Dickinson* a gentleman who wrote a Series of Letters Calld the **Farmers* Letters which were almost universaly admird For explaining the Rights of Taxation and the **Constitution* of Pennsylvania" (ibid.).

11. Fergusson, *Lania to a Friend,* 41. Fergusson was in London at the time of the Stamp Act's passage. She reported in this second transcription that Fothergill had relayed the news that "you were yesterday made a Slave of" (40). Presumably, she thought Fothergill would find "The Dream" of interest in light of that conversation. She suggested that this second transcription related to her decision to send the poem to Elias Boudinot, the former Continental Congress president and the brother of her dearest friend, Annis Boudinot Stockton. A transcription of her letter to Boudinot introduces this copy of the poem (37–38).

12. For more about the salon's participants, see Stabile, introduction to *Most Learned Woman,* 2–3, and Ousterhout, *Most Learned Woman,* 122. All of Fergusson's biographers discuss the salon; see Rush, "An Account," 523, and Wharton, *Salons,* 13–24. Rush's florid description is oft-quoted: "These evenings were, properly speaking, of the attic kind. The genius of Miss Graeme evolved the heat and light that animated them. One while she instructed by the stores of knowledge contained in the historians, philosophers, and

poets of ancient and modern nations, which she called forth at her pleasure; and again she charmed by a profusion of original ideas, collected by her vivid and widely expanded imagination, and combined with exquisite taste and judgment into an endless variety of elegant and delightful forms. Upon these occasions her body seemed to evanish, and she appeared to be all mind" (523).

13. Cohen, *Networked Wilderness,* 7.

14. Brooks, *Common Pot,* 12. A number of other Native studies scholars have also influenced my thinking about publication, writing, and literacy. For example, Boone's "Aztec Pictorial Histories" challenges our limited alphabetic understanding of writing by examining other kinds of writing in Mesoamerica and the Andes. Rasmussen's *Queequeg's Coffin* explains that European colonists "marveled" at the host of "indigenous ways to record and transmit information." Acknowledging that examples such as pictographs are also forms of writing, she considers a "vast and rich tableau in which the inter-animation between different forms of writing plays an important role in shaping literary production" (20). Newman's *On Records* highlights how colonial encounter called into question the nature of records, memory, and inscription: "What authority do certain material forms, such as wampum (Algonquian or Iroquoian shell beads), or landmarks, or relics, contribute to spoken recollections? Is alphabetic writing a reliable repository for memory, or does it distort memory by alienating it from necessary interpretive context?" (2–3). Round's *Removable Type* offers a book history of early Native print that considers multiple timelines, including indigenous oral and graphic communication: "Native people were already employing a wide array of sign systems prior to the arrival of Europeans" (11). In assembling an approach to literacy, Bross and Wyss's *Early Native Literacies* includes essays and primary material that range from manuscripts and printed texts to basketry and grave goods. For more examples of rich new analytical approaches, see the essays in Cohen and Glover, *Colonial Mediascapes,* particularly chap. 9: Rath, "Hearing Wampum."

15. See, for example, Gustafson, *Eloquence is Power,* and Jackson, "Talking Book." Elsewhere, Gustafson critiques early American public sphere scholarship for "neglecting the persistent importance of verbal arts such as oratory, and at the same time assuming a sharp divide between printed texts and oral performances" ("American Literature," 465). Though I find Native studies to be the field with the most established and robust reconsideration what early American publication means in its oral, material, performative, and scriptive valences, there is a significant and rapidly expanding conversation about the meaning of publication beyond that field. For example, Amory and Hall's *Colonial Book* frequently invokes the specter of scribal publication in which copies were made by hand rather than press. In his chapter on the early Chesapeake, Hall admits that a history of the book suffers from scribal publication's ephemerality, placing gaps in our knowledge of what circulated. Further contemplating our necessarily contingent view of the early American book and publication history, he explains: "Texts were also 'published' by the age-old method of being read aloud. When colonists used the word 'publish,' it usually signified this mode of communication" ("Chesapeake," 57). Cohen and Stein's collection *Early African American Print Culture* responds to Jackson's call for more work in the area and testifies to the rich yet understudied cultures of early African American print, which until recently was mostly understood through the "talking book," a trope first noted by Paul Edwards and made central by Henry Louis Gates. See Edwards's edition of *Life of Olaudah Equiano,* and Gates, *Signifying Monkey.* Though

concerned with an Anglo-African rather than an African American, Mattes's "Penman's Devil" delineates the play between print and handwriting in Ignatius Sancho's letters, thereby locating this reconsideration of publication and its forms in a broader Atlantic world. Medieval studies has also considered the question of when written English-language texts became associated with reliability and truth. See, for example, Clanchy's seminal *From Memory to Written Record.* This longer view reminds us that print was, in the eighteenth century, something of an arriviste among publication technologies.

16. Gustafson, "American Literature," 475.

17. *Publisher* may seem a more apt word than *author,* but it admits too much confusion. For a famous example of the large, long-standing, and varied conversation that troubles and contextualizes the meaning of authorship, see Foucault's essay "What Is an Author?" in *Language,* which considers the ideological function of the author in discourse (113–38). More recent highlights include Brewer, "Tactility," and Garvey, *Writing with Scissors.* Garvey's entire book is fascinating, but her introduction provides a strong overview, surveying scrapbooks, commonplace books, and newspaper reprints, all of which are forms in which "the reader becomes the author" (26). While she refers to scrapbook *makers* (not *authors*) and lingers on what she terms the anonymity (rather than author) function (39–47), she also pointedly notes: "Clipping and saving the contents of periodicals in scrapbooks is a form of active reading that shifts the line between reading and writing" (47). Blayney's *First Folio* is a strong reminder that even our most traditional understandings of literary authorship are suspect.

18. Decker, *Epistolary Practices,* 4.

19. Altman, *Epistolarity,* 13.

20. Ibid., 118. For Altman, an interpersonal bond "necessarily structures meaning" in an epistolary novel, whether or not both sides of a correspondence are included in the narration (118). She includes certain well-known multicorrespondent examples, such as Samuel Richardson's *Pamela* (1740), Pierre Choderlos de Laclos's *Les Liaisons Dangereuses* (1782), and Hannah Webster Foster's *The Coquette* (1797). Yet one side of the exchange may be extratextual, as in Crèvecoeur's *Letters from an American Farmer* (1781). Altman also cites diary novels addressed to specific individuals, such as Denis Diderot's *La Religieuse* (1796), though she applies *epistolary* only to those in which the addressee alters the form and meaning of the work (88–92).

21. McLuhan, *Understanding Media,* 8.

22. Bolter and Grusin, *Remediation,* 45.

23. The incorporation of letters into virtually every genre attests to epistolarity's portability and availability. Without a doubt, the eighteenth-century letter maintained, even intensified, in vigor, paralleling the emerging republic. As literacy spread, so did correspondence. For evidence of its cultural importance, see Bannet's *Empire of Letters,* which documents more than fifty distinct examples of letter writing manuals in the eighteenth century and posits that their "influence" "rivaled" that of popular novels such as Richardson's *Clarissa* (ix, 316–22). The epistolary novel and the verse epistle dominated their respective classes. Letters are so ubiquitous in other genres—travelogues, advice books, natural histories, and so on—that to many their presence has seemed scarcely worth noting.

24. *Republican* here is the adjectival form of *republic.* In this book, I do not enter into or distinguish between philosophies of republicanism and liberalism.

25. Anderson, *Imagined Communities,* 37.

26. Habermas, for example, asserts that in the eighteenth century "the public very much assumed its specific form" from the "bourgeois reading public" and "remained rooted in the world of letters" (*Structural Transformation,* 85). In a chapter section titled "The Model Case of British Development," he cites newspapers, periodicals, and pamphlets as well as Jonathan Swift's *Gulliver's Travels* and Alexander Pope's *Dunciad* as exemplars of the public sphere's formative literary technology (60).

27. Warner, *Letters,* 40. Warner elaborates on anonymity in subsequent publications; see, for example, the section "*A public is a relation among strangers,*" in *Publics and Counterpublics* (74–76).

28. Anderson, *Imagined Communities,* 7.

29. This suggestion of a temporal relationship between local and national identities mirrors a similar one that some have observed in Habermasian public sphere theory, wherein the private sphere is understood to be the precursor to the public sphere. Dillon, for example, critiques Habermas's theory because it aligns women with the private sphere and therefore misunderstands them as prepolitical (*Gender of Freedom,* 19–25). Challenges to a before-and-after model also appear in scholarship about the Enlightenment and religious superstition and enthusiasm. See, for example, Seeman, *Pious Persuasions,* chap. 6.

30. Of course, real participants in the public sphere did not always match the imagined reader. While some believe that the gender diversity of the reading and writing public was ignored in favor of a supposedly universal male subject, others argue that identifying women solely with the private sphere was necessary and ongoing. For example, Dillon, building on the work of feminist political philosophers, brands the public sphere as masculine while identifying the constitutive role of both genders in its emergence and maintenance. While women were found frequently in the public sphere, their presence, she argues, primarily "addressed the value (if not the sacred nature) of women's association with domesticity and privacy" (*Gender of Freedom,* 4). Women as subjects and agents entered the literary (not political) public sphere to confirm the domestic as their pure and proper abode and thereby reaffirm its ideological distinction from the public (3). Although Dillon distinguishes between liberalism and republicanism, her point still stands: the public sphere reifies women's embodied particularity (1–48). For other critiques of public sphere exclusivity, see Landes, *Women and the Public Sphere,* and Eley, "Nations Publics, and Political Cultures."

31. The occasional inclusion and even influence of women did not transform the public sphere into a gender-neutral space. Speaking about the English public sphere, Cowan reminds us that the "presence of women in the coffeehouses cannot be taken as clear-cut evidence of their equal participation" ("What Was Masculine about the Public Sphere?" 128).

32. A host of important feminist scholars theorize about women's gendered embodiment (for example, Simone de Beauvoir, Luce Irigaray, and Judith Butler). See Bordo, *Unbearable Weight,* 1–42, for an overview of those theories and their connection to contemporary American culture. For a powerful review of theories on women's bodies, liberalism, and the ideological functions of gender, see Dillon, *Gender of Freedom,* 11–19.

33. Dillon, *Gender of Freedom,* 34.

34. I am more concerned with the neighborhood as experienced by early Americans rather than theorizing the concept of neighbor; yet as Žižek notes, the neighbor can be a figure of both "imaginary *semblable*/double" and "an inert, impenetrable, enigmatic

presence": the latter, "alien traumatic kernel forever persists in my Neighbor" (Žižek et al., *Neighbor,* 140).

35. Kaye, *Joining Places,* 4.

36. Schneider refers to this aspect of letter writing as "sociotextual" (*Culture of Epistolarity,* 15). For other studies of letters, see Cook, *Epistolary Bodies,* and Decker, *Epistolary Practices.*

37. Since the mid-2000s, scholars of early America have been engaging in fascinating discussions about cartography and what Brückner terms *geographic literacy,* which he sees as an increasingly important version of literacy in the colonial Americas: "Over the course of the eighteenth century [geography's] signs, symbols, and rhetoric became an everyday language by which men and women not only spoke and wrote about each other but came to symbolically represent themselves" (*Geographic Revolution,* 13–14). See also the essays in Brückner, *Early American Cartographies.*

38. I searched for *neighb*rhood** to account for variations in spelling. I had more than 85,000 hits when including those for *neighb*r.* Given the recent popularity of Actor-Network-Theory (ANT) I also tried *netw*rk** as an alternative. However, *network* is not an early American concept, and I only had 235 hits in the same database, which were generally references to actual nets (that is, net work) or character-recognition errors for the words *New York* and *Newark.* Additionally, *network* suggests, to me, a certain evenness across nodes, whereas *neighborhood* gestures to diversity and imbalance, precisely the kinds of bondedness with which relational publication is concerned. See Latour, *Reassembling the Social,* for a thorough and entertaining overview of ANT.

39. Robinson, *Virginia Treaties,* 82.

40. Ibid., 84.

41. Hazard, *Minutes,* 2:15. See Spady, "Colonialism," for a discussion of these articles in the context of Penn's rhetoric. Though he does not hone in on the word *neighborhood,* he convincingly cautions that Lenape and Haudenosaunee understandings of the implications of such diplomatic relations were quite different.

42. Hazard, *Minutes,* 3:274.

43. "Protocol demanded that friendly visitors stop at the wood's edge before entering a village. The concept is so distinct that it is best rendered in English as one word—*woodsedge.* There they shouted to announce themselves, upon which a party came out to escort them into the village. *To be at the wood's edge,* therefore, was a manner of announcing one's readiness to treat" (Jennings et al., "Glossary," 124). Richter considers the wood's edge in the context of town layout and diplomatic ceremony (*Ordeal of the Longhouse* 17–20, 41–42).

44. Waselkov, "Indian Maps," 207. I elaborate on this aspect of southeastern indigenous cartography in chap. 1.

45. Mather, *Wonders,* title page.

46. It is fascinating to see the ways in which other virtuosos of republican print sought to enfold the neighborhood into a national model. Paine, for example, presented a hierarchy of fraternal identifications: "It is pleasant to observe by what regular gradations we surmount the force of local prejudice, as we enlarge our acquaintance with the world. A man born in any town in England divided into parishes, will naturally associate most with his fellow parishioners (because their interests in many cases will be common) and distinguish him by the name of *neighbour;* if he meet him but a few miles from home, he drops the narrow idea of a street, and salutes him by the name of *townsman;* if he travel

out of the county, and meet him in any other, he forgets the minor divisions of street and town, and calls him *countryman,* i.e. *country-man;* but if in their foreign excursions they should associate in France or any other part of *Europe,* their local remembrance would be enlarged into that of *Englishmen.* And by a just parity of reasoning, all Europeans meeting in America, or any other quarter of the globe, are *countrymen;* for England, Holland, Germany, or Sweden, when compared with the whole, stand in the same places on the larger scale, which the divisions of street, town, and county do on the smaller ones; distinctions too limited for continental minds" (*Common Sense,* 16). For him, distance and scale make "distinctions" illegible; yet due to their gender, women bring distinction with them, even when encountering their male neighbor on a distant continent.

47. Crèvecoeur, *Letters,* 55.

48. Ibid., 54.

49. I agree with others who contend that the divide between public and private is messy, even fictitious. If, however, we could map the public and the private, then a neighborhood geographically would include both. I refer to public and private in this subjunctive way, replacing *private* with *domestic* to call to mind the interior of actual homes and calling *public* what lies outside the door. Even this distinction remains messy and fictitious as a home's walls were no guarantor of privacy. See D'Emilio and Freedman, *Intimate Matters,* 29–30.

50. Kaye, *Joining Places,* 1.

51. For a clear overview of the term *affect-nation* and its relation to contemporary scholarship, see Coviello, *Intimacy in America,* 169–75. On masculinity, American nationalism, and feeling, see Hendler, *Public Sentiments.* On intimacy and the work of empire, see, for example, Povinelli, *Empire of Love,* 1–25. She is particularly interested in intimacy as it relates to sexuality.

52. While anonymity remained fundamental after the eighteenth century, the public sphere (always the *liberal, bourgeois* public sphere, even if those Habermasian qualifiers were frequently dropped) broke into *publics* and *counterpublics.* See Warner, *Publics and Counterpublics,* and Fraser, "Rethinking the Public Sphere."

53. See Berlant, introduction to *Intimacy,* 1, and Coviello, *Intimacy in America,* 3–9. For women, the trauma of prohibition—consistently ideological but also occasionally material, as when vocal women experience mockery, expulsion, and assault—pervades American literature. Since the nation's founding in the eighteenth century, women have remained on the periphery, unable to convincingly or consistently insist on their intimate affiliation. In the nineteenth century, their pursuit of public intimacy and influence was redirected away from full political participation toward consumption, idealized feminine companionship, and extrapolitical activism via societies, clubs, church groups, and so on (Berlant, *Female Complaint,* 5–8; Ryan, "Gender and Public Access," 267–74). I consider this subject more fully in the afterword.

54. Berlant, introduction to *Intimacy,* 2.

55. Warner, *Publics and Counterpublics,* 120.

56. In *Intimacy in America,* Coviello ponders what would happen "were we to define intimacy as, at base, an affective exchange understood to be reciprocal and recursive." Later in the paragraph, he declares that intimacy "may . . . designate a kind of connectedness between persons whose proper vehicle is feeling." Between these two possible definitions (which are the ones he uses for the remainder of the book), he refers to kinds of intimacy that do not clearly belong to either: "lifelong proximity" and "domesticity"

(6). These modes draw attention to the conditional nature of his definitions, especially when we consider the neighborhood. At times forced and often uneven, "lifelong proximity" and "domesticity" are not always affective; and feeling can be ancillary or incidental to their existence. Thus, the neighborhood leads us to ponder what other kinds of reciprocal and recursive exchange occur between persons whose intimacy transpires under these subcategories.

57. See Zboray and Zboray, *Everyday Ideas,* for a fascinating study of exchange and relationality. Focusing on antebellum New England, it argues that "readers refashioned ideas gleaned from literature into webs of local knowledge that were spun out through social ties. Insofar as ideas themselves became everyday, common social experience became literary as genre conventions structured thinking and interpersonal expression. Literary experience unfolded in often dense networks of kin, friends, and neighbors, deeply imbuing it with social relations and implicating it in them. Basically, literature supported family life and socializing" (xvii–xviii).

58. Fergusson uses the phrase twice in "The Dream," at the beginning and the end, effectively framing the moment of message delivery with a geographic (Atlantic coast) and relational invocation.

59. For a discussion of the royal and American postal systems, see John, *Spreading the News,* 25–27. Offices were located primarily in port cities because their main users were merchants and politicians.

60. Early modern English author Margaret Cavendish famously referred to her manuscript writings as "Paper Bodies," an evocative phrase (*CCXI Sociable Letters,* 296).

61. For a lucid explanation of the architectural dimensions of writing, especially for women, see Stabile, *Memory's Daughters,* chap. 2.

62. Most scholars connect letter writing to an elite or a rising middle class. For example, Shields contends that the performative civility of belletristic coteries brings "into being" a "sensus communis" wherein "distinctions" are "put aside" to "establish fraternal or sororal familiarity" (*Civil Tongues,* xviii, xx). In *Empire of Letters,* Bannet focuses on letter manuals and their importance in creating imperial and regional identities. She uncovers the practical importance of correspondence generally when she observes that letter manuals disseminate "a single standard language, method and culture of polite communication" (x). Monaghan's *Learning to Read and Write,* though not concerned with letter writing per se, identifies a link between a free colonial class identity and writing instruction: introduction to disciplined writing included a subtextual education in self-expression and self-determination (273). Even as it was a marker of class, competence in letter writing reproduced and extended colonization. Dierks's *In My Power* amasses an impressive array of examples and equates Euro-Americans' "exclusionary possession of social and cultural resources to cultivate skills, to sustain family connections, and to pursue economic opportunities" with a "covert mode of power" that contributed to the victimization and exploitation of Native Americans and Africans (1).

63. Pinckney, *Letterbook,* 35.

64. Ibid., 8.

65. Indigo cultivation was labor-intensive. The species with which Lucas experimented was *Indigofera tinctoria,* a native of India and Africa and grown in the West Indies, where the French had developed it as a profitable crop. A 1747 British pamphlet explains that it requires land that is "as clean as possible from Weeds," has been "well ploughed, and harrowed, to break the Clods, and make it fine, before the Seed is sown" (*Further*

Observations, 15). To plant the seeds, one "make[s] Drills about half an Inch deep, either with a Hoe or a drill Plow, at about a Foot and a half distance from each other, and scatter[s] the Seeds thin in the Drills, then draw[s] the Earth over the Seeds, so as to bury them about half an Inch deep" (16). During the approximately two-month growing period, the planter kept the indigo moist and the ground free of weeds. When mature, the plant was cut at the base of the stalk, and a second crop would be ready in another six or seven weeks. In her experiments, Lucas would have striven for a crop large enough for her to determine an ideal method of local cultivation, to yield seed, and to produce a reasonable quantity for processing and thus verifying the plants' quality. A later letter reveals that one of her earliest crops produced about "a hundred bushels" (approximately eight hundred gallons). Her disappointment in what was to her a meager harvest indicates that she was working with substantial quantities (Pinckney, *Letterbook,* 16). Pettit's *America's Indigo Blues* provides a thorough overview of indigo cultivation and preparation; see, in particular, chaps. 3 and 4.

66. Jensen, *English Historical Documents,* 489.

67. See Brooks, *Common Pot,* 220–24, for more on Native letters, especially as tools of "traveling communication," information relay, and diplomacy.

68. McCallum, *Letters,* 228.

69. Ibid., 229–30. For an image and analysis of the younger Simon's letter, see Wyss, "Writing Back to Wheelock." For Wyss, the daughter's letters are "a poignant reminder that whatever promise education held out to young Native women in the eighteenth century, in the end it offered a structure through which they could define only what they would not be rather than what they could be" (98).

70. See Daybell, "Scripting," for a discussion of early modern women's use of the petition. See Kerber, *Women of the Republic,* 85–99, for women's use of the petition during the Revolution, though she concludes that it rhetorically required them to perform weakness and subservience. Brooks argues that Native petitions resemble wampum, "corresponding to formal messages from one nation to another" (*Common Pot,* 224).

71. Kerber, *Women of the Republic,* 85.

72. Belinda, "Petition of 1782," 187.

73. Ibid., 188.

74. Belinda was granted an annual income, though she only received it twice: once after her 1782 petition and again in 1787, when she petitioned again. For another discussion of Belinda's petitions, see Harris, *Executing Race,* 69–79.

75. See, for example, the minutes of the Monthly Meeting of Women Friends in Philadelphia, 1768–81, and of the Burlington Quarterly Meeting of Women Friends, 1686–1845, hereafter cited as PWMM and BWQM. The Philadelphia minutes note reading the London Yearly Meeting epistle of 1772 (PWMM, 233). The Burlington minutes note reading the same epistle twice in 1773, in the second month (February) and the eighth month (August), "by particular Desire" (BWQM, 115).

76. These reports relayed information about membership, worship attendance, temperance, slave ownership, discipline, education, and so on.

77. The minutes are available on microfilm at Swarthmore and Haverford colleges. Citations here refer to the microfilm copy of the Philadelphia Women's Yearly Meeting minutes, 1681–1814, hereafter referred to as PWYM.

78. Ibid., 268.

79. Ibid., 276–77.

80. Ibid., 277.

81. BWQM, 138.

82. About four Monthly Meetings were affiliated with the Burlington Quarterly Meeting ("Friends' Meetings in America," 29).

83. A manuscript dates the correspondence to the 1760s, but the letters may have been written as early as 1746, when Harrison's father died. See letters among Hannah Griffitts, Hannah Harrison, and Mary Norris.

84. For a discussion of Fairhill's construction and architecture, see Reinberger and McLean, "Isaac Norris's Fairhill."

85. Kerber recalls the long history of petitioning when she refers to oral and written petitions collectively as a "most archaic mode" (*Women of the Republic,* 85).

86. Native studies has also engaged in a spirited debate regarding an oral-written divide. See Teuton, *Deep Waters,* for a comprehensive history and response. Also see Ong, *Orality and Literacy.*

87. Conscious of the likelihood of a wider audience, Esther Edwards Burr and Sarah Prince, who kept and exchanged detailed and at times confessional epistolary journals, saved certain confidences for their "privacies": secret letters sent via "trusted friends" and "burned as soon as they were read" (Burr, *Journal,* 48, n. 9).

88. For a study of belletristic culture and the pleasures of manuscript and letter exchange, see Shields, *Civil Tongues.*

89. Franklin, *Autobiography,* 119–20. Franklin's plan was inspired by his familiarity with Philadelphia's sole newspaper, the "wretchedly manag'd" *American Weekly Mercury,* published by Andrew Bradford but printed by Franklin (119).

90. Franklin, *Papers,* 1:12.

91. Ibid., 113.

92. See Klepp, *Revolutionary Conceptions,* especially chap. 6, for a discussion of this incident in the context of early American contraceptive history.

93. Franklin, *Papers,* 115.

94. Ibid., 123.

95. Ibid., 124. These entertaining lampoons distracted readers from Keimer's novel yet uninspired *Universal Instructor,* which struggled to find "enough filler" (Franklin, *Autobiography,* 120; Lemay, *Life,* 414.). By the end of the year, Franklin and his partner George Meredith had assumed responsibility for the paper. In his *Autobiography,* Franklin crows that Keimer "offer'd" it to him for a "Trifle" (120). The *Pennsylvania Gazette,* in his possession, "prov'd in a few Years extreamly profitable" (120).

96. While Franklin was indisputably the force launching these barbs, it is impossible to prove definitively that Careful and Shortface were his inventions. However, his authorship has been widely and reasonably presumed. For examples, see the introductory headnote of Labaree et al. (Franklin, *Papers,* 112), the Library Company of Philadelphia's digital exhibit *Benjamin Franklin,* and Klepp's suggestive comments on his female pseudonyms ("Benjamin Franklin and Women," 246). Franklin wrote Busy-Body nos. 1–5 and 8. His fellow Junto member, Joseph Breintnall wrote the others (Lemay, *Life,* 378). The Patience letter is from no. 4.

97. Warner, *Letters,* 82. Warner is the scholar most associated with this interpretation of Franklin. He identifies in Franklin's early years the emergence of a philosophy of letters as objects: "Just as the young Franklin arranged paper and type, and just as the good writer arranges words and expression, and just as the rational thinker arranges thought, so also rational man arranges discourse" (81).

98. Warner acknowledges this paradox but glosses this and other moments of youthful extravagant femaleness by shifting discussion to the endurance and variety of Franklin's personae over a long career (ibid., 86–88).

99. Franklin, *Papers,* 112.

100. Ibid., 113.

101. Ibid., 123–24.

1. Coosaponakeesa's Colonial Neighborhood

1. Coosaponakeesa went by Mary Musgrove, Mary Mathews, Mary Bosomworth, and variant spellings of Coosaponakeesa. When speaking of her generally, I use the name she was using at the end of her life, Coosaponakeesa. When speaking about a particular moment or text, I use the name she preferred at that time.

2. *Mico* is the Creek term for a *talwa*'s (town's) peace leader. Each talwa had a separate leader for war concerns, called the *tastanagi thlako* (war chief). The mico had more power than the tastanagi thlako did and acted as the primary leader of the talwa (Lankford, "Red and White," 57–58).

3. Candler, *Proceedings,* 262.

4. Ibid.

5. Ibid., 263.

6. Baine, "Myths," 432. Tuckabatchee was located at the bend of the Tallapoosa River in Georgia where it moves northward. Baine's article and the first three chapters of Hahn's *Life and Times* provide the most thorough accounts of Coosaponakeesa's early life, correcting other authors who have repeated the fabrications of Coosaponakeesa and her third husband, Thomas Bosomworth, as well as those of some of Georgia's historians. Hahn's biography, in particular, is a welcome corrective to the often confused and fragmentary narratives of her life. For more on her father, Edward Griffin, see 14–25. Hahn calls her mother his "Coweta wife," as the details of her life and residence are uncertain (18).

7. In 1732, Yamacraw mico Tomochichi requested that South Carolina provide his town with a trading post. Oglethorpe chose Savannah as the site for the first Georgian settlement during a preliminary trip in January 1733, during which Coosaponakeesa and her husband helped enlist Tomochichi's agreement. See Juricek, *Georgia Treaties,* 2–3, 7.

8. Ibid., 140.

9. For detailed participant biographies and discussions of the Bosomworth Controversy, see Fisher, "Mary Musgrove," and Hahn, *Life and Times.* For a succinct overview, see Green, "Mary Musgrove." For an example of a filing that includes multiple memorials and affidavits, see Candler, *Original Papers, Trustees,* 465–502.

10. These documents became more accessible to scholars in the early twentieth century, when editors began to compile and publish them. See Candler et al., eds., *Colonial Records.*

11. In choosing the word *emblematic,* I follow David A. Chang's lead. At the panel "Indigenous History: Speaking to Core Issues in Early American History" at the June 2015 joint conference of the Society of Early Americanists and the Omohundro Institute for Early American History and Culture, he responded to a question about a particular Native Hawaiian's representativeness, saying that, while not representative, the man was emblematic.

12. For an overview of scholarship about Native women, gender roles, and leadership, see Shoemaker, introduction to *Negotiators of Change.*

13. Shoemaker, "Rise or Fall," 39.

14. For more on the Lady of Cofitachequi and Opossunoquonuske, see Hudson, *Knights of Spain,* 174–83, and Smith, *Writings,* 6. Documenting the unbroken persistence of Native women's sociocultural authority has been integral to twentieth-century tribal recognition cases, such as the one successfully pursued by the Mohegan tribe of Connecticut. See Fawcett-Sayet, "Sociocultural Authority."

15. Like Coosaponakeesa and many other Native women, Pocahontas used different names at different points in her life, including Amonute, Matoaka, and Rebecca Rolfe. Pocahontas, meaning "little mischievous one," was the name she used publicly as a girl, although it is probably the least accurate one when discussing the woman she became. For discussions of her name, see Rountree, "Pocahontas," 15–16; Allen, *Pocahontas,* 18; and Gilliam, "His Dearest Daughter's Names."

16. Because there was not enough time for a painting, van de Passe sketched her first and later produced the engraving. See Rountree, *Pocahontas,* 180.

17. Allen asserts that this fan marked Pocahontas as a Beloved Woman, "a significance perhaps known only to her and the Powhatan members of her party" (*Pocahontas,* 295). Perdue's *Cherokee Women* explains, "The Cherokees used the term *beloved* to apply to women and men who were repositories of spiritual knowledge and power" (206, n. 92).

18. See Townsend, *Pocahontas,* 151–54, for a more extensive discussion of this portrait.

19. Van de Passe produced a series of royal portraits that were collected, along with others, in *Baziliωlogia: A Booke of Kings.* This rare seventeenth-century book, of which no complete copy exists, is a miscellany of engravings of English monarchs and royal consorts. The Delabere and Fife copies include *Matoaka als Rebecca,* but it was probably not part of the original series of twenty-six (Levis, *Baziliωlogia,* 3–4). Portraits of women other than Queen Anne appear in the book, but none were engraved by van de Passe. However, he did also craft some silver and gold medallions that depicted royal figures such as Elizabeth I and Charles, Prince of Wales. See Veldman, *Crispijn de Passe and His Progeny,* 243–46.

20. Garber argues that early modern cross-dressing signaled a general crossing of boundaries, especially class, as the period's sumptuary laws "attempted to mark out as visible and above all *legible* distinctions of wealth and rank within a society undergoing changes that threatened to blur or even obliterate such distinctions" (*Vested Interests,* 25–26).

21. On viewing the trip to England as a marketing campaign for the Virginia Company, see Rountree, *Pocahontas,* 176.

22. Townsend, *Pocahontas,* 154.

23. Ibid., 152. Townsend notes that some elite women wore men's hats, but that doing so made them "subject to criticism for being unfeminine." She also argues that the simple hat resembles those worn by "bourgeois Puritans" (152).

24. Smith, *Writings,* 34.

25. In her biography, Allen contends that Pocahontas was a medicine woman, spy, and diplomat.

26. See *Catalogus Impressorum,* 168, and *English Part,* 4. John Chamberlain also possessed a copy of the engraving, though his was one of the originals produced by van de Passe. He wrote of the portrait: "Here is a fine picture of no fayre Lady and yet with her

tricking up and high stile and titles you might thincke her and her worshipfull husband to be sombody, yf you do not know that the poore companie of Virginia out of theyre povertie are faine to allow her fowre pounds a weeke for her maintenance" (McClure, *Letters,* 56–57).

27. Kidwell, "Indian Women," 98.

28. An understanding of Native women as cultural mediators necessarily relies on communication technologies. As LeMaster reminds us, southeastern Native women "served as translators, messengers, and providers of hospitality and, in their roles as wives, gave white men access to Indian kinship systems. They traveled with diplomatic delegations and shaped political decisions" (*Brothers,* 13).

29. Portable examples of media include Anishinaabe birchbark scrolls, Nahua codices, Haudenosaunee wampum, Pomo baskets, and Kiowa calendars. See Dewdney, *Sacred Scrolls;* León-Portilla, *Broken Spears,* 25–49; Fenton, *Great Law,* 224–39; Sarris, *Keeping Slug Woman Alive,* 51–62; and Mooney, *Calendar History.* For a collection of essays on early Native literacies in New England, see Bross and Wyss, *Early Native Literacies.*

30. Bolter and Grusin, *Remediation,* 45, 11–12.

31. Cohen and Glover, *Colonial Mediascapes,* 7–8.

32. Brooks, *Common Pot,* 9.

33. Ibid.

34. Ibid., 12.

35. Ibid., 13.

36. Justice, "Go Away Water!," 150.

37. According to Braund, "clans were composed of matrilineages that possessed a common, though distant and usually mythical, ancestor" (*Deerskins and Duffels,* 11). For an in-depth discussion of kinship, clans, and matrilineages, also see Hudson, *Southeastern Indians,* 184–257.

38. Mihesuah, *Indigenous American Women,* 44; Mann, *Iroquoian Women,* 118–19.

39. Landes, *Ojibwa Woman,* 133–35.

40. Van Kirk, *Many Tender Ties,* 66.

41. Ibid. Also see Van Kirk, "Thanadelthur."

42. Van Kirk, *Many Tender Ties,* 68.

43. Ibid., 69.

44. Ibid., 68–69.

45. Fraser, *Third Report,* 171–72. McKee separately confirmed the conversation but insisted he had made no commitment. Agushaway is another name for Egushwa (or Gushgushagwa), the Ottawa war chief who some saw as Pontiac's successor (Horsman, "Egushwa"). Interestingly, elsewhere Egushwa warned his brethren about the "*pen and ink witch-craft*" of treaties (Calloway, *Pen and Ink Witchcraft,* 106).

46. Fraser, *Third Report,* 172.

47. Ibid., 173. Brooks reasons that Native petitions can be like prayers or like satirical protest. If like prayers, which for an Oneida woman such as Ainse might assume obligation on the part of the power being appealed to, then the colonial government would be obligated to "relieve [the petitioners'] suffering" (*Common Pot,* 225).

48. Mann, *Iroquoian Women,* 16.

49. The board, after hearing her petition, granted her the land, though McKee, as deputy superintendent of Indian affairs, later overruled that decision.

50. Goeman's *Mark My Words* elucidates contemporary Native women's use of spatial remappings through literature to recover Native space, seeing it as integral to decolonization.

51. See Hudson, *Creek Paths,* 4–5. Due to their status as economic crossroads and their domestic compositions, Coosaponakeesa's trading posts and Cowpen plantation reflect an intimate mingling. She and her husbands possessed slaves and indentured servants. See, for example, Hahn, *Life and Times,* 72–74, 85.

52. See Waselkov, "Indian Maps," for an analysis of this and similar maps.

53. Juricek, *Colonial Georgia,* 7.

54. Braund, *Deerskins,* 42.

55. Ibid., 25.

56. For a discussion of Coosaponakeesa's transition to life in Pon Pon, a Carolina frontier town in Saint Bartholomew's Parish, see Hahn, *Life and Times,* chap. 2. For a discussion of Indian education in the Carolinas, see Szasz, *Indian Education,* 129–47. Coosaponakeesa may have been first taught by Ross Reynolds, a parish schoolmaster, and later by Nathaniel Osborn, an SPG missionary.

57. Juricek, *Georgia Treaties,* 141.

58. For the SPG's instructions, see *Collection of Papers.*

59. *Collection of Papers,* 17.

60. Tyerman, *Oxford Methodists,* 80.

61. Her relationship with Christianity soured after the death of her three sons. A Muskogee-English-German vocabulary, the likely product of Ingham's education, is in the Moravian Archive in Bethlehem, Pennsylvania. See Hahn, *Life and Times,* 105–6.

62. Gallay, "Origins," 376.

63. Ibid., 377.

64. Ibid., 379.

65. Candler, *Original Papers, Trustees,* 234.

66. See Schmidt, "'Grand Prophet.'"

67. Much recent scholarship—such as that of Brooks, Wyss, and Bross—insists on the authenticity of Native Christians' professions of faith and resists a view of Native converts as somehow less "Indian." They identify what is Native about Natives' Christianity. While it is unclear to what extent Coosaponakeesa's conversion was genuine, her strategic professions of a Christian identity suggest that Christianity offered a way to reconceptualize territorial sovereignty and natural rights.

68. Gordon, *Journal,* 35.

69. For firsthand descriptions of this encounter, see Coleman and Ready, *Original Papers, Correspondence,* 15–17, and Gordon, *Journal,* 35–36. The descriptions do not mention the presence of Coosaponakeesa, only her husband John Musgrove, at the first encounter. It is unclear whether she first greeted the colonists there or at her trading post shortly after. As Hahn discusses, her absence from this portion of the record reflects English colonizers' gendered expectations. He ponders whether Coosaponakeesa would have remained in the background if Musgrove had lived (*Life and Times,* 91).

70. Candler, *Proceedings,* 272.

71. According to *The Oxford English Dictionary,* a petticoat could be a skirt worn externally or underneath another skirt or dress. It could also be a short, tight-fitting undercoat worn by men or women for warmth, though this definition was increasingly rare by 1733. By the eighteenth century, a shift meant a woman's "body-garment" or

"underclothing." While traditional winter dress for Creek women was a short deerskin skirt and a fur or cloth coat, Yamacraw women dressed similarly to Coosaponakeesa. In a letter to his wife, Georgian colonist Thomas Causton, present at the landing, related, "The [Yamacraw] Queen and her Daughters wear Common printed Calicoe, Jacket and Petticoat without any Head Cloaths" (Juricek, *Georgia Treaties,* 10).

72. Osnabrig is also a cloth acquired by trade. This coarse, durable cloth is made from linen and used for clothing, tents, sacks, and so on. American slaves were often given osnabrig clothing.

73. Coosaponakeesa mentions Governor Robert Johnson's recommendation of her to Oglethorpe during a 1752 letter to the South Carolina council. See McDowell, *Documents,* 264.

74. Because Creek culture continues to thrive and adapt, my discussion of eighteenth-century specifics is written in the past tense. However, dualities remain core components to Creek ideology.

75. Because red and white occur at various structural points, many Creek men would transition between red and white mindsets, relating to a situation through not only personal character and desires but also assigned roles. "The point is not to be red or white, but red and white" (Lankford, "Red and White," 78).

76. Hudson, *Southeastern Indians*, 187.

77. Braund, "Guardians," 242. A small number of women achieved the official status of Beloved Woman or chief after being recognized for achieving peace.

78. Lankford, "Red and White," 77.

79. Piker, *Okfuskee,* 46.

80. The Red Coat King, whose name suggests a warlike attitude to colonial encounter, was in fact a staunch peacemaker, a Fanni Mico whose role was to mediate between his natal and adopted communities. The coat itself was "a garment that British diplomats reserved for leading headmen" (ibid., 25). For more on the role of the Fanni Mico, see 22–23, 48–52. One wonders how tenuous the Yamacraws may have perceived that moment of peace to be. Having experienced firsthand the costly Tuscarora and Yamasee wars of the 1710s—caused in part by traders' abuse of Indians throughout the region—and now seeing their interpreter in red, the observing Yamacraws would have conceivably recalled the potential for economic mistreatment. Musgrove herself may have been even more sensitive to such costs, as she resided in Saint Bartholomew's Parish during the wars, a place that "bore the brunt of Indian attacks" (Hahn, *Life and Times,* 53).

81. Juricek, *Georgia Treaties,* 15.

82. Ibid., 4.

83. In his introduction to these early documents, Juricek describes how "this treaty was closely patterned after the Creek treaty negotiated in 1717 by Oglethorpe's friend and collaborator, Governor Johnson of South Carolina." Article 4, in which the two groups lay out terms for future transfers of territory from Creeks to English colonists, has no counterpart in the 1717 treaty. Juricek also reasons, "If [Coosaponakeesa] was not the chief interpreter for the formal conference, she evidently was the interpreter for the land agreement" (ibid.)

84. Ibid., 15.

85. Unsurprisingly, given English cultural attitudes, not all English settlements honored this agreement, which led to conflict throughout the early years of the colony. Part of the Bosomworth Controversy included Creek anger about colonists' encroachment

on the so-called Yamacraw tract, the portion of land adjacent to Savannah that had been verbally delineated and reserved for the Yamacraws.

86. This distinction would not have been wholly foreign to the Georgian colonists. As Worster explains, "In traditional European society, land had ultimately belonged to the Crown. No individual could assert absolute, total authority over any part of it as long as it was in a final sense the Crown's, and the Crown was supposed to hold it as representative of all people living through all time" (*Wealth of Nature,* 97).

87. These negotiations were unsuccessful, probably due to the absence of Oglethorpe and inexperience of those he left in charge. See Sweet, *Negotiating for Georgia,* 61–66.

88. Whatever her motives, she did not write this letter in her capacity as interpreter because Jones had that role. Perhaps she didn't speak Choctaw, though she might have communicated with them using a trade language. Though dialectically distinct, Creek (or Muskogee) and Choctaw are branches of the Muskogean language family. See Hardy, introduction to "Part Two: The Muskogean Language Family."

89. Coleman and Ready, *Original Papers, Correspondence,* 63.

90. Ibid. According to the British translation and account, the Choctaw "king" said, "We are very glad that the English have taken notice of us. We have wanted an opportunity to make peace: but being come a great way we were not able to bring any presents. I belong to a great Nation and all my People are ready to confirm what I say, we are very glad you have sent so good a Man as Thomas Jones [official Georgia representative] to us. We are surrounded with White People and the French are building Forts which we do not like. We are come to see who are our friends and whose Protection we may rely on. We desire a trade very much that a Path may be kept betwixt you and us. And that you may see we come with good hearts we have brought our Women with us" (Juricek, *Georgia Treaties,* 36).

91. Coleman and Ready, *Original Papers, Correspondence,* 63.

92. Ibid.

93. Ibid. While troubling, her mention of alcohol as well as her own participation in its trade points to the contested and complex nature of Native alcohol consumption. Though there is no substantive history of its consumption by the Creeks, Ishii's study of its consumption by Cherokees in the colonial and preremoval eras considers its role in a changing economy and identifies its importance in politics and rituals. She also argues that its strategic use was a component of Cherokee sovereignty claims (see *Bad Fruits*). Archaeologists working at the site of the Cowpen, Coosaponakeesa's plantation outside Savannah, discovered unbroken bottles that contain traces of rum (Hahn, *Life and Times,* 3, 89).

94. For a historiographical analysis of this letter, see Juricek, *Georgia Treaties,* 28–29.

95. Coleman and Ready, *Original Papers, Correspondence,* 64.

96. This letter also highlights the important and helpful diplomatic role that Thomas Jones played. He was a Creek relation, of mixed-descent like Coosaponakeesa was, and a neighbor in Saint Bartholomew's Parish during her childhood and after her marriage. See Hahn, *Life and Times,* 94.

97. See Corkran, *Creek Frontier,* 48–60, and Sweet, *Negotiating for Georgia,* 15–20. For Creek leaders at this time, texts were a tangential part of that repertoire. Talks and gift exchanges continued to be the most integral practices in their diplomacy, though they were probably familiar with the creation of wampum to record formal agreements, a practice of certain Native nations in the northeast—for instance, the Haudenosaunee.

For more on Creek diplomacy and its relationship to English diplomacy, see Juricek, *Colonial Georgia,* 5–10. For more on wampum, see Richter, *Ordeal of the Longhouse,* especially 47–49; Murray, *Indian Giving,* 116–40; and Snyderman, "Functions of Wampum." I discuss wampum at some length in the introduction.

98. Lyons views Native treaty signatures as "a sign of consent in a context of coercion" (*X-Marks,* 1).

99. A memorial is a document expressing facts in support of a petition.

100. This memorial was not her first. In 1742 she petitioned for an overdue corn bounty on behalf of her deceased husband, Jacob Mathews, and in 1745 she submitted what appears to be the first memorial in the larger monetary and land recognition case. That one is no longer extant. See Candler, *Colonial Records,* 487.

101. Juricek, *Georgia Treaties,* 140.

102. Ibid., 143.

103. Ibid., 140.

104. There is some question as to whether Coosaponakeesa and the "Old Emperor," Brims, were blood relatives. Baine explains that translations of familial terms from Creek to English are "imprecis[e]" and argues that Coosaponakeesa's "pretensions to Creek aristocracy were false" ("Myths," 429–30). Also see Hudson, *Southeastern Indians,* 189. If Baine is correct, then this moment, in which Coosaponakeesa finesses differences in kinship terms, stresses her deftness at adapting Creek rhetorics of kinship. Hahn's biography argues that such moments attest to Coosaponakeesa's mother's "close relat[ion] to Coweta's chiefs, granting her infant girl, by birthright, a privileged place in Coweta society" (*Life and Times,* 14).

105. Juricek, *Georgia Treaties,* 140.

106. Ibid.

107. Hudson, *Southeastern Indians,* 200.

108. Juricek, *Georgia Treaties,* 141.

109. For example, Bosomworth narrated her essential role in keeping the Spanish at bay: "That after the War with Spain the services of the Indians were so frequently required that no Advantage could Possably be made by the Trade there; that she Constantly employed her Interest to bring Down her Friends and Relations from the Nation to fight against his Majestys Enemies which since the War they have so much Annoyed that they have been a strong Barrier and Defence of the Country against the Designs of the Spaniards as must be universally Allowed by every Unprejudiced Person" (ibid., 143).

110. Ibid., 144–45.

111. Womack, *Red on Red,* 29.

112. Ibid., 54. Womack is explicating Creek storytelling, politics, and the red-white duality by referring to Lankford, "Red and White."

113. Candler, *Proceedings,* 263.

114. Ibid., 264.

115. Ibid.

116. Ibid., 270–71.

117. Ibid., 274–75.

118. Ibid., 258, my emphasis. The word *spirited* may suggest alcohol to the modern reader; but according to the *Oxford English Dictionary,* its use in that context didn't emerge until 1822.

119. Coleman and Ready, *Original Papers of Governor John Reynolds,* 173.

120. Bosomworth's response to this particular accusation had perhaps been preplanned. Several years before, Georgia's president, William Stephens, had mocked Creek complaints about colonists' timber theft when, after expressing his "desir[e]" for "justice," requested that Bosomworth "Order any *christian* person to . . . make Oath to the truth of the facts" (ibid., 202). Thus, she knew she must tack between being Christian and Creek to maintain credibility and independence.

121. Candler, *Proceedings,* 295–96.

2. Vexing Motherhood and Interracial Intimacy

1. Though Osborn did not note where Berkley was, she was probably referring to the one in Massachusetts because she also notes that her relative is "near Neighbour to the Rev mr [T]obey" (letter, 4 June 1754). Samuel Tobey was a minister in Berkley, Massachusetts, which was roughly thirty miles from Osborn's home (Sanford, *History,* 6–9).

2. Norton, "My Resting Reaping Times," 527. In her article, Norton discusses and transcribes an Osborn letter to Joseph Fish that details her long-standing morning ritual of prayer and writing. For the original, see Osborn, letter, 28 February–7 March 1767.

3. Osborn, diary, 190. Osborn's manuscript diaries are short on punctuation. When quoting to provide chronology and events, I have inserted punctuation for the sake of clarity. When quoting to elucidate her affective and spiritual state, I have eschewed such edits, staying true to her powerfully fluid expression.

4. Ibid., 190–91.

5. Ibid., 191.

6. Ibid., 192.

7. Ibid.

8. Ibid., 193.

9. The most prevalent form of life writing in eighteenth-century New England was the spiritual autobiography, a highly formulaic subgenre. Because many include or rely on conversion narratives, which Congregationalists had to submit to their church in oral or written form to attain full membership, they were often arguments that reinforced understandings of community and the requirements of belonging. Osborn's was no exception. Spiritual diaries, on the other hand, are episodic. In his comparison of spiritual autobiographies and diaries, Shea insists on a "division of duties" between the forms and argues that a diary "would fail . . . if the writer could not bring himself to view his most abhorrent self" (*Spiritual Autobiography,* 142). Thus, in contrast to the consistent argument in favor of the author's conversion found in the period's spiritual autobiographies and conversion narratives, a spiritual diary might have explicitly or implicitly argued for the uncertainty of one's spiritual conversion and revealed ongoing evidence of sin, unworthiness, and doubt. The primary audience was God, and the author might be more pressed than in a spiritual autobiography or conversion narrative to write with humility and honesty in the face of an omnipotent and all-knowing reader. As Imbarrato's study of early American autobiography concludes, because "the individual self is barely distinct from the larger social community," life writing from the period sought to simultaneously "enhance spiritual commitment and improve community welfare" (*Declarations of Independency,* xiii).

10. For extensive biographies of Osborn, see Osborn, *Memoirs,* 5–83, and Kujawa, "Religion, Education, and Gender." Brekus has recently published a meticulously re-

searched monograph that segments Osborn's chronology into themes and positions her in the context of early American evangelicalism; see *Sarah Osborn's World,* xiv–xv, 1–5, 333–35, for brief overviews of her life and death.

11. See Brekus for the archival evidence that suggests how and when Osborn acquired Bobey (*Sarah Osborn's World,* 174).

12. The curriculum included reading, writing, religion, and needlework. For a discussion of the school, its impact on Osborn's finances, her educational philosophy, and student demographics, see Kujawa, "Religion, Gender, and Education," 145–51. For a discussion of Osborn's work as an instructor, especially of needlework, see Ring, *Let Virtue,* 46–50. Brekus notes that Osborn is absent from Newport's tax lists (*Sarah Osborn's World,* 1).

13. This date comes from death and burial records at the Newport Historical Society.

14. It is possible that businessman Henry Osborn owned Phillis before his 1742 marriage to Sarah and that she became her mistress thereafter. It is also possible that the Osborns owned Phillis at the time of Bobey's birth in 1744, the same year Osborn opened her second school, and that they sold her for financial reasons, though this is unlikely, as evidenced by Osborn's suggestion that Bobey was a present from friends (see n. 16). They may have loaned her at some point as well. Brekus notes a suggestive sentence about Phillis from Osborn's 1757 diary: "This was my servant but is she now thine?" (*Sarah Osborn's World,* 202).

15. Phillis was married to a fellow slave, Gosper, and was the mother of another child whose name is unknown (ibid.).

16. Osborn, letter, 4 June 1754. Osborn's reasons for raising the helpless infant Bobey are also unknown, but a contributing factor may have been the death of her only son, Samuel, which roughly coincided with Bobey's birth. Brekus notes that Bobey was a surprise gift from friends, perhaps an attempt to "ease her grief" (*Sarah Osborn's World,* 174).

17. I infer that Bobey was sent to her former brother-in-law, based on a letter to Fish in which she tells him she plans to do so. Although Fish was her first choice, he was already in possession of a boy and probably had no need of another (Osborn, letter, 4 June 1754).

18. There are two known Timothy Allens who resided in Newport during this period. One died in 1769 at the age of forty-six, according to death and burial records at the Newport Historical Society. The other, a gold- and (probably) silversmith, died in 1792 at the age of seventy-nine. This second Allen probably owned Phillis because the father of Osborn's closest friend, Susanna Anthony, was also a gold- and silversmith. See advertisement, *Newport Mercury,* 21 May 1792, 2. Brekus similarly identifies Allen the silversmith as Phillis's owner (*Sarah Osborn's World,* 202).

19. See First Church's 1757 baptismal records at the Newport Historical Society. Brekus recounts Osborn's active advocacy of Phillis's First Church membership, accompanying her to speak with its minister, the Reverend Vinal, and meeting with her master to get his approval (*Sarah Osborn's World,* 201–2).

20. Melish, *Disowning Slavery,* 54.

21. Bailyn, *Ideological Origins,* 232–45.

22. Minkema and Stout, "Edwardsean Tradition," 45. For another study that relates revolutionary politics to abolitionist evangelicals, see Essig, *Bonds of Wickedness.* For an overview of the period's pro- and antislavery arguments, see Melish, *Disowning Slavery,*

50–83; Mason, *Slavery and Politics,* 9–41; and Nash, "Slaves and Slaveholders," 3–23. Other New Divinity theologians who published antislavery tracts include Levi Hart and Jonathan Edwards, Jr.

23. See, for example, Davis, *Problem of Slavery,* and Sweet, "More Than Tears."

24. See, for example, Carey, *British Abolitionism,* especially chaps. 2 and 4.

25. In contrast, studies of early American sexuality are often attentive to cross-boundary analysis, perhaps because in that conversation intimacy often operates as a synonym for sexuality and sex acts and thus encompasses rape and coercion in addition to pleasure, desire, and the erotic. See D'Emilio and Freedman, *Intimate Matters,* 3–52; Block, *Rape and Sexual Power;* Godbeer, *Sexual Revolution;* and Lyons, *Sex among the Rabble.* Straub's work on intimacy between servants and their employers in eighteenth-century Britain is similarly fascinating, but her insistence on the permeability of the British servant class attests to the impermeabilities of the boundary between Phillis and Osborn (*Domestic Affairs,* 3–4).

26. Osborn's extant manuscripts include her multivolume diary (housed at the Newport Historical Society, the Beinecke Library at Yale University, the Connecticut Historical Society, and the Trask Library Special Collections at Andover Newton Theological School) and various letters (housed at the American Antiquarian Society). For printed writings, see *Nature,* an anonymously published religious tract; *Memoirs* (1799), a posthumous publication edited by Hopkins that includes the memoirs she wrote at age thirty, a biography, and extracts from her diaries; and *Familiar Letters,* a compilation of letters by Osborn and her friend Susanna Anthony, edited by Hopkins's widow. Though literary scholars have rarely analyzed these texts, they have attracted students of history and religion. For studies of Osborn's relationships with male religious leaders, see Lacey, "Bonds of Friendship," and Kujawa, "Path of Duty Plain," 75–89. For a study of Osborn, the Enlightenment, and early American evangelicalism, see Brekus, *Sarah Osborn's World,* and "Sarah Osborn's Enlightenment." For considerations of the radicalism of her work and its often subtle resistance to gender and racial norms, see Norton, "My Resting Reaping Times," and Crane's more skeptical *Ebb Tide,* 97. In 2012, when I published a version of this chapter (see Wigginton, "Vexing Motherhood"), no other scholar had discussed Phillis. Since then, Brekus has reviewed the proposed sale of Bobey and concludes that Phillis and Gosper were only "bit players" in Osborn's "religious drama." She reasons that Osborn's "anguished debate over selling Bobey was the first step in a slow, halting journey toward a new vision of race, slavery, and the meaning of the gospel" (*Sarah Osborn's World,* 242, 243).

27. Osborn, diary, 195.

28. Ibid., 196.

29. Ibid., 199.

30. Ibid., 196.

31. On family slavery in New England, see Piersen, *Black Yankees,* 25–36.

32. Robertson, "Africa into the Americas?," 18.

33. Dill, "Our Mothers' Grief," 419.

34. Not all enslaved women found motherhood empowering. Some sought autonomy through contraception, abortion, and even infanticide. See Morgan, *Laboring Women,* especially chap. 4.

35. Some may argue that Osborn would have seen her relationship as sororal not maternal, due to the women's membership in the same church and female society. Yet

her use of infantilizing language to describe black Christians suggests that she found it difficult to view Phillis in the same light as she did white women.

36. Ulrich, *Good Wives,* 158.

37. Ibid.

38. Osborn, *Memoirs,* 66.

39. In a widely read eighteenth-century pamphlet, Mather urged his readers to glorify themselves and God by converting the enslaved persons they had bought and instructed masters to teach their slaves that the Fifth Commandment required them to be "dutiful" to their owners just as it required white Christians to honor their fathers and mothers (*Negro Christianized,* 28).

40. Osborn, diary, 195.

41. Osborn, *Nature,* 5.

42. Ibid., 6.

43. Here, Osborn displayed the sensuality and physicality that Juster indicates is most characteristic of women's spirituality (*Disorderly Women,* 66). Also see Dillon, "Nursing Fathers," 137–39.

44. Bulkeley, *Gospel-Covenant,* 50. Osborn retold the parable in her diary (*Memoirs,* 346–48). For more sermons expounding on the bride of Christ metaphor, see Pearse, *Best Match,* and Mather, *Glorious Espousal.* The church was also referred to as the bride of Christ. See Edwards, *Church's Marriage,* in which he refers to the parable as well as a number of other biblical passages.

45. See Morgan, "Puritan's Marriage"; Masson, "Typology of the Female"; Greven, *Protestant Temperament,* 124–40; Hughes, "Meat Out of the Eater"; Schweitzer, *Work of Self-Representation;* Porterfield, *Female Piety;* and Dillon, "Nursing Fathers." Other Christians, especially women mystics, had been turning to this idiom for centuries. For discussions of female mystics and sexualized Christ imagery, see the essays in Bynum, *Fragmentation and Redemption.*

46. Osborn and Anthony, *Familiar Letters,* 50.

47. Osborn, letter, 1 November 1754.

48. Osborn, letter, 10 December 1755.

49. Ibid.

50. Osborn's word choices evoke the shape and force of a phallus. They may also refer to the biblical story of Esther, who gains a political voice when her husband, the king of Persia, holds out his scepter to her. My thanks to Catherine Brekus for suggesting the possible allusion.

51. For the more usual interpretation of the earthquake as a sign of God's anger, see Williams, *Duty of a People,* a sermon originally delivered in November 1755; and Burt, *Earthquakes,* a sermon published in Newport. One of Fish's letters to Osborn may have chided her for the tone of this letter, for she refers to his description of her as "fraught with Pride" (Osborn, letter, 17 December 1756).

52. Edwards, *Treatise,* 328.

53. Porterfield, *Female Piety,* 90, 93.

54. Juster, *Disorderly Women,* 74.

55. For an extended consideration of how another evangelical woman, Experience Richardson, practiced an adapted orthodox faith, see Seeman, *Pious Persuasions,* 180–203.

56. The children of one of Henry Osborn's sons moved in with Sarah after their father died in 1759. Another son died at about the same time, and she intermittently helped

support that son's widow and children, even though they did not live with her (Osborn, letter, 3 May 1759).

57. Osborn, *Memoirs,* 32–33.

58. Ibid., 33–34.

59. Ibid., 258–59.

60. See ibid., 270; and Osborn, letter, 10 May 1761.

61. Osborn, diary, 198.

62. Ibid., 200.

63. Ibid., 202.

64. These entries tack between positive (often figured as drowning and torrents) and privative (often figured as dry and barren) sin. For brief discussions of this distinction, see Delbanco, *Puritan Ordeal,* 23–27, and Hughes, "Meat Out of the Eater," 109–10.

65. Osborn, diary, 205.

66. Ibid., 207–9.

67. Osborn did use "we" at points in this entry, referring to herself and her husband as Bobey's joint legal owners, but the much higher frequency of "me" and "I" testifies to her passionate and particular sense of maternal possession.

68. Osborn, diary, 213, 215.

69. A 1774 census of Newport shows that the Osborn household included one male over age sixteen (Henry Osborn), two white women over age sixteen (Sarah Osborn and probably Susanna Anthony), and six black people (*Census,* 24).

70. Osborn, letter, 21 April 1765.

71. My interpretation of these moments in the letter accords with Norton's "My Resting Reaping Times," 520.

72. Osborn, *Memoirs,* 82.

73. For a transcription of the letter, see Norton, "My Resting Reaping Times."

74. Ibid., 522.

75. Ibid., 523.

76. Ibid., 526. Oddly, despite the suggestion here that singing occurred only in meetings with children, young people, and servants, Osborn had just mentioned that singing was a portion of Friday night meetings of church "Brethren" (525–26).

77. Ibid., 525.

78. Ibid.

79. As Piersen argues, the unilineal nature of kinship in Africa meant that people of African descent could not simply reinstate kinship ties if they gained freedom in America: "Even if the slaves had been able to return to African kinship forms, such extended families would have taken generations to rebuild" (*Black Yankees,* 87).

80. My argument in this section builds on Patterson's definition of slavery in *Slavery and Social Death,* 5.

81. See Hopkins, *Sketches.*

82. Osborn, letter, 29 July 1769.

83. Park, *Memoir,* 99. Park was Hopkins's nineteenth-century biographer. In his preface, he reports that the sources of "many of the facts" were "surviving parishioners or personal friends of Dr. Hopkins" [vii]. His paragraph-long account of Osborn's and Hopkins's relationship suggests that the neighborhood provided much of his information about it.

84. Kujawa, "Religion, Education, and Gender," 289.

85. There are few extant writings from the final decades of Osborn's life. Due to illness, she found it difficult to write and at times to attend church services. For more on her health, see Brekus, *Sarah Osborn's World,* 89–91.

86. Grimsted, "Anglo-American Racism," 381. For discussions of the relationship between Osborn and Hopkins's abolition work, see Grimsted, "Anglo-American Racism," 378–83; Kujawa, "Path of Duty," 75–89; and Kujawa, "Religion, Education, and Gender," 289–310.

87. Grimsted, "Anglo-American Racism," 381. Brekus has been more reluctant than either Kujawa or Grimsted to view Osborn as antislavery (*Sarah Osborn's World,* 268–69; 395, n. 59).

88. Minkema and Stout attribute Hopkins's change of heart to his "firsthand witness" of the "violent and brutalizing business of the [Newport's] slave trade" ("Edwardsean Tradition," 52).

89. Wheatley's first published poem, "On Messrs Hussey and Coffin," appeared in the *Newport Mercury.* She also sent several volumes of her book to Tanner, designating one for Mrs. Mason, a member of the female society and Osborn's caretaker in her final years.

90. See Osborn, letters, 29 July 1769, 26 October 1769.

91. The seeming contradiction between Osborn's public recognition of black people's spiritual humanity and her childish treatment of them fits well with Boulukos's study of the transatlantic grateful slave trope in the eighteenth century. See *Grateful Slave,* especially 7–8.

3. The Consolation of Phillis Wheatley's Elegies

1. For Wheatley's 1772, 1773, 1779, and 1784 book proposals (only 1772 and 1779 contain extensive lists), see Wheatley, *Complete Writings,* 165–70. The titles listed in the proposals were not always the same as those given to published or manuscript versions. For example, by the time she published "Thoughts on Being Brought from Africa to America" in her book, the title had been truncated to "On being brought from AFRICA to AMERICA," by which it is now more familiarly known.

2. Though I remain skeptical, Bly's "Wheatley's ON THE AFFRAY" and Robinson's "Phyllis Wheatley" argue that an anonymous piece published in March 1770 in Boston's *Evening Post* is Wheatley's missing poem. Here is the anonymous poem:

> With Fire enwrapt, surcharg'd with sudden Death,
> Lo, the pois'd Tube convolves its fatal breath!
> The flying Ball with heaven-directed Force,
> Rids the Spirit of the fallen corse.
> Well sated Shades! let no unwomanly Tear
> From Pity's Eye, disdain in your honour'd Bier;
> Lost to their View, surviving Friends may mourn,
> Yet on thy Pile shall Flames celestial burn;
> Long as in *Freedom's* Cause the wise contend,
> Dear to your unity shall Fame extend;
> While to the World, the letter'd *Stone* shall tell,
> How *Caldwell, Attucks, Gray,* and *Mav'rick* fell.
> (Bly, "Wheatley's ON THE AFFRAY," 177)

3. Willis, "Phillis Wheatley," 165.

4. For an account noting Attucks's race, see "THE Town of Boston affords a recent and melancholy Demonstration . . . ," *Boston Gazette, and Country Journal,* 12 March 1770, [2].

5. Zobel, *Boston Massacre,* 292.

6. Rowe, *Letters and Diary,* 199.

7. Seider (or Snider) was an eleven-year-old boy shot by loyalist Ebenezer Richardson only a few weeks earlier during another violent street protest, and his funeral had been a similarly public event (Zobel, *Boston Massacre,* 175–79). Wheatley wrote an elegy for him and listed the poem in her 1772 book proposal: see "On the Death of Mr. Snider Murder'd by Richardson" (*Complete Writings,* 77–78, 165). However, like "On the Affray in King-Street," it was not included in the published book, *Thoughts on Various Subjects, Religious and Moral* (1773). The poem survives in manuscript at the Library Company of Philadelphia. See Kuncio, "Some Unpublished Poems," 288, n. 3.

8. Ramsay, *History,* 90–91.

9. Ibid., 91. Ramsay apparently did not see the irony in this statement: Attucks was probably a runaway slave (Kachun, "From Forgotten Founder," 250–51).

10. For discussions of early American funerary practices in New England, see Earle, *Customs and Fashions,* 364–87; Coffin, *Death in Early America;* Dethlefsen and Deetz, "Death's Heads"; Fitts, *Inventing,* 157–62; Jamieson, "Material Culture"; Piersen, *Black Yankees,* 75–78; and Wells, "Tale of Two Cities." For a history of Boston's burying grounds, see Shurtleff, *Topographical and Historical Description,* 182–293.

11. *Report,* no. 14, 53.

12. *Report,* no. 13, 87.

13. *Report,* no. 8, 176. The selectmen passed additional statutes regarding funerals for persons of color. In 1734, they set the price for the burial of black persons at seven shillings and sixpence, two and a half shillings less than the price for a white adult but still a half-shilling more than the price for a white youth between the ages of six and twelve (*Report,* no. 13, 262).

14. *Report,* no. 13, 283. For a brief discussion of these two laws, see Piersen, *Black Yankees,* 77–78.

15. *Report,* no. 14, 53.

16. See Brooks, "Our Phillis," for a discussion of the ways in which white women in particular directed her practice.

17. Brooks, "Our Phillis," 8.

18. See Gilroy, *Black Atlantic,* 68; Roach, *Cities of the Dead,* especially chaps. 2 and 3; Holland, *Raising the Dead;* Holloway, *Passed On;* Wardi, *Death;* and Luciano, *Arranging Grief,* especially chap. 4.

19. Roach, *Cities of the Dead,* 60.

20. Seeman, *Death in the New World,* 5.

21. Ibid., 6.

22. Carretta's inclusion of the word *genius* in the subtitle of his biography, *Phillis Wheatley,* recalls eighteenth-century references to the poet. She is called a genius in several proposals and advertisements for her first book (see, for example, 80–85, 98). To contemporary readers, a genius is a person of superb intellect and capability. However, according to *The Oxford English Dictionary,* this meaning arose only after 1749. Late eighteenth-century readers would have read it first as an allusion to Wheatley's natural (as opposed to cultivated) abilities, especially when it was used to indicate something that she possessed: "the strength of her own Genius" (80).

23. Earle, *Customs and Fashions,* 364. For a detailed discussion of colonial New England elegies and mourning rituals, see 364–87.

24. Ibid., 364.

25. Cavitch, *American Elegy,* 34.

26. See Rigsby, "Form and Content," for a discussion of Wheatley's elegiac style in terms of form. Levernier's "Style As Protest" and Shields's "Phillis Wheatley's Struggle" analyze her elegiac style, asserting that it is more content than form and expresses a consistent emancipatory message.

27. Brooks, "Our Phillis," 8. *Commission* here does not mean payment or any official or contractual agreements for poetry writing. Of course, coercion and compensation were a tricky business in a slave society. Carretta confirms that, while it is extremely likely that Wheatley was asked to write elegies, we have no actual records of anyone doing so (personal communication, July 2015). However, we do have evidence that she was asked to compose two non-elegy poems (Carretta, *Phillis Wheatley,* 84–85, 130–31).

28. Ellison, *Cato's Tears,* 114.

29. Wheatley, *Complete Writings,* 44.

30. Ibid.

31. Ibid., 16.

32. Ibid., 16–17.

33. Ibid., 17.

34. Ibid., 37–38.

35. Ibid., 37.

36. Ibid., 38.

37. Ibid., 38–39.

38. Ibid., 38.

39. Ibid., 17. Eighteenth-century Americans constantly monitored against excessive grief. Men were particularly pressing about this issue, especially when addressing female readers. See Eustace, *Passion Is the Gale,* 293–310.

40. In "Seduction," Thorn discusses how Wheatley's elegies for children consistently turn to seductive reversals of juvenile death literature to "destabilize dyadic oppositions not only of black and white, slave and free, but also of parent and child, active and passive, even life and death" (202).

41. Carretta posits that Wheatley's youth gave her relative freedom aboard the slave ship (*Phillis Wheatley,* 10).

42. In "Wheatley's 'On the Death,'" Bly notes the parallels between Nancy and Wheatley and asserts that Wheatley herself "is the subject of the poem's subtext" (11).

43. Wheatley, *Complete Writings,* 50.

44. Ibid., 38.

45. Bassard points out that the verb *snatch* appears three times in Wheatley's writings (*Spiritual Interrogations,* 63). One is her memorable reference to being "snatch'd" from Africa, in her poem to the Earl of Dartmouth, written soon after the elegy to Charles (Wheatley, *Complete Writings,* 40). Another is in "To MAECENAS," her poem to an unidentified patron or literary foreparent: "I'll snatch a laurel from thine honour'd head, / While you indulgent smile upon the deed" (10).

46. Wheatley, *Complete Writings,* 13.

47. Patterson, *Slavery,* 5–10.

48. Ibid., 5.

49. Ibid. Jamieson identifies the "mortuary context as a place within slave culture where in some cases 'freedoms' were allowed by slave owners" ("Material Culture," 41).

50. Carretta, *Phillis Wheatley,* 1.

51. Pruitt, *Massachusetts,* 38. See Carretta, *Phillis Wheatley,* 21–22, for a discussion of the indentured servant, Abner Wade.

52. For a brief discussion of elegies' circulation, see Henson, "Form and Content," 11. For additional analyses of the Puritan funeral elegy (the form adopted by Wheatley), see Hammond, *American Puritan Elegy,* and Scheick, "Tombless Virtue." Many other scholars have also analyzed the form. For a discussion of American elegies through Walt Whitman, see Cavitch, *American Elegy.* For a discussion of feminism and elegies, see Schenck, "Feminism." For treatments of eighteenth-century women authors and elegies, see Hawley, "Charlotte Smith's *Elegiac Sonnets,*" and Backscheider, *Eighteenth-Century Women Poets,* 268–315. For a broad treatment of the elegiac form, see Sacks, *English Elegy.*

53. For examples of early African American elegies in addition to those by Wheatley, see Lucy Terry's 1746 "Bars Fight" (Holland, *History,* 360); George Moses Horton's pre-1865 "Death of an Old Carriage Horse" and "Death of Gen. Jackson—An Eulogy" (*Black Bard,* 136); James Monroe Whitfield's 1853 "To Cinque" (*Works,* 49); and Ann Plato's 1841 "Reflections, Written on Visiting the Grave of a Venerated Friend" and 1841 "I Have No Brother" (*Essays,* 95–97). For another interesting juxtaposition, see Jupiter Hammon's 1782 "A Poem for Children with Thoughts on Death" (Wheatley, *Complete Writings,* 208–11).

54. Shields, *Civil Tongues,* 219.

55. Cavitch, *American Elegy,* 180. Cavitch cites Wheatley's poetry as an exemplar of this facet of African American elegies, contending that her poetry's presence in nineteenth-century African American periodicals links her to a black elegiac tradition (195).

56. Roach, *Cities of the Dead,* 5.

57. Smallwood, *Saltwater Slavery,* 131. Bassard's *Spiritual Interrogations* asserts that Wheatley's elegies were a form of "self-ventriloquism" in which the author "desire[d] to speak beyond the 'grave' of separation to those she left behind for a 'better' world" (70).

58. Seeman, *Death in the New World,* 188.

59. Piersen, *Black Yankees,* 77.

60. Brown, *Reaper's Garden,* 66–69. For a rather dismissive discussion of the practice in sixteenth-century Africa, see Marees, *Description,* 180. For a firsthand account of the practice in nineteenth-century Jamaica, see Phillippo, *Jamaica,* 244.

61. McCaskie, "Death," 427. The Yoruba, Asante, and Tio are some of the West African cultures that held forms of this belief (Jamieson, "Material Culture," 51). McCaskie and Jamieson, an archaeologist, point to Hertz, *Death,* as the anthropological source for studies into this form of mortuary practice. Wheatley was likely from West Africa.

62. For discussions of mediumship, ancestral possession, and the re-creation of spiritual inquisitions in colonial Brazil, see Sweet, *Recreating Africa,* 139–52, 176–78.

63. Wheatley, *Complete Writings,* 52.

64. Ibid.

65. See Krüger-Kahloula, "Homage."

66. See Hansen and McGowan, *Breaking Ground.*

67. McHenry, *Forgotten Readers,* 47.

68. Wheatley confirms sending five books in a 6 May 1774 letter to Tanner (*Complete Writings,* 156–57).

69. See Hammons's poems "AN ADDRESS to Miss PHILLIS WHEATLY" and "A Poem for Children with Thoughts on Death" (Wheatley, *Complete Writings,* 204–11). In the first, he repeatedly refers to her journey "from distant shore" "o'er the raging main" (205–6). Those "left behind" in Africa resemble the "thousands" who "range about the street" and disregard "heaven's joys" (206–7).

70. See ibid., 59–60, and Carretta, *Phillis Wheatley,* 100–101.

71. Carretta, *Phillis Wheatley,* 79.

72. In *History of Printing,* Thomas documents the presence of several black workers in Boston and Philadelphia print shops (294–95, 333–35, 338). Though none appears to have been employed by Ezekiel Russell, the primary printer involved in the Boston publication of Wheatley's works, a black carver did produce woodcuts in Thomas Fleet's shop. Fleet published the *Boston Evening Post,* which printed "*On the Death of Doctor* SAMUEL MARSHALL" in 1771 and a book proposal in 1779 (Wheatley, *Complete Writings,* 119, 167). Undocumented black workers may have been employed by other printers or people involved in the print trade, such as booksellers.

73. Piersen, *Black Yankees,* 15–18, 163.

74. For a discussion of this community and its leader, Sarah Osborn, see chap. 2.

75. For writings that explicitly or implicitly argue against chattel slavery, see Wheatley's two biblical paraphrases and her February 1774 letter to Samson Occom (*Complete Writings,* 19–25, 33–34, 152–53). For examples of poems that argue against political tyranny, see "To the Right Honourable WILLIAM, Earl of DARTMOUTH," "America," "On the Death of Mr. Snider Murder'd by Richardson," and "LIBERTY AND PEACE, A POEM" (39–40, 75–76, 77–78, 101–2).

76. For a powerful counterargument to a providential view of slavery, see free black Antiguan Elizabeth Hart Thwaites's letter on slavery (Moore et al., *Transatlantic Feminisms,* 299–308).

77. Wheatley, *Complete Writings,* 40.

78. Ibid., [3].

79. Carretta, *Phillis Wheatley,* 33.

80. Wheatley, *Complete Writings,* 33.

81. Ibid., 34.

82. Henry, *Exposition,* 190.

83. Scheick, *Authority,* 125.

84. Norris, *Collection,* 44–46; Henry, *Exposition,* 190–92; Wesley and Wesley, *Hymns,* 140–42. Versions of Norris's *Collection* and Henry's *Exposition* were available to Boston readers. For example, Cox and Berry, booksellers on King Street (where the Wheatleys also lived), list both in their circa 1772 *Catalogue* (14, 20). For a discussion of Henry's influence on Wesleyian hymns, see Routley, "Charles Wesley."

85. Brooks, *American Lazarus,* 9.

86. Here, I am inspired by Scott's *Extravagant Abjection,* which identifies "a history of humiliating defeat, a useless history which must be in some way overturned or overcome," as "animat[ing]" many strands of black diasporic rhetoric and politics (4).

87. Brooks, *American Lazarus,* 105.

88. Marrant, "Narrative," 117–20, 125–26. For a biography and brief discussion of Marrant's writing, see Saillant and Brooks, introduction to *"Face Zion Forward,"* 17–27.

89. Marrant, "Funeral," 162.

90. Ibid., 176.

91. Ibid., 171.

92. Ibid., 165.
93. Saillant and Brooks, introduction to *"Face Zion Forward,"* 10.
94. Marrant, "Funeral," 167.
95. Saillant and Brooks, introduction to *"Face Zion Forward,"* 26; Wheatley, *Complete Writings,* 159.
96. For another example of black Christians and print, see Rezek's "Orations." This essay explores antebellum orations and attests to black authors' and orators' use of print "to constitute a counterpublic imagined as limitless and unending" (655).
97. Wheatley, *Complete Writings,* 153–54.
98. Roach, *Cities of the Dead,* 2.
99. Carretta, *Phillis Wheatley,* 190.
100. Ibid. The Granary Burial Ground was certainly the closest to her funeral, held at the home of her neighbor "Mr. Todd," but her "gravesite, like that of most of her contemporaries of African descent, was unmarked and remains unknown." For more on Wheatley's last years, see ibid., 172–96. Carretta explains that there are no records to confirm the widely accepted contention (started by nineteenth-century memoirist Margaretta Matilda Odell) that Wheatley had three children, the last of whom died with her (177). A meticulous biographer, he does note moments in the archive that hint that she may have borne one or more children; for instance, he refers to an unrhymed poetic prayer that may or may not be Wheatley's composition (184–85).
101. Caretta, introduction to *Complete Writings,* xxxv.

4. Unions of the Soul

1. See Soderlund, *William Penn,* for a documentary history of the first charter and its negotiation and application. Friends did periodically consider moving to a royal government, but that consideration involved retaining and even extending their control of the colony. In the 1760s, there was a vigorous campaign to switch to a royal government, with Franklin and Joseph Galloway its most vocal and famous proponents. The Stamp Act crisis all but ended the campaign, as it made Pennsylvanians skeptical that they would retain their colonial privileges under a royal government. See Hutson, "Campaign."
2. For a concise overview of the Society of Friends' relation to the American Revolution, see Mekeel, "Relation." Early on, there were efforts to grant Friends liberty of conscience in certain matters, but the Philadelphia Yearly Meeting's vocal support for peace created an unstable distinction. For example, in his appendix to *Common Sense,* a response to the Yearly Meeting's *Ancient Testimony,* Paine reasons that the Meeting's public espousal of peace unjustifiably usurps the political voice of "the whole body of the Quakers" (45). He suspects that they are "partial ministers" and sneers, "If ye really preach from conscience, and mean not to make a political hobby-horse of your religion, convince the world thereof, by proclaiming your doctrine to our enemies, *for they lik[e] wise bear ARMS*" (46).
3. See the introduction, 17-18.
4. For a discussion of Moore's familial network in Philadelphia and her husband's medical practice, see Wulf, "*Milcah Martha Moore's Book,*" 8–10, 15. In a 1780 letter, Moore referred to the couple's continuing presence at Meetings, despite official prohibition: "We had been frequently assured by many of our friends, that our attending their

meetings of business, gave offence to none of them" (Smith, *Letters,* 243). Moore was not able to rejoin the Society until after her husband's death in 1801. Despite the repercussions of their marriage, they were apparently a devoted couple. They had no children.

5. Though scholars are uncertain about when Moore began her book, the entries themselves (the latest was composed in 1778, but earlier poems are mixed in with later entries) indicate that the bulk of its transcription coincided with the revolution. See Wulf, "*Milcah Martha Moore's Book,*" 37–38. In addition to work by the authors I discuss in this chapter, it includes entries by her acquaintance Benjamin Franklin; Patrick Henry, the rhetorically savvy revolutionary; and Jonathan Odell, a New Jersey Loyalist. Prose entries are frequently letters, some of which had been printed in periodicals or copied into others' commonplace books. Significantly, one is a series of excerpts from Fergusson's travel diary, kept during a visit to Europe. This travel diary was "the stuff of oral legend" and praised in print by Benjamin Rush (Ousterhout, *Most Learned Woman,* 1, 81–82). However, Moore's transcriptions of the diary, and of many of the poems, are the only remnants extant today—which is why Blecki and Wulf felt compelled to edit and publish her commonplace book (see their preface to *Moore's Book,* xi). The original is housed at the Haverford College Library, Quaker Collections, Edward Wanton Smith Collection, Ms. 955.

6. For an overview of commonplace books from classical to modern times, see Havens, *Commonplace Books.* For an example of an analysis of commonplace books in the Renaissance, see Moss, *Printed Commonplace-Books.* For a study of two eighteenth-century American commonplace books, see Lockridge, *On the Sources.* For a broad rather than deep study, see Miller, *Assuming the Positions,* which delves into the Virginia Historical Society's commonplace book collection. For a study of commonplace books in nineteenth-century American popular culture, see Gernes, "Recasting."

7. Ousterhout titles her biography of Fergusson *The Most Learned Woman in America,* thereby recalling Fergusson's now unknown reputation as an eighteenth-century literary intellect. She takes her title from Wharton's compendium, *Salons Colonial and Republican* (1900). It is unclear if Moore and Fergusson were personally acquainted, though they clearly knew of and admired each other's literary talents. See Wulf, "*Milcah Martha Moore's Book,*" 53–55, for more on their relationship. Moore's transcription of Fergusson's writing demonstrates her regard, and, according to Wulf, Fergusson published a poem, "Lines on reading Martha Moore's Selections" (1788), about *Miscellanies.*

8. For other criticism that discusses literary sorority and writings in Moore's circle, see Stabile, *Memory's Daughters,* and Vietto, *Women and Authorship,* 19–36. For discussions of some of Wright's poems not found in *Moore's Book,* see Blecki and Treese, "Susanna Wright's 'The Grove,'" and Cowell, "'Womankind Call Reason.'" For analyses of the Fergusson writings transcribed into *Moore's Book,* see Parrish, "Women's Nature," 219–22. Kelley references Moore's circle as an informal precursor to female academies in *Learning,* 115–17, 133–34. For monographs which deal directly or partially with women's writing during the era, see Norton, *Liberty's Daughters;* Kerber, *Women of the Republic;* Dillon, *Gender of Freedom;* Vietto, *Women and Authorship;* and Harris, *Executing Race.* In the introduction to this book, I discuss "The Dream," a Fergusson poem not in *Moore's Book.* See also Wigginton, "Letters."

9. Shields, *Civil Tongues,* xiv. For another excellent example, see Teute, "Loves of the Plants."

10. Shields explains his admittedly brief considerations of religious belletristic discourse:

"Christian belletrism could not resolve the contradiction inherent in yoking the sublime, a profoundly individual experience of elevation and terror, with the polite, a profoundly social experience of the sensus communis" (*Civil Tongues,* 236). While Moore may not have explicitly considered the "contradiction" that he identifies, her book suggests that the sublime and the polite were not irreconcilable.

11. Frost, *Quaker Family,* 12.

12. Barclay, *Apology,* 47.

13. This belief in spiritual equality resulted in unadorned worship and a governance structure founded on radical consensus. During Meetings, decisions about discipline and policy occurred though the "sense of the Meeting," a process through which both individualism and authoritarianism could be avoided (Barbour and Frost, *Quakers,* 40). The Society structured Meetings through the weekly Local or Particular Meeting, the Monthly Meeting, the Quarterly Meeting, and the Yearly Meeting. Because each successive Meeting represented several Meetings from the level below, it also represented the "sense" of a larger group of Friends. The Yearly Meeting, therefore, was the highest decision-making body for its constituent Local, Monthly, and Quarterly Meetings. The most prestigious Yearly Meeting was London; Philadelphia was the most prestigious in the colonies (77). In addition to an unadorned worship, Quakerism advocated a lifestyle that emphasized four testimonies: equality, simplicity, integrity, and peace. The simple lifestyle was visible in the plain dress of many Friends. Unadorned worship occurred during Meetings in which Friends gathered and, without hymns or other embellishments, quietly waited to individually experience the inward light of Christ. During the Meetings, some Friends did feel compelled by that inward light to speak. For an introduction to Society of Friends theology in the seventeenth and eighteenth centuries, see Frost, *Quaker Family,* chap. 1; Barbour and Frost, *Quakers,* especially 3–47 and 95–136; and Hamm, *Quakers in America,* 13–36. For a brief discussion of the testimonies' sources, meanings, and applications, see Barbour and Frost, *Quakers,* 41–46.

14. Horn, "Texted Authority," 298.

15. Higginson, *Brief Relation,* sig. a2.

16. For a fascinating library, see the Fox-Abraham-Shipley tract collection at the Library Company of Philadelphia, collected by early Quaker matriarch and patron Margaret Askew Fell Fox (1614–1702). Her grandson, Englishman John Abraham, gifted the set to Philadelphian Elizabeth Shipley in 1750. It was later acquired by Robert Waln and presented to the Library Company in 1834. Perhaps Abraham thought it would be of interest to the American Shipley because its first several texts deal with Quaker persecution in seventeenth-century New England. Before its presentation to Shipley, the library was bound and paginated, though it is unclear when and by whom. The Library Company separated and cataloged its contents in about 1900, but they can be identified and placed in order through their acquisition numbers: 2252.Q.[X] where [X] refers to a tract's likely position in the collection. For notes regarding the collection's provenance, see marginalia in the Library Company's copy of Howgill, *Popish Inquisition* (call no. Am 1659 How 2252.Q.1).

17. Shields, *Civil Tongues,* xiv.

18. See ibid., xviii–xx. In her study of friendship in early America, Schweitzer argues for its intricacy. Historicizing friendship, she explains that "equality and likeness are requirements for and thus constitutive elements of perfect friendship, which produce a fiction or illusion of interchangeability." With its definition and requirements visible in

the writings of the period's elite white men, she questions how "women and people of color" could use friendship to "produce rhetorical equality" (*Perfecting Friendship*, 28). Therefore, friendship as an affective relationship contains elements of predictability and pliancy; one is friends with those who are similar, *and* one can decide who is similar by defining which traits matter to friendship.

19. For a lucid overview of the rise of sensibility and the importance of visiting in Philadelphia Quaker culture, see Klepp and Wulf, introduction to Sansom's *Diary*.

20. See Schweitzer, *Perfecting Friendship*, 27–71, for a powerful introduction to early American friendship philosophy.

21. Schweitzer writes, "But friendship's insistence on likeness can also be a means of neutralizing differences and hierarchy and producing spiritual equality" (ibid., 16). A number of other scholars have also focused on friendship as a union of likeness and its flexibility in establishing communal borders. On the relationship of masculine friendship to antebellum American nationalism, see Nelson, *National Manhood;* Crain, *American Sympathy;* and Coviello, *Intimacy in America.* Bray's *Friend* presents a pre-affectionate conception of friendship that complicates our assumptions about friendship and likeness. On women's friendship in particular, see Todd, *Women's Friendship;* Haggerty, *Unnatural Affections;* Donoghue, *Passions;* and Love, *Feeling Backward.* Todd surveys women's friendship in eighteenth-century novels, categorizing different types, including what she calls *vertical friendship.* Haggerty and Donoghue situate women's friendship within a larger recovery of eighteenth-century queer relations. Love turns to Willa Cather to consider the "death of female romantic friendship" (*Feeling Backward,* 25).

22. PWYM, 164, 183.

23. Ibid., 164. Notes about surveillance, reportage, and discipline pervade the minutes of the Monthly Meeting. For example, see PWMM, 10–12.

24. All Friends were not created equal, as evidenced by the Society's increasingly active disapproval of slavery but its lack of black Friends. Philadelphia operated a separate "Meeting for Negroes," established in 1756 and not reincorporated until 1805; the first black Friend, Abigail Franks, was not "received" until 1784 (Hamm, *Quakers in America,* 170). Philadelphia abolished this Meeting, apparently because by this time independent African American churches were operating in the city (see Cadbury, "Negro Membership"). Long before it strongly advocated against slave owning, the Society encouraged slave owners to be responsible for the religious education of their slaves and to provide for the religious education of free black people. Black persons could attend Weekly Meetings. A number of Philadelphia Friends had been outspoken against slavery in the colony's early years but were viewed largely as troublemakers (Marietta, *Reformation,* 111–12). In this regard, the new climate of reform was much more open to abolition within the community. Between 1754 and 1774, a strict official stance against slaveholding and trade gradually emerged, as did an environment of decreasing leniency toward violators. With the support of Society leadership, John Woolman published his famous pamphlet, *Some Considerations on the Keeping of Negroes,* in 1754. In 1755, the Philadelphia Yearly Meeting officially ordered Friends to stop participating in the slave trade. In 1758, the Meeting decided to exclude Friends who practiced slave trading from business meetings. In 1774, it resolved "to completely disown any Friend who bought, sold, or transferred slaves" and provided instructions for gradual emancipation (Marietta, *Reformation,* 120). However, discipline was not entirely successful. As Nash has shown, in the Philadelphia area, more Friends than non-Friends were slaveholders: "The evidence

is substantial, then, that when faced with a direct choice between forgoing the human labor they needed or ignoring the principles enunciated by their leaders and officially sanctioned by the Society through its Quarterly and Yearly Meetings, the rank and file of Philadelphia Friends chose the latter course" ("Slaves and Slaveholders," 254). In 1776, the Society decided to disown those who still would not manumit their slaves. Whether for this reason or another, the advent of the American Revolution marked the point at which many Philadelphia Friends finally obeyed.

25. My conception of friendship here is indebted in part to Derrida's *Politics of Friendship,* which queries singularity and universality through friendship, and Gandhi's *Affective Communities,* which considers friendship as a technology of resistance and affiliation without egalitarianism.

26. Blair, *Too Much to Know,* 73. Also see Erasmus, *On Copia,* 67–68. In contrast to Erasmus, Locke's "A New Method of Common-Place-Book" proposed using a special index to organize the book under various subjects (*Works,* 441–59). His text went through several reprints and editions. Although many faithfully followed such models, eighteenth-century commonplace books had the "same great variety of subject matter and hodgepodge of organizational techniques encountered in exemplars from the sixteenth and seventeenth centuries" (Havens, *Commonplace Books,* 81). While eighteenth-century compilers could choose from a range of styles, organization remained a concern. Even inattentiveness to organization indicates an attitude toward transcription and content. Some compilers perhaps copied more for enjoyment than usefulness.

27. See Blecki and Wulf, preface to *Moore's Book,* xiv–xvi, for a succinct biography. Also see Smith, *Letters,* 202–3.

28. See Wulf, "*Milcah Martha Moore's Book,*" 18–19, for a discussion of the difference between the sisters' experiences.

29. Marietta, *Reformation,* 4.

30. Ibid., 10.

31. See Barbour and Frost, *Quakers,* 95–97, 130–31, and Marietta, *Reformation,* 83–86.

32. In a 1681 letter to James Harrison, Penn famously referred to the colony as a "holy experiment" that he hoped would be "an example . . . to the nations" (Soderlund, *William Penn,* 77). He published a frame of government in 1682 that "provided for liberty of conscience," "guaranteed trials by jury," "a stringent moral code," and made "no provision for militia or defense" for the colony (Barbour and Frost, *Quakers,* 75–76).

33. Barbour and Frost, *Quakers,* 130; for discussions of mid-eighteenth-century discipline and reformation, see 107–36, and Marietta, *Reformation.* Marietta's detailed study of the reformation indicates that about 40 percent of disciplinary offenses were marriage offenses, for which Moore, too, was disowned.

34. See Marietta, *Reformation,* especially 131–86.

35. Ibid., 83.

36. British troops under General Howe occupied Philadelphia from September 1777 to June 1778.

37. Moore, letter to Hannah Moore.

38. In a 1780 letter to her brother-in-law George Dillwyn, Moore made her longest extant remarks on the couple's disownment:

> The state of separation we have long been in, has, indeed, my dear brother, given me a good deal of uneasiness at times, and I have most earnestly wished to commit it wholly to the wise Disposer of all things, who is greatly careful over his creatures, and can preserve through every difficulty. He was promised as a 'Repairer of breaches, and a restorer of paths to dwell in,'

> and I make not the least doubt he will order for the best. I think that I can, with the greatest sincerity say that I am entirely resigned, let the event be what it may; and having done what I looked upon to be a duty, with respect to the acknowledgements, must leave the rest to him, who has been good to me many ways, and who, I believe and humbly trust, will not look upon this deviation as unpardonable.
>
> It has often been my earnest prayer that he would be pleased to support us in Christian patience under this, and every other discouragement and disappointment we may meet with, however great. (Smith, *Letters,* 243)

39. This peculiarity was unbearable because of its isolation. As a sect, Quakers prided themselves on their communal peculiarity, one that set them apart collectively.

40. During the war, Morris determined to remain in Burlington, New Jersey, despite its location along the Delaware River, a thoroughfare for British, Hessian, and American forces. Her journal is an important historical document. See Smith, *Letters,* 210–37, for a substantial portion of the journal; also see Gilroy, "Margaret Morris."

41. Smith, *Letters,* 239.

42. Ibid., 210.

43. Hannah Griffitts, whose work comprises the most substantial portion of *Moore's Book,* also read, composed, and circulated a host of elegies for pious Friends. Her poem "On reading some pious Memorials of the Dead" (circa 1777) finds solace for present sufferings in mortality (Moore, *Moore's Book,* 290–91). In 1785, she compiled a portfolio of such elegies and wrote another verse, "On Transcribing the following Memorials of the Pious Dead," which reiterates the imperfections of present society and calls on the "offspring" of her subjects to emulate their elders' example. For her, poetic composition and collection worked together to provide spiritual comfort and guidance. Garvey's study of nineteenth-century scrapbooks indicates that Americans "in positions of relative powerlessness used their scrapbooks to make a place for themselves and their communities by finding, sifting, analyzing, and recirculating writing that mattered to them" (*Writing with Scissors,* 4).

44. *Moore's Book* is not Moore's only extant manuscript book from this period. The others are a small devotional, begun in 1776 and containing personal prayers, and a large commonplace book, undated and encompassing texts written by or about noteworthy Friends. (I refer to this as her testimony book.) The devotional seems to refer to her and Charles's separation from other Friends, possibly due to the war or to their disownment. Individual entries in the testimony book date from the 1680s to the 1770s. Many can be found in other contemporaneous commonplace books. For example, see a family transcription of *Abigail Griffitts' Book* (1792), available at www.wellsclan.us/History/abigail/APB%20Preface.htm and to be used for reference purposes only. (Abigail Griffitts was married to Hannah Griffitts's first cousin James.) Entries in both books include Mary Horner's "Dream" and Robert Jordan's "Of Musick." The other two Moore manuscript books also reside in the Haverford College Library's Quaker Collection. Moore kept a third commonplace book that she shared widely. The document proved so suitable for schoolchildren that, "at the request of her friends," she published it as an educational miscellany in 1787 (Moore, *Miscellanies,* iii). Containing excerpts by authors such as Alexander Pope, Joseph Addison, and Edward Young, this published work is markedly different from *Moore's Book,* though the manuscript version circulating in earlier years may have included additional or alternative entries. *Miscellanies* was reprinted at least eight times and was used in schools for several decades. Probably referring to the miscellany manuscript but perhaps to *Moore's Book* or the testimony book, a 1776 letter (most likely from Moore sister and transcribed in the nineteenth century by Thomas

Stewardson) explains how the book was "unveil[ed]" to neighbors and urges Moore to "be less covetous, my Patty, of the choice flowers thee has picked from reading" (letter to Milcah Martha Moore).

45. Moore's care with this book is especially visible in comparison to the "loose" organization of her testimony book (Blecki, "Reading *Moore's Book*," 63). Though Blecki also compares the arrangements of *Moore's Book* and the devotional, I do not; in my view, the latter resembles a spiritual diary more than a commonplace book. Its organization and topoi would necessarily be less important than the inspiration and requirements of the moment.

46. Ibid., 64–65. My own comparison of several poems shows that Moore did transcribe carefully but also made changes in capitalization, abbreviations, and, less frequently, punctuation.

47. This last aspect contrasts with Moore's *Miscellanies*. In that publication, she apologizes for frequently not listing authors and excuses her lapse by mentioning that she copied the "extracts" "some years ago." Because she had "collected" only for "her own perusal and amusement," it was no longer "in her power to supply the omission" (iii).

48. For more on how commonplacing as well as other compilation and note-taking activities protected against loss, see Blair, *Too Much to Know,* especially 12–13, 55–61, 73. With the exception of schoolgirls, commonplacing Friends were likely to be deliberate in their transcription and arrangement because they were generating a material object. In his discussion of Friends as producers, Herman declares that "Quaker material culture" shared the themes of "kinship, community, craft, and consensus" (introduction to *Quaker Aesthetics,* 149). Material objects could be used to "achiev[e] and articulat[e] consensus" among Friends (153). He explains that craftsmanship permitted Friends to mark their social distinctiveness and status: "There is the sense that Quakers elevated the art of craftsmanship in the production of their material world. . . . Craftsmanship functioned as a kind of surrogate value system for fashion; that is, craft was the proper vehicle for the expression of worldly attainment" (151). Like friendship, a commonplace book in such a tradition could arrange structures of mutual bondedness. While I focus here on Quaker conceptions of craft, a consideration of commonplace books as material objects connects to scholarly conversations about collecting, nostalgia, and memory making. For a study of collecting, see Pearce, *On Collecting.* For a study of nostalgia, see Stewart, *On Longing.* For a study of memory making that focuses on Moore's literary circle, see Stabile, *Memory's Daughters,* although her argument emphasizes the nostalgia of such productions. While I am persuaded that eighteenth-century women's commonplace books did "creat[e] landscapes of memory," I attend more to the immediacy of such texts for their authors and readers (15). *Moore's Book* invites engagement with the present.

49. Brown, *Pilgrim,* 63. Brown uses the example of Joseph Tompson to elucidate these paired reading practices and the practice of perusal (60–67).

50. Moore, *Moore's Book,* 115.

51. Ibid.

52. Ibid., 115–16. The quotation marks around the concluding couplet appear to indicate emphasis rather than citation.

53. Ibid., 117.

54. Blecki and Wulf, preface to *Moore's Book,* xvi. For a more detailed biography of Wright and her family, see Schaefer, *Wright's Ferry Mansion,* 1:25–70.

55. Wulf, "*Milcah Martha Moore's Book*," 27.

56. Blecki identifies five sections in *Moore's Book*, and I generally concur with her divisions. The first section preserves Susanna Wright's poetry and honors her poetic correspondence with Hannah Griffitts (entries 1–26), the second acts as a transition (entries 27–29), the third is a set of poems by Griffitts (entries 30–47), the fourth is a series of mostly prose texts by a variety of Friends and non-Friends (entries 48–70), and the final is another set of mostly Griffitts's poems (entries 71–126) ("Reading *Moore's Book*," 67–69).

57. Moore, *Moore's Book*, 119.

58. The poem may follow "An Essay on Friendship" because it is the earliest Wright poem chronologically, or Moore may have deliberately juxtaposed the two texts. Given what information we have about their dates, the Wright poems (other than the closing poetic exchange) appear to be arranged chronologically. Moore's transcription includes a biblical epitaph, Matthew 12:40: "For as Jonah was 3 Days & 3 Nights in the Whales Belly, so shall the Son of Man be 3 Days & 3 Nights in the Heart of the Earth." The biblical verse uses the story of Jonah to prefigure Jesus' resurrection, another kind of rehearsal. The actual story of Jonah appears in the book of Jonah in the Old Testament.

59. Wright's 1784 death notice, printed in the *Pennsylvania Gazette*, eloquently eulogizes her: "Possessed of an elevated understanding, improved by acquired knowledge to an eminent degree, she was distinguished by her superior benevolence, evinced by a multitude of pious and charitable offices done in the course of her long life, towards those within her beneficent sphere" (Schaefer, *Wright's Ferry*, 1:65).

60. Moore probably transcribed every poem she had of Wright's, so these are not the only topics. However, it is clear that they were abiding concerns of the poet.

61. Moore, *Moore's Book*, 140.

62. Ibid., 141.

63. Ibid., 142.

64. Ibid., 144.

65. Ibid., 146. It is likely that "On Friendship" is addressed to Norris. They were friends, and their extant letters evince deep familiarity and intellectual rapport (see Norris papers).

66. Roughly speaking, of the twenty-four Wright poems, fifteen are about mortality, three address theology generally, three address friendship, and three are on miscellaneous subjects. Many that are not entirely about friendship do mention friendship or concern friends.

67. Moore, *Moore's Book*, 131.

68. Ibid., 141.

69. Ibid., 144–45.

70. Of course, piety and friendship are not equally vital. In Moore's view, piety precedes friendship; if a choice is necessary, one should choose the former over the latter. While the poems I have discussed suggest this point, it is most forcefully borne out by the contents of Moore's devotional book. The small volume contains few pieces, most of which were probably written by her because she mentions no other author and some refer to her own circumstances. The book is dated 1776, meaning that it was composed while Moore was disowned by the Society and, most likely, while she was living in Montgomery County. In keeping with the devotional style, it focuses on solitary contemplation. For example, the first entry, "Happiness," rejects worldly gratifications:

"Nothing short of eternal Life can be called Happiness, the Smiles of the World and its poor perishing Delights are not worth one serious thought. My Soul longs after purer Pleasures,—after more sweet and unmix'd Enjoyments.—Seek the Lord then, Oh! my Soul, and rejoice in him alone." Here, happiness is specifically spiritual. Because *Moore's Book* submits that the joy of friendship arises from the piety of its members, friendship for Moore may have been satisfying because it contained a suggestion of those "purer Pleasures" that awaited her in the "eternal Life" of heaven. Numerous passages in the devotional reveal the preeminent importance of friendship. For example, in one entry, she criticized herself for dwelling on her and her husband's isolation:

> Let me not repine at being thus disown'd by them nor suffer a resentful Breath to escape me, or an unkind Thought to arise in my Heart but may I rather love them the more, & rejoice in Tribulation, as it may be a happy Means of my drawing still nearer to thee (whom I humbly trust we have not offended past Forgiveness)—Oh! what a glorious exchange will it be, if by l[o]sing the Name, we should [be] brought to inherit the Substance, & be join'd & united more firmly than ever to the Lord, in a durable everlasting Fellowship, that the World cannot disturb. (Moore, devotional book, n.d.)

While this entry clearly exposes Moore's desire to belong to community, it also exposes her ability to find consolation for friendship's absence in prayer. The preference for piety, even solitary piety, over friendship is therefore elaborated both in the transcription of Wright's "A Meditation" and in Moore's most personal contemplations.

71. Moore, *Moore's Book,* 147–48.

72. Ibid., 149.

73. Ibid., 150.

74. Griffitts's choice of Venera, or Venus, is unusual. The muses, especially their chief Calliope and their mother Mneme (memory), were more frequently invoked as poetic inspirations. Eighteenth-century Britons and Anglo-Americans associated Venus with sexual pleasure and eroticism, and most references to her include some discussion of sexuality. For example, Gautruche refers to "*Sicca Venera* near Carthage, an infamous place dedicated to this Goddess, where the Women did freely abandon themselves to their Lusts, and to the pleasure of Men for a Reward" (*Poetical History,* 103). Cicero's *Major de Senectute* does directly address sexuality and old age, and Franklin, whose literary circles were similar to Griffitts's, published a translation of that work in 1744 (see Cicero, *M. T. Cicero's Cato Major*). According to this translation, attributed to James Logan (Franklin's friend, Griffitts's and Moore's relation, and a correspondent of Wright's), "it is alledged that Old Age is not sensible to that Titillation of Pleasure, that is found in the other Parts of Life; which is certainly true: But at the same time it has this great Advantage to ballance it, that it does not so much as wish to have it. *Sophocles* said well, who, when he was asked at a great Age, whether he had yet any Acquaintance with *Venus,* answered, Heavens forbid! I thank the Gods I am got rid of that Tyranny" (99). Contrary to Sophocles, who is grateful to be done with Venus's "Tyranny" in his old age, Griffitts suggests that Venus and perhaps one's relationship to the erotic are some of the sole consolations at the end of a long life.

75. Moore, *Moore's Book,* 150.

76. Ibid., 151.

77. Note the replacement of Griffitts's female eroticism with phallic imagery. Here, time seems to strip away the masculine energy of authorship, revealing a more feminine experience of the soul's communion with the divine. Of course, while Wright's words argue that the quill of her authorship is unable to access the vigor of its past inspirations,

the poem's existence belies them. This first section's exclusive use of women's authorship gives women particular authority. Moore's religious culture esteemed women as important figures for spiritual instruction, permitting them to leave their husbands and children to travel as sanctioned itinerant preachers throughout the transatlantic region. Moreover, the governmental structure of the Society of Friends progressively included separate Women's Meetings in which women administered those areas deemed appropriate for their control. In fact, Friends saw the hierarchical relationship between men and women as an earthly experience that would disappear in the afterlife, and they philosophically if not always practically "stressed the unity of genders" (Larson, *Daughters of Light,* 20). Moore clearly agreed with the Society's esteem for women's spirituality and leadership. In a 1785 letter, she described a visit from Jemima Wilkins, a Friend and preacher. She and her husband allowed Wilkins to use their orchard as a meeting space, brought over benches from their school, and hosted her at their home (see Moore, letter, 22 March 1785). Moreover, almost half the entries in the testimony book were authored by women, including the first four. For a discussion of women's authorization to speak publicly, see Fell's *Women's Speaking Justified* and Larson's *Daughters of Light,* 30–34, 227–30. Bacon's *Mothers of Feminism* provides a history of the Society of Friends' proto-feminism and feminism.

78. Moore, *Moore's Book,* 151.

79. Born in 1727, Griffitts was about thirty years younger than Wright. Moore's copies of Wright's poems and Griffitts's responses may have come from a correspondence between the two women that lasted from 1762 to 1764. Four of Griffitts's letters to Wright are in the Norris papers, box 12, folders 44–47. Her letters are consistently effusive in their praise for Wright and deprecate her own poetic talents, though she notes the enclosure of her own verse with these letters. The final letter, dated 5 August 1764, expresses dismayed hurt that Wright has determined to cease their correspondence.

80. Generally, the explicitly political texts acknowledge colonial rights, value freedom, and deplore British oppression but also protest the violence of revolution and point out the hypocrisy of patriots' tyranny over those who disagree. Therefore, the poems reflect a neutral and pacifist stance toward the American Revolution and "capture . . . the sentiments of many Quakers" (Wulf, "*Milcah Martha Moore's Book,*" 41). Examples of overtly political entries include "On the Right Honble Willm. Pitt Esqr. by a Female" (*Moore's Book,* 152), "The female Patriots. Address'd to the Daughters of Liberty in America" (172–73), and "New Jail" (198–99).

81. Out of such occasional lingering emerges an example of what Brown terms "thick style" (*Pilgrim,* 31–34, 62–64).

82. Thomas Paine was raised as a Friend, a fact that may have exacerbated Griffitts's contempt for his stirring revolutionary tract. For a discussion of the influence of Friendly ideology on his writings, see Kashatus, *Conflict,* 1–34.

83. Moore, *Moore's Book,* 255. "Sylvania" is poetic shorthand for Pennsylvania.

84. Ibid., 256.

85. "Declaration," 1.

86. Friendship does not preclude criticism. Rather, these women were troubled by the form that disagreement was taking in the revolutionary climate. As described in "An Essay on Friendship," a friend who is wrong is "reprove[d] . . ./. . . with the tenderness of love" (Moore, *Moore's Book,* 118).

87. Ibid., 256.

88. Ibid.

89. Ibid., 257.

90. For a brief biography of Morris, see Larson, *Daughters of Light,* 313. Larson lingers frequently on Morris; see especially chap. 3. Her book narrates the long tradition of preaching women, describing female Friends' call to ministry as "primarily an internal experience that gave women the certainty that they had been divinely chosen" (76). See also Evans and Evans, "Memoir."

91. Moore, *Moore's Book,* 254.

92. Blecki believes such moments asked the reader to "ponder" whether "the 'good' had left for another world" while "the 'bad' or 'malicious' were still actively (and dangerously) present in colonial America" ("Reading *Moore's Book,*" 67). Adding to the elegy's authority would be the reader's likely familiarity with it. It was a text used in at least one Society of Friends school. In her study of unmarried women in eighteenth-century Philadelphia, Wulf observes that at least two female students attending a Philadelphia school run by the unmarried Friends Rebecca Jones and Hannah Catherill were given this poem to transcribe into their copybooks as part of their education (*Not All Wives,* 47–48). Reading a poem from and about women known to the author, the reader might have felt united to the community during the act of reading. The poem immediately before the Morris poem, "To S. Fothergill on his leaving Philada. June 4th. 1756," only adds to this endorsement because it aligns Morris's piety with that of another eminent Friend. Samuel Fothergill was a celebrated preacher and leader who visited America from 1754 through 1756. During the Seven Years War (1756–63), he advocated pacifism. The North American community of Friends greatly admired him, and his texts were published and circulated. For another transcription of the Morris elegy, see *Catherine Haines.* Haines's commonplace book also includes entries by Joseph Addison, Phillis Wheatley, John Dryden, Mary Leapor, and Alexander Pope, thereby situating Griffitts's work among these widely printed authors. For a brief biography of Fothergill, see Winchester, "Samuel Fothergill."

93. Moore, *Moore's Book,* 246–47.

94. Ibid., 247, 250. Moore attributed "Ladies Lamentation" to Europa but also indicated that it was "by the same" author as the prior entry, "Beware the Ides of March." Blecki proposes that Europa is another Griffitts pseudonym and that its use was "appropriate" because the poems present "opposite position[s]" ("Reading *Moore's Book,*" 92). It's a curious moment.

95. Moore, *Moore's Book,* 250.

96. Women were encouraged to participate in politics during the colonial tea boycott that began in response to the Townshend Act of 1767 (see Norton, *Liberty's Daughters,* 157–63). Female Friends such as Griffitts, Moore, and Wright appear to have sympathized with the tea boycott (perhaps because it was peaceful resistance). For additional entries on the topic of tea, see "The female Patriots" (Moore, *Moore's Book,* 172–73) and "Wrote extempore on Tea" (299).

97. As Wulf notes, documenting a direct connection between Moore and Fergusson is difficult, especially because Fergusson's circle "was composed primarily of Anglicans" ("*Milcah Martha Moore's Book,*" 31). Fergusson held a heterosocial salon at her home from approximately 1765 to 1775. For a discussion of her literary salon, see Stabile's introduction to *Most Learned Woman,* 1–15. Despite the separation between Moore's and Fergusson's literary circles, they did share "socioeconomic status and geographic proximity"

and also, most likely, friends and acquaintances (Shields, *Civil Tongues*, 120–40). While *Moore's Book* also includes "A few Extracts from E[lizabeth] G[raeme]'s Journal" early in the book (200–217), these two poems are the only other entries by Fergusson, and their insertion in the midst of a long stretch of Griffitts's poetry is somewhat abrupt. This stretch spans entries 71–125. Insertions are entries 89–90, 101–3, 106–7, and 111–14 (and possibly 82, Europa's "Ladies Lamentation"). The final entry, 126, is also not by Griffitts.

98. Moore's note about Cupid: "A favorite Lap-Dog." Thus, the only masculine presence is a small obedient dog.

99. Moore, *Moore's Book*, 259.

100. Though I do not address the topic here, the subtle eroticism of the poem and its connection to female friendship deserves analysis. For evocative examples of such an analysis, see Moore, *Sister Arts*.

101. See Moore, *Moore's Book*, 266–67, 288–89. These poems are by Griffitts.

102. Parrish, "Women's Nature," 219.

103. Another example is Griffitts's "The voluntary Retreat 1772" (Moore, *Moore's Book*, 182–84). Hester "Hetty" Griffitts was her first cousin. Interestingly, Fergusson's "The Invitation" is addressed to Amanda, Hester Griffitts's pseudonym.

104. Moore juxtaposed Hester Griffitts's poem with "New Jail. Philadelphia Jany. 1st. 1776.," a poem about the jailing of two New Jersey Friends for advocating pacifism. In the poem, the men's isolation is a sign of persecution and their "justest Cause" (ibid., 198). Even the prison's "confin[ement]" will not stop their commitment to "Freedom, Government, & Laws" (199). This arrangement offers a brief poetic respite and then returns the reader to the demands of friendship.

105. Ibid., 239. This poem as well as the next two, "A moral Sonnet" and "The Query," are by Griffitts.

106. Ibid., 240.

107. Ibid., 240–41.

108. Ibid., 239.

Afterword

1. Bannet, *Empire of Letters*, 194.

2. Katteuha, "Cherokee Women," 181.

3. In *Eastern Band*, Cherokee scholar Carney notes that Katteuha may have met Franklin on her diplomatic journeys and may have recalled his "outspoken support of Canasatego, the Onondaga sachem who had spoken for the Six Nations at the Treaty of Lancaster, Pennsylvania, in the summer of 1744" (28). For a discussion of Katteuha's possible identities, see Justice, "Katteuha (Cherokee)," 861.

4. Katteuha, "Cherokee Women," 181.

5. The letter reads, "Indorsed by Kaattahee, Scolecutta, and Kaattahee, Cherokee Indian Women" (ibid., 182). Kaattahee (and the other Cherokee names, including Katteuha) may be a title rather than a name. When it was printed in the *Pennsylvania Archives*, the editor followed it with another document, noting the presentation of diplomatic gifts. That second document suggests that Kaattahee is Corn Tassel, also known as Onitositah and Old Tassel, a powerful and peace-minded Cherokee leader, and that Scolecutta is Hanging Maw, his war chief. If this is true, the above endorsement should be read as "[and] Cherokee Indian Women." My interpretation takes into account both

possibilities. For both documents, see Hazard, *Pennsylvania Archives,* 181–82. The interpreters may have transcribed Katteuha's words to produce this letter; their names are printed in the *Pennsylvania Archives* version: "Moses Price & Tom Ben, Linchester" (182). Price was of mixed heritage and had established residence in the Nation (see Sturtevant, "Cherokee Frontiers," 66–71). For a review of the escalating violence and the Franklinites' 1788 betrayal and murder of Old Tassel and Hanging Maw, see Woodward, *Cherokees,* 103–9.

6. Katteuha, "Cherokee Women," 181. Franklin's correspondence includes these letters as well as correspondence with John Sevier, governor of the temporary outlaw state of Franklin, and Cornstalk, the aforementioned Cherokee diplomat. See the unpublished 1787 volumes of the Franklin papers (www.franklinpapers.org). For a history of the state of Franklin, see Barksdale, *Lost State.* Cornstalk may be Corn Tassel. See n. 4.

7. Katteuha, "Cherokee Women," 182.

8. For more on Cherokee complementary pairings, see Justice, *Our Fire,* 27–31.

9. For more on Cherokee women's collaborative oratory and diplomacy, see Moulder, "'By Women.'" For more on Beloved Women, see Perdue, *Cherokee Women,* 206, n. 92; and Justice, *Our Fire,* 29–33, 229, n. 34.

10. For more on Logan and colonial Pennsylvania, see Tolles, *James Logan.* He is a fascinating but often neglected historical figure. For treatments of specific aspects of his life and writings, see Wolf's *Library* and "Romance" and Lokken's "Social Thought." For an essay on Logan's correspondence with Susanna Wright, see Blecki and Treese, "Susanna Wright's 'The Grove.'"

11. Logan, "Selections," 1. Here, Deborah Norris Logan quotes Erskine's *Armata,* published in 1817, the year she began the transcription part of her project.

12. Armstrong and Logan, *Correspondence,* viii.

13. Ibid., vii–viii. This citation is to the preface to the 1870 published version, which quotes Logan's words in their entirety, with the exception of a few in the final line. The published version, edited by Armstrong, is not a printed replica of her manuscripts. For example, he inserts two documents at the beginning and includes additional prefatory material and notes. The manuscript books are housed at the American Philosophical Society, Philadelphia, Pennsylvania (see Logan, "Selections," 3–4).

14. Logan was prone to such majestic genealogical projects. See, for example, her manuscript "The Bank of the United States: Formerly the Norris House and Garden," which was more about her childhood home than about the bank, its architectural replacement. Stenton Park in Philadelphia holds the manuscript, but a published version is available as Logan, *Norris House.* Stabile discusses this manuscript extensively (*Memory's Daughters,* 1–8).

15. Stockton, *Only for the Eye,* 304.

16. Ibid., 305.

17. For a fuller discussion of this letter, see Wigginton, "Late Night Vindication."

18. Foster, *Coquette,* 50. While referred to as a letter, Sanford's longest note to Wharton is quite brief. He leaves it with a servant after her mother will not let him see her daughter. Fearing Wharton is about to choose his rival, he entreats, "Let me conjure you to meet me in your garden" (90). The text is transcribed into a much longer letter that Wharton sends to Lucy Sumner, recounting Boyer's discovery of Sanford and Wharton's meeting and his subsequent outraged rejection. The contents of Sanford's several other billets do not appear in the text, with one exception. Again writing to Sumner,

Wharton transcribes, "Will Miss Wharton condescend a few moments with her once favored Sanford? He is but too sensible that he has forfeited all claim to the privilege. He therefore presumes not to request it on the score of merit, or of former acquaintance; but solicits it from her benevolence, and pity" (117).

19. Ibid., 22.

20. Ibid., 116. Sanford quotes Epistle II of Pope's *An Essay on Man* (*Poems,* 518, ll. 63–64), lines that consider the ill consequences of self-love unbalanced by reason. Indeed, there is something diaristic and masturbatory about Sanford's letters, directed to an otherwise never seen or described character, who never responds.

21. Ibid., 127.

22. Ibid., 150. A host of scholarship considers the topics of epistolary and narrative forms, reading practices, and Wharton's shifting presence. See Davidson, *Revolution,* especially 185–232; Smith-Rosenberg, "Domesticating Virtue"; Fizer, "Signing"; Harris, "Hannah Webster Foster's *The Coquette*"; Lukasik, "Breeding"; and Mower, "Bodies." Waterman's impressive archival discoveries of the letters of Elizabeth Whitman, the notorious real-life model for Wharton, are the subject of his essay "Coquetry and Correspondence."

23. See Looby, *Voicing America,* 14, for more on the relation between diversity and American nationalism. Nelson's argument foregrounds individualism and capitalism as part of fraternal citizenship because white manhood "relocate[s] men's affiliations away from more locally conceived identities" (*National Manhood,* ix; also see 16–19).

24. For additional reproductions and discussions of this engraving, see Cahill, "Liberty," 70–72, and Knott, *Sensibility,* 196–97.

25. "PHILADELPHIA, May 7, CIVIC FESTIVAL," n.p. Richard Godbeer relates this same article to the idealized role of friendship in the new republic (*Overflowing,* 155).

26. Berlant, introduction to *Intimacy,* 1.

27. Nelson, *National Manhood,* ix.

28. Coviello, *Intimacy in America,* 6.

29. Schweitzer, *Perfecting Friendship,* 13.

30. Ibid., 16.

31. Godbeer, *Overflowing,* 12.

32. Nation as fantasy is powerfully explored in Berlant, *Anatomy of National Fantasy.* Anderson's (*Imagined Communities*) and Nelson's (*National Manhood*) use of the word *imagined* in their titles also encourage a sense of the national fantastic.

33. Foster, *Coquette,* 158.

34. In one example, a basket was sent from the Mohegan minister and leader Samson Occom in Brotherton to his sister Lucy in Mohegan, "a record of their journey" (Fitzgerald, "Cultural Work," 53).

35. Tantaquidgeon and Fawcett, "Symbolic Motifs," 99–101.

36. See Fitzgerald's "Cultural Work" for a concise analysis of one such basket. Relying on the writings of Mohegan anthropologist and medicine woman Tantaquidgeon and her successor Fawcett to interpret the basket's decorations, Fitzgerald repudiates anthropologist Ann McMullen's readings of similar baskets and Laurel Thatcher Ulrich's attention to the newspaper lining of another. (The basket in plate 5 is similarly lined with a newspaper.) However, I think one should not choose between reading the basket as reconciliatory or admonishing. Though here I note its surface, I contend that there is something consequential about basketry's enclosure of print. See Tantaquidgeon

and Fawcett, "Symbolic Motifs"; McMullen, "Looking for People"; and Ulrich, *Age of Homespun,* 340–73.

37. Dickinson, *Manuscript Books,* 548.

38. See Rosenthal, "White Blackbird," for a discussion of Harper's play on the tragic mulatta.

39. See Harper, *Iola Leroy,* 99–108 and 120–27, for accounts of Iola's and her brother's epistolary pathways to their mixed-race revelations. Iola identifies her maternal uncle, Robert, by singing at his hospital bedside a lullaby learned from her mother and originally sung by his (140–42). That same song foregrounds his and Iola's reunification with Iola's grandmother (179–83). The novel also opens with coded messages, as slaves invite their fellows to secret meetings (7).

40. See Berlant, "Queen of America," for a juxtaposition of Iola's testimony of forced movement with Anita Hill's testimony of sexual harassment. Foreman's "'Reading Aright'" offers an instructive reading of *Iola Leroy* that attends to its multiple registers and rhetorics.

41. For more on Punderson, see Ulrich, *Age of Homespun,* 228–47, especially 237–39; and Schoelwer and Steinway, *Connecticut Needlework,* 86–88.

42. Though not part of the exhibit, as it was in Brooklyn, Punderson's needlework was also cited as the inspiration for Smith's 2008 installation, *Her Home,* at Museum Haus Esters in Krefeld, Germany. See Hentschel, *Kiki Smith,* 29–30, for an analysis of the relation between Punderson's work and *Her Home.* Many of the same pieces were displayed in *Sojourn.*

43. Both reviewers and Smith herself have focused on her play with the annunciation as a way to think about how the exhibition commented on women artists and the creative act. See Rosenberg, "On Being"; Valdez, "In Conversation"; and "Go See—New York."

BIBLIOGRAPHY

Advertisement, *Newport Mercury*, 21 May 1792, n.p.

Allen, Paula Gunn. *Pocahontas: Medicine Woman, Spy, Entrepreneur, Diplomat.* New York: Harper, 2003.

Altman, Janet Gurkin. *Epistolarity: Approaches to a Form.* Columbus: Ohio State University Press, 1982.

Amory, Hugh, and David D. Hall, eds. *The Colonial Book in the Atlantic World.* Vol. 1 of *A History of the Book in America.* Chapel Hill: University of North Carolina Press, 2007.

Anderson, Benedict. *Imagined Communities: Reflections on the Origin and Spread of Nationalism.* Rev. ed. London: Verso, 1991.

Armstrong, Edward, and Deborah Norris Logan, eds. *Correspondence Between William Penn and James Logan, Secretary of the Province of Pennsylvania, and Others. 1700–1750.* Vol. 1. Philadelphia: Lippincott, 1870.

Backscheider, Paula. *Eighteenth-Century Women Poets and Their Poetry: Inventing Agency, Inventing Genre.* Baltimore: Johns Hopkins University Press, 2005.

Bacon, Margaret Hope. *Mothers of Feminism: The Story of Quaker Women in America.* San Francisco: Harper and Row, 1986.

Bailyn, Bernard. *The Ideological Origins of the American Revolution.* Enlarged ed. Cambridge: Belknap, 1992.

Baine, Rodney M. "Myths of Mary Musgrove." *Georgia Historical Quarterly* 76 (1992): 428–35.

Bannet, Eve Tavor. *Empire of Letters: Letter Manuals and Transatlantic Correspondence, 1680–1820.* Cambridge: Cambridge University Press, 2005.

Barbour, Hugh, and Jerry William Frost. *The Quakers.* Westport, Conn.: Greenwood, 1988.

Barclay, Robert. *An Apology for the True Christian Divinity.* 6th ed. Newport, R.I.: Franklin, 1729.

Barksdale, Kevin T. *The Lost State of Franklin: America's First Secession.* Lexington: University Press of Kentucky, 2009.

Bassard, Katherine Clay. *Spiritual Interrogations: Culture, Gender, and Community in Early African American Women's Writing.* Princeton: Princeton University Press, 1999.

Beauvoir, Simone de. *The Second Sex,* translated by Constance Borde and Sheila Malovany-Chevallier. New York: Vintage, 2011.

Belinda. "Petition of 1782." In *Transatlantic Feminisms in the Age of Revolutions,* edited by Lisa L. Moore, Joanna Brooks, and Caroline Wigginton, 187–88. New York: Oxford University Press, 2012.

Berlant, Lauren. *The Anatomy of National Fantasy.* Chicago: University of Chicago Press, 1991.

———. *The Female Complaint: The Unfinished Business of Sentimentality in American Culture.* Durham, N.C.: Duke University Press, 2008.

———. Introduction to *Intimacy,* edited by Lauren Berlant, 1–8. Chicago: University of Chicago Press, 2000.

———. "The Queen of America Goes to Washington City: Harriet Jacobs, Frances Harper, Anita Hill." *American Literature* 65, no. 3 (1993): 549–74.

Blair, Ann M. *Too Much to Know: Managing Scholarly Information before the Modern Age.* New Haven: Yale University Press, 2010.

Blayney, Peter W. M. *The First Folio of Shakespeare.* Washington: Folger Library, 1991.

Blecki, Catherine La Courreye. "Reading *Moore's Book:* Manuscripts vs. Print Culture, and the Development of Early American Literature." In *Milcah Martha Moore's Book: A Commonplace Book from Revolutionary America,* by Milcah Martha Moore, edited by Catherine La Courreye Blecki and Karin A. Wulf, 59–106. University Park: Pennsylvania State University Press, 1997.

Blecki, Catherine La Courreye, and Lorett Treese. "Susanna Wright's 'The Grove': A Philosophic Exchange with James Logan." *Early American Literature* 38, no. 2 (2003): 239–55.

Blecki, Catherine La Courreye, and Karin A. Wulf. Preface to *Milcah Martha Moore's Book: A Commonplace Book from Revolutionary America,* by Milcah Martha Moore, edited by Catherine La Courreye Blecki and Karin A. Wulf, xi–xx. University Park: Pennsylvania State University Press, 1997.

Block, Sharon. *Rape and Sexual Power in Early America.* Chapel Hill: University of North Carolina Press, 2006.

Bly, Anthony T. "Wheatley's ON THE AFFRAY IN KING STREET." *Explicator* 56, no. 4 (1998): 177–80.

———. "Wheatley's 'On the Death of a Young Lady of Five Years of Age.'" *Explicator* 58, no. 1 (1999): 10–13.

Bolter, Jay David, and Richard Grusin. *Remediation: Understanding New Media.* Cambridge: MIT Press, 2000.

Boone, Elizabeth Hill. "Aztec Pictorial Histories: Records without Words." In *Writing without Words: Alternative Literacies in Mesoamerica and the Andes,* edited by Elizabeth Hill Boone and Walter D. Mignolo, 50–76. Durham, N.C.: Duke University Press, 1994.

Bordo, Susan. *Unbearable Weight: Feminism, Western Culture, and the Body.* Berkeley: University of California Press, 1993.

Boulukos, George. *The Grateful Slave: The Emergence of Race in Eighteenth-Century British and American Culture.* Cambridge: Cambridge University Press, 2008.

Braund, Kathryn E. Holland. *Deerskins and Duffels: The Creek Indian Trade with Anglo-America, 1685–1815.* Lincoln: University of Nebraska Press, 1993.

———. "Guardians of Tradition and Handmaidens to Change: Women's Roles in Creek Economic and Social Life During the Eighteenth Century." *American Indian Quarterly* 14 (1990): 239–58.

Bray, Alan. *The Friend.* Chicago: University of Chicago Press, 2003.

Brekus, Catherine A. "Sarah Osborn's Enlightenment: Reimagining Eighteenth-Century Intellectual History." In *The Religious History of American Women: Reimagining the Past,* edited by Catherine A. Brekus, 108–41. Chapel Hill: University of North Carolina Press, 2007.

———. *Sarah Osborn's World: The Rise of Evangelical Christianity in Early America.* New Haven: Yale University Press, 2013.

Brewer, David A. "The Tactility of Authorial Names." *Eighteenth Century* 54, no. 2 (2013): 195–213.

Brooks, Joanna. *American Lazarus: Religion and the Rise of African-American and Native American Literatures.* New York: Oxford University Press, 2003.

———. "Our Phillis, Ourselves." *American Literature* 82, no. 1 (2010): 1–18.

Brooks, Lisa. *The Common Pot: The Recovery of Native Space in the Northeast.* Minneapolis: University of Minnesota Press, 2008.

Bross, Kristina, and Hilary E. Wyss, eds. *Early Native Literacies in New England: A Documentary and Critical Anthology.* Amherst: University of Massachusetts Press, 2008.

Brown, Matthew. *The Pilgrim and the Bee: Reading Rituals and Book Culture in Early New England.* Philadelphia: University of Pennsylvania Press, 2007.

Brown, Vincent. *The Reaper's Garden: Death and Power in the World of Atlantic Slavery.* Cambridge: Harvard University Press, 2010.

Brückner, Martin, ed. *Early American Cartographies.* Chapel Hill: University of North Carolina Press, 2011.

———. *The Geographic Revolution in Early America: Maps, Literacy, and National Identity.* Chapel Hill: University of North Carolina Press, 2006.

Bulkeley, Peter. *The Gospel-Covenant, or, the Covenant of Grace Opened.* London: Simmons, 1651.

Burlington Women's Quarterly Meeting Minutes (BWQM), 1686–1845. Haverford College Library, Quaker Collection, Haverford, Pennsylvania.

Burr, Esther Edwards. *The Journal of Esther Edwards Burr, 1754–1757,* edited by Carol F. Karlsen and Laurie Crumpacker. New Haven: Yale University Press, 1984.

Burt, John. *Earthquakes, the Effects of God's Wrath. A Sermon Preached at Bristol, the Lord's Day after a Very Terrible Earthquake, Which Was on Tuesday, November*

18, 1755. a Few Minutes after Four O'clock in the Morning. Newport, R.I.: Franklin, 1755.

Butler, Judith. *Bodies That Matter: On the Discursive Limits of "Sex."* New York: Routledge, 1993.

Bynum, Caroline Walker. *Fragmentation and Redemption: Essays on Gender and the Human Body in Medieval Religion.* New York: Zone, 1991.

Cadbury, Henry J. "Negro Membership in the Society of Friends." *Journal of Negro History* 21, no. 2 (1936): 151–213.

Cahill, Edward. "Liberty of the Imagination in Revolutionary America." In *American Literature's Aesthetic Dimensions,* edited by Cindy Weinstein and Christopher Looby, 39–55. New York: Columbia University Press, 2012.

Calhoun, Craig J., ed. *Habermas and the Public Sphere.* Cambridge: MIT Press, 1997.

Calloway, Colin G. *Pen and Ink Witchcraft: Treaties and Treaty Making in American Indian History.* New York: Oxford University Press, 2013.

Candler, Allen D., ed. *Colonial Records of the State of Georgia.* Vol. 1 of *The Colonial Records of the State of Georgia.* Atlanta: Franklin, 1904.

———, ed. *Original Papers, Correspondence, Trustees, General Oglethorpe and Others, 1741–1742.* Vol. 23 of *The Colonial Records of the State of Georgia.* Atlanta: Byrd, 1914.

———, ed. *Original Papers, Trustees, President and Assistants, and Others, 1750–1752.* Vol. 26 of *The Colonial Records of the State of Georgia.* Atlanta: Byrd, 1916.

———, ed. *Proceedings of the President and Assistants from October 12, 1741, to October 30, 1754.* Vol. 6 of *The Colonial Records of the State of Georgia.* Atlanta: Franklin, 1906.

Carey, Brycchan. *British Abolitionism and the Rhetoric of Sensibility: Writing, Sentiment and Slavery,1760–1807.* New York: Palgrave Macmillan, 2005.

Carney, Virginia Moore. *Eastern Band Cherokee Women: Cultural Persistence in Their Letters and Speeches.* Knoxville: University of Tennessee Press, 2005.

Carretta, Vincent. Introduction to *Complete Writings,* by Phillis Wheatley, edited by Vincent Carretta, xiii–xlvii. New York: Penguin, 2001.

———. *Phillis Wheatley: Biography of a Genius in Bondage.* Athens: University of Georgia Press, 2011.

Catalogue of a Very Large Assortment of the Most Esteemed Books In Every Branch of Polite Literature, Arts and Sciences . . . Which Are to Be Sold by Cox & Berry At Their Store in King-Street, Boston. [Boston], ca. 1772.

Catalogus Impressorum Librorum Bibliothecæ Bodlejanæ in Academia Oxoniensi, 1674.

Catherine Haines [commonplace book], 1775. Ms. 975A. Haverford College Library, Quaker Collection, Haverford, Pennsylvania.

Cavendish, Margaret. *CCXI Sociable Letters Written by the Thrice Noble, Illustrious, and Excellent Princess, the Lady Marchioness of Newcastle.* London: Wilson, 1664.

Cavitch, Max. *American Elegy: The Poetry of Mourning from the Puritans to Whitman.* Minneapolis: University of Minnesota Press, 2007.

Census of the Inhabitants of the Colony of Rhode Island and Providence Plantations, Taken by Order of the General Assembly, in the Year 1774. Providence: Knowles, Anthony, 1858.

Cicero, Marcus Tullius. *M. T. Cicero's Cato Major, or His Discourse of Old-Age: With Explanatory Notes.* Philadelphia: Franklin, 1744.

Clanchy, M. T. *From Memory to Written Record: England, 1066–1307.* 3rd ed. Malden, Mass.: Wiley-Blackwell, 2013.

Clarke, Noah T. *The Thacher Wampum Belts of the New York State Museum.* Albany: State University of New York, 1929.

Coffin, Margaret. *Death in Early America: The History and Folklore of Customs and Superstitions of Early Medicine, Funerals, Burials, and Mourning.* Nashville, Tenn.: Nelson, 1976.

Cohen, Lara Langer, and Jordan Alexander Stein, eds. *Early African American Print Culture.* Philadelphia: University of Pennsylvania Press, 2012.

Cohen, Matt. *The Networked Wilderness: Communicating in Early New England.* Minneapolis: University of Minnesota Press, 2009.

Cohen, Matt, and Jeffrey Glover, eds. *Colonial Mediascapes: Sensory Worlds of the Early Americas.* Lincoln: University of Nebraska Press, 2014.

Coleman, Kenneth, and Milton Ready, eds. *Original Papers, Correspondence to the Trustees, James Oglethorpe, and Others, 1732–1735.* Vol. 20 of *The Colonial Records of the State of Georgia.* Athens: University of Georgia Press, 1982.

———, eds. *Original Papers of Governor John Reynolds, 1754–1756.* Vol. 27 of *The Colonial Records of the State of Georgia.* Athens: University of Georgia Press, 1982.

Collection of Papers, Printed by Order of the Society for the Propagation of the Gospel in Foreign Parts. London, 1706.

Cook, Elizabeth Heckendorn. *Epistolary Bodies: Gender and Genre in the Eighteenth-Century Republic of Letters.* Stanford: Stanford University Press, 1996.

Corkran, David H. *The Creek Frontier, 1540–1783.* Norman: University of Oklahoma Press, 1967.

Corry, John Pitts. "Some New Light on the Bosomworth Claims." *Georgia Historical Quarterly* 25 (1941): 195–224.

Coulter, E. Merton. "Mary Musgrove, 'Queen of the Creeks': A Chapter of Early Georgia Trouble." *Georgia Historical Quarterly* 11 (1927): 1–30.

Coviello, Peter. *Intimacy in America: Dreams of Affiliation in Antebellum Literature.* Minneapolis: University of Minnesota Press, 2005.

Cowan, Brian. *The Social Life of Coffee: The Emergence of the British Coffeehouse.* New Haven: Yale University Press, 2005.

———. "What Was Masculine about the Public Sphere? Gender and the Coffeehouse Milieu in Post-Restoration England." *History Workshop Journal* 51 (2001): 127–57.

Cowell, Pattie. "'Womankind Call Reason to Their Aid': Susanna Wright's Verse Epistle on the Status of Women in Eighteenth-Century America." *Signs* 6, no. 4 (1981): 795–800.

Crain, Caleb. *American Sympathy: Men, Friendship, and Literature in the New Nation.* New Haven: Yale University Press, 2001.

Crane, Elaine Forman. *Ebb Tide in New England: Women, Seaports, and Social Change, 1630–1800.* Boston: Northeastern University Press, 1998.

Crèvecoeur, J. Hector St. John de. *Letters from an American Farmer, Describing Certain Provincial Situations, Manners, and Customs, and Conveying Some Idea of the State of the People of North America.* Philadelphia: Carey, 1793.

Davidson, Cathy N. *Revolution and the Word: The Rise of the Novel in America.* Expanded ed. New York: Oxford University Press, 2004.

Davis, David Brion. *The Problem of Slavery in the Age of Revolution, 1770–1823.* Ithaca: Cornell University Press, 1975.

Daybell, James. "Scripting a Female Voice: Women's Epistolary Rhetoric in Sixteenth-Century Letters of Petition." *Women's Writing* 13, no. 1 (2006): 3–22.

Decker, William Merrill. *Epistolary Practices: Letter Writing in America before Telecommunications.* Chapel Hill: University of North Carolina Press, 1998.

"Declaration by the Representatives of the United States of America, in General Congress Assembled." *Pennsylvania Evening Post.* 6 July 1776.

Delbanco, Andrew. *The Puritan Ordeal.* Cambridge: Harvard University Press, 1991.

D'Emilio, John, and Estelle B. Freedman. *Intimate Matters: A History of Sexuality in America.* 2nd ed. Chicago: University of Chicago Press, 1997.

Derrida, Jacques. *Politics of Friendship,* translated by George Collins. London: Verso, 1997.

Dethlefsen, Edwin, and James Deetz. "Death's Heads, Cherubs, and Willow Trees." In *Passing: The Vision of Death in America,* edited by Charles O. Jackson, 48–59. Westport, Conn.: Greenwood, 1977.

Dewdney, Selwyn H. *The Sacred Scrolls of the Southern Ojibway.* Toronto: University of Toronto Press, 1975.

Dickinson, Emily. *The Manuscript Books of Emily Dickinson,* edited by R. W. Franklin. Vol. 1. Cambridge: Belknap, 1981.

Dierks, Konstantin. *In My Power: Letter Writing and Communications in Early America.* Philadelphia: University of Pennsylvania Press, 2009.

Dill, Bonnie Thornton. "Our Mothers' Grief: Racial Ethnic Women and the Maintenance of Families." *Journal of Family History* 13, no. 4 (1988): 415–31.

Dillon, Elizabeth Maddock. *The Gender of Freedom: Fictions of Liberalism and the Literary Public Sphere.* Stanford: Stanford University Press, 2004.

———. "Nursing Fathers and Brides of Christ: The Feminized Body of the Puritan Convert." In *A Centre of Wonders: The Body in Early America,* edited by Janet Moore Lindman and Michele Lise Tarter, 127–44. Ithaca: Cornell University Press, 2001.

Dimock, Wai-Chee. "Scales of Aggregation: Prenational, Subnational, Transnational." *American Literary History* 18, no. 2 (2006): 219–28.

Donoghue, Emma. *Passions between Women: British Lesbian Culture, 1668–1801.* New York: HarperCollins, 1995.

Earle, Alice Morse. *Customs and Fashions in Old New England.* New York: Scribner, 1894.

Edwards, Jonathan. *The Church's Marriage to Her Sons, and to Her God: A Sermon Preached at the Instalment of the Rev. Mr. Samuel Buel as Pastor of the Church and Congregation at East-Hampton on Long-Island, September 19. 1746.* Boston: Kneeland and Green, 1746.

———. *A Treatise Concerning Religious Affections, in Three Parts.* Boston: Kneeland and Green, 1746.

Edwards, Paul, ed. *The Life of Olaudah Equiano, or Gustavas Vassa, the African.* London: Dawson, 1969.

Eley, Geoff. "Nations, Publics, and Political Cultures: Placing Habermas in the Nineteenth Century." In *Habermas and the Public Sphere,* edited by Craig Calhoun, 289–339. Cambridge: MIT Press, 1992.

Ellison, Julie. *Cato's Tears and the Making of Anglo-American Emotion.* Chicago: University of Chicago Press, 1999.

English Part of the Library of the Late Duke of Lauderdale, Being a Catalogue of Choice English Books in Divinity, History, Geography, Law, Poetry and Miscellany. [London]: [Hall?], 1690.

Erasmus, Desiderius. *On Copia of Words or Ideas,* translated by Donald B. King and H. David Rix. Milwaukee: Marquette University Press, 1999.

Erskine, Thomas. *Armata: A Fragment.* 2nd ed. London: Murray, 1817.

Essig, James D. *The Bonds of Wickedness: American Evangelicals against Slavery, 1770–1808.* Philadelphia: Temple University Press, 1983.

Eustace, Nicole. *Passion Is the Gale: Emotion, Power, and the Coming of the American Revolution.* Chapel Hill: University of North Carolina Press, 2008.

Evans, William, and Thomas Evans, eds. "Memoir of Sarah Morris, a Minister of the Gospel in the Religious Society of Friends." In *The Friends' Library: Comprising Journals, Doctrinal Treatises, and Other Writings of Members of the Religious Society of Friends,* 4:478–80. Philadelphia: Rakestraw, 1842.

Fawcett-Sayet, Melissa. "Sociocultural Authority: The Mohegan Land Case." In *Rooted Like the Ash Trees: New England Indians and the Land,* edited by Richard G. Carlson, 52–53. Naugatuck, Conn.: Eagle Wing, 1987.

Fell, Margaret. *Women's Speaking Justified, Proved and Allowed by the Scriptures.* London, 1666.

Fenton, William Nelson. *The Great Law and the Longhouse: A Political History of the Iroquois Confederacy.* Norman: University of Oklahoma Press, 1998.

Fergusson, Elizabeth Graeme. *Lania to a Friend.* In *Papers, 1752–1799.* Vol. 1. Ms. 13298.Q. Library Company of Philadelphia, Pennsylvania.

———. *Poemata Juvenalia.* In *Papers, 1752–1799.* Vol. 2. Ms. 13298.Q. Library Company of Philadelphia, Pennsylvania.

Fisher, Doris. "Mary Musgrove: Creek Englishwoman." Ph.D. diss., Emory University, 1990.

Fitts, Robert K. *Inventing New England's Slave Paradise: Master/Slave Relations in Eighteenth-Century Narragansett, Rhode Island.* New York: Garland, 1998.

Fitzgerald, Stephanie. "The Cultural Work of a Mohegan Painted Basket." In *Early Native Literacies in New England: A Documentary and Critical Anthology,* edited by Kristina Bross and Hilary E. Wyss, 52–56. Amherst: University of Massachusetts Press, 2008.

Fizer, Irene. "Signing As Republican Daughters: The Letters of Eliza Southgate and *The Coquette.*" *Eighteenth Century* 34, no. 3 (1993): 243–63.

Fliegelman, Jay. *Declaring Independence: Jefferson, Natural Language, and the Culture of Performance.* Stanford: Stanford University Press, 1993.

Foreman, P. Gabrielle. "'Reading Aright': White Slavery, Black Referents, and the Strategy of Histotextuality in *Iola Leroy.*" *Yale Journal of Criticism* 10, no. 2 (1997): 327–54.

Foster, Hannah Webster. *The Coquette,* edited by Cathy N. Davidson. New York: Oxford University Press, 1986.

Foster, Michael K. "Another Look at the Function of Wampum in Iroquois-White Councils." In *The History and Culture of Iroquois Diplomacy: An Interdisciplinary Guide to the Treaties of the Six Nations and Their League,* edited by Francis Jennings, 99–114. Syracuse: Syracuse University Press, 1995.

Foucault, Michel. *Language, Counter-Memory, Practice: Selected Essays and Interviews,* edited by Donald F. Bouchard, translated by Donald F. Bouchard and Sherry Simon. Ithaca: Cornell University Press, 1980.

Franklin, Benjamin. *The Autobiography of Benjamin Franklin,* edited by Leonard W. Labaree, Ralph L. Ketchum, Helen C. Boatfield, and Helene H. Fineman. New Haven: Yale University Press, 2003.

———. *The Papers of Benjamin Franklin,* edited by Leonard W. Labaree, J. Bell Whitfield, Jr., Helen C. Boatfield, and Helene H. Fineman. Vol. 1. New Haven: Yale University Press, 1959.

Fraser, Alexander. *Third Report of the Bureau of Archives for the Province of Ontario.* Toronto: Cameron, 1906.

Fraser, Nancy. "Rethinking the Public Sphere: A Contribution to the Critique of Actually Existing Democracy." In *Habermas and the Public Sphere,* edited by Craig Calhoun, 109–42. Cambridge: MIT Press, 1992.

"Friends' Meetings in America, 1772." *Bulletin of Friends' Historical Society of Philadelphia* 4, no. 1 (1911): 28–30.

Frost, Jerry William. *The Quaker Family in Colonial America: A Portrait of the Society of Friends.* New York: St. Martin's, 1973.

Fur, Gunlög. *A Nation of Women: Gender and Colonial Encounters among the Delaware Indians.* Philadelphia: University of Pennsylvania Press, 2009.

Further Observations Intended for Improving the Culture and Curing of Indigo, &c. in South-Carolina. London, 1747.

Gallay, Allan. "The Origins of Slaveholders' Paternalism: George Whitefield, the Bryan Family, and the Great Awakening in the South." *Journal of Southern History* 53, no. 3 (1987): 369–94.

Gandhi, Leela. *Affective Communities: Anticolonial Thought, Fin-de-Siècle Radicalism, and the Politics of Friendship.* Durham, N.C.: Duke University Press, 2006.

Garber, Marjorie. *Vested Interests: Cross-Dressing and Cultural Anxiety.* New York: Routledge, 1997.

Garvey, Ellen Gruber. *Writing with Scissors: American Scrapbooks from the Civil War to the Harlem Renaissance.* New York: Oxford University Press, 2012.

Gates, Henry Louis. *The Signifying Monkey: A Theory of African-American Literary Criticism.* Reprint. New York: Oxford University Press, 1989.

Gautruche, Pierre. *The Poetical History: Being a Compleat Collection of All the Stories Necessary for a Perfect Understanding of the Greek and Latin Poets.* London: Collins, 1701.

Gernes, Todd S. "Recasting the Culture of Ephemera." In *Popular Literacy: Studies in Cultural Practices and Poetics,* edited by John Trimbur, 107–27. Pittsburgh: University of Pittsburgh Press, 2001.

Gillespie, Michele. "The Sexual Politics of Race and Gender: Mary Musgrove and the Georgia Trustees." In *The Devil's Lane: Sex and Race in the Early South,* edited by Catherine Clinton and Michele Gillespie, 187–201. New York: Oxford University Press, 1997.

Gilliam, Charles Edgar. "His Dearest Daughter's Names." *William and Mary Quarterly* 2nd ser. 21, no. 3 (1941): 239–42.

Gilroy, Amanda. "Margaret Morris." In *American Women Prose Writers to 1820,* edited by Carla Mulford, Angela Vietto, and Amy E. Winans, 245–53. Detroit: Thomson Gale, 1999.

Gilroy, Paul. *The Black Atlantic: Modernity and Double Consciousness.* Cambridge: Harvard University Press, 1993.

Godbeer, Richard. *The Overflowing of Friendship: Love between Men and the Creation of the American Republic.* Baltimore: Johns Hopkins University Press, 2009.

———. *Sexual Revolution in Early America.* Baltimore: Johns Hopkins University Press, 2004.

Goeman, Mishuana. *Mark My Words: Native Women Mapping Our Nations.* Minneapolis: University of Minnesota Press, 2013.

Gordon, Peter. *The Journal of Peter Gordon, 1732–1735,* edited by E. Merton Coulter. Athens: University of Georgia Press, 1963.

"Go See—New York: Kiki Smith 'Sojourn' at the Brooklyn Museum through September 12, 2010." *ArtObserved.* www.artobserved.com.

Green, Michael D. "Mary Musgrove: Creating a New World." In *Sifters: Native American Women's Lives,* edited by Theda Perdue, 29–47. New York: Oxford University Press, 2001.

Greven, Philip. *The Protestant Temperament: Patterns of Child-Rearing, Religious Experience, and the Self in Early America.* New York: Knopf, 1977.

Griffitts, Hannah. "On Transcribing the Following Memorials of the Pious Dead," 1785. Poe Collection, no. 2067, folder 2. Historical Society of Pennsylvania, Philadelphia.

Grimsted, David. "Anglo-American Racism and Phillis Wheatley's 'Sable Veil,' 'Length'ned Chain,' and 'Knitted Heart.'" In *Women in the Age of the American Revolution,* edited by Ronald Hoffman and Peter J. Albert, 338–444. Charlottesville: University of Virginia Press, 1989.

Groesen, Michael van. *The Representations of the Overseas World in the De Bry Collection of Voyages (1590–1634).* Boston: Brill, 2008.

Gross, Robert A., and Mary Kelley, eds. *An Extensive Republic: Print, Culture, and Society in the New Nation, 1790–1840.* Vol. 2 of *A History of the Book in America.* Chapel Hill: University of North Carolina Press, 2010.

Gustafson, Sandra M. "American Literature and the Public Sphere." *American Literary History* 20, no. 3 (2008): 465–78.

———. *Eloquence Is Power: Oratory and Performance in Early America.* Chapel Hill: University of North Carolina Press, 2000.

Haas, Angela M. "Wampum As Hypertext: An American Indian Intellectual Tradition of Multimedia Theory and Practice." *Studies in American Indian Literatures* 19, no. 4 (2007): 77–100.

Habermas, Jürgen. *The Structural Transformation of the Public Sphere: An Inquiry into a Category of Bourgeois Society,* translated by Thomas Burger and Frederick Lawrence. Cambridge: MIT Press, 1991.

Haggerty, George E. *Unnatural Affections: Women and Fiction in the Later 18th Century.* Bloomington: Indiana University Press, 1998.

Hahn, Steven C. *The Life and Times of Mary Musgrove.* Gainesville: University Press of Florida, 2012.

Hall, David D. "The Chesapeake in the Seventeenth Century." In *The Colonial Book in the Atlantic World,* edited by Hugh Amory and David D. Hall, 55–82. Vol. 1 of *A History of the Book in America.* Chapel Hill: University of North Carolina Press, 2007.

Hamm, Thomas D. *The Quakers in America.* New York: Columbia University Press, 2003.

Hammond, Jeffrey. *The American Puritan Elegy: A Literary and Cultural Study.* Cambridge: Cambridge University Press, 2000.

Hansen, Joyce, and Gary McGowan. *Breaking Ground, Breaking Silence: The Story of New York's African Burial Ground.* New York: Holt, 1998.

Hardy, Heather K. Introduction to "Part Two: The Muskogean Language Family" in *Native Languages of the Southeastern United States,* edited by Heather K. Hardy and Janine Scancarelli, 69–74. Lincoln: University of Nebraska Press, 2005.

Harper, Frances E. W. *Iola Leroy, or Shadows Uplifted.* New York: Oxford University Press, 1988.

Harris, Sharon M., ed. *American Women Writers to 1800.* New York: Oxford University Press, 1996.

———. *Executing Race: Early American Women's Narratives of Race, Society, and the Law.* Columbus: Ohio State University Press, 2005.

———. "Hannah Webster Foster's *The Coquette:* Critiquing Franklin's America." In *Redefining the Political Novel: American Women Writers, 1797–1901,* edited by Sharon M. Harris, 1–22. Knoxville: University of Tennessee Press, 1995.

Havens, Earle. *Commonplace Books: A History of Manuscripts and Printed Books from Antiquity to the Twentieth Century.* New Haven: Yale University, Beinecke Rare Book and Manuscript Library, 2001.

Hawley, Judith. "Charlotte Smith's *Elegiac Sonnets:* Losses and Gains." In *Women's Poetry in the Enlightenment: The Making of a Canon, 1730–1820,* edited by Isobel Armstrong and Virginia Blain, 184–98. Houndsmill, U.K.: Palgrave Macmillan, 1999.

Hazard, Samuel, ed. *Minutes of the Provincial Council of Pennsylvania, from the Organization to the Termination of the Proprietary Government.* 10 vols. Harrisburg: Fenn, 1838.

———. *Pennsylvania Archives. Selected and Arranged from Original Documents in the Office of the Secretary of the Commonwealth.* Vol. 11. Philadelphia: Severns, 1855.

Hendler, Glenn. *Public Sentiments: Structures of Feeling in Nineteenth-Century American Literature.* Chapel Hill: University of North Carolina Press, 2001.

Henry, Matthew. *An Exposition of the Prophetical Books of the Old Testament.* Vol. 4. London: Clark, 1725.

Henson, Robert. "Form and Content of the Puritan Funeral Elegy." *American Literature* 32, no. 1 (1960): 11–27.

Hentschel, Martin. *Kiki Smith: Her Home.* Bielefeld, Germany: Kerber Art, 2008.

Herman, Bernard L. Introduction to Part II of *Quaker Aesthetics: Reflections on a Quaker Ethic in American Design and Consumption, 1720–1920,* edited by Emma Jones Lapsansky and Anne A. Verplancke, 149–55. Philadelphia: University of Pennsylvania Press, 2003.

Hertz, Robert. *Death and the Right Hand,* translated by Rodney Needham and Claudia Needham. London: Cohen and West, 1960.

Higginson, Francis. *A Brief Relation of the Irreligion of the Northern Quakers.* London: T.R., 1653.

Hirsch, Alison Duncan. "'The Celebrated Madame Montour': 'Interpretress' across Early American Frontiers." *Explorations in Early American Culture* 4 (2000): 81–112.

Holland, Josiah Gilbert. *History of Western Massachusetts. The Counties of Hampden, Hampshire, Franklin, and Berkshire.* Vol. 2, part 3. Springfield, Mass.: Bowles, 1855.

Holland, Sharon Patricia. *Raising the Dead: Readings of Death and (Black) Subjectivity.* Durham, N.C.: Duke University Press, 2000.

Holloway, Karla F. C. *Passed On: African American Mourning Stories.* Durham, N.C.: Duke University Press, 2002.

Hopkins, Samuel. *Sketches of the Life of the Late, Rev. Samuel Hopkins, D.D.* Hartford, Conn.: Hudson and Goodwin, 1805.

Horn, Matthew. "Texted Authority: How Letters Helped Unify the Quakers in the Long Seventeenth Century." *Seventeenth Century* 23, no. 2 (2008): 290–314.

Horsman, Reginald. "Egushwa." *Dictionary of Canadian Biography.* www.biographi.ca.

Horton, George Moses. *The Black Bard of North Carolina: George Moses Horton and His Poetry,* edited by Joan R. Sherman. Chapel Hill: University of North Carolina Press, 2000.

Howgill, Francis. *The Popish Inquisition Newly Erected in New-England, Whereby Their Church Is Manifested to Be a Daughter of Mysterie Babylon, Which Did Drink the Blood of the Saints, Who Bears the Express Image of Her Mother, Demonstrated by Her Fruits.* London: Simmons, 1659.

Hudson, Angela Pulley. *Creek Paths and Federal Roads: Indians, Settlers, and Slaves and the Making of the American South.* Chapel Hill: University of North Carolina Press, 2010.

———. "Imagining Mary Musgrove: 'Georgia's Creek Indian Princess' and Southern Identity." In *Feminist Interventions in Early American Studies,* edited by Mary C. Carruth, 112–25. Tuscaloosa: University of Alabama Press, 2006.

Hudson, Charles. *Knights of Spain, Warriors of the Sun: Hernando de Soto and the South's Ancient Chiefdoms.* Athens: University of Georgia Press, 1997.

———. *The Southeastern Indians.* Knoxville: University of Tennessee Press, 1976.

Hughes, Walter. "'Meat Out of the Eater': Panic and Desire in American Puritan Poetry." In *Engendering Men: The Question of Male Feminist Criticism,* edited by Joseph A. Boone and Michael Cadden, 102–21. New York: Routledge, 1990.

Hutson, James H. "The Campaign to Make Pennsylvania a Royal Province, 1764–1770, Part I." *Pennsylvania Magazine of History and Biography* 94, no. 4 (1970): 427–63.

Imbarrato, Susan Clair. *Declarations of Independency in Eighteenth-Century American Autobiography.* Knoxville: University of Tennessee Press, 1998.

Irigaray, Luce. *This Sex Which Is Not One,* translated by Catherine Porter and Carolyn Burke. Ithaca: Cornell University Press, 1985.

Ishii, Izumi. *Bad Fruits of the Civilized Tree: Alcohol and the Sovereignty of the Cherokee Nation.* Lincoln: University of Nebraska Press, 2008.

Jackson, Leon. "The Talking Book and the Talking Book Historian: African American Cultures of Print—The State of the Discipline." *Book History* 13 (2010): 251–308.

Jacobs, Wilbur R. "Wampum, the Protocol of Indian Diplomacy." *William and Mary Quarterly* 3rd ser. 6, no. 4 (1949): 596–604.

Jamieson, Ross W. "Material Culture and Social Death: African-American Burial Practices." *Historical Archaeology* 29, no. 4 (1995): 39–58.

Jennings, Francis, William N. Fenton, Mary A. Druke, and David R. Miller, eds. "Glossary of Figures of Speech in Iroquois Political Rhetoric." In *The History and Culture of Iroquois Diplomacy: An Interdisciplinary Guide to the Trea-*

ties of the Six Nations and Their League, 115–24. Syracuse: Syracuse University Press, 1985.

Jensen, Merrill, ed. *English Historical Documents: American Colonial Documents to 1776.* New York: Oxford University Press, 1962.

John, Richard R. *Spreading the News: The American Postal System from Franklin to Morse.* Cambridge: Harvard University Press, 1995.

Juricek, John T. *Colonial Georgia and the Creeks: Anglo-Indian Diplomacy on the Southern Frontier, 1733–1763.* Gainesville: University of Florida Press, 2010.

———, ed. *Georgia Treaties, 1733–1763.* Vol. 11 of *Early American Indian Documents: Treaties and Laws, 1607–1789*, edited by Alden T. Vaughan. Frederick, Md.: University Publications of America, 1989.

Juster, Susan. *Disorderly Women: Sexual Politics and Evangelicalism in Revolutionary New England.* Ithaca: Cornell University Press, 1994.

Justice, Daniel Heath. "'Go Away Water!': Kinship, Criticism, and the Decolonization Imperative." In *Reasoning Together: The Native Critics Collective*, edited by Craig S. Womack, Daniel Heath Justice, and Christopher B. Teuton, 147–68. Norman: University of Oklahoma Press, 2008.

———. "Katteuha (Cherokee)." In *The Heath Anthology of American Literature*, edited by Paul Lauter et al. 7th ed. Boston: Houghton Mifflin, 2013.

———. *Our Fire Survives the Storm: A Cherokee Literary History.* Minneapolis: University of Minnesota Press, 2006.

Kachun, Mitch. "From Forgotten Founder to Indispensable Icon: Crispus Attucks, Black Citizenship, and Collective Memory, 1770–1865." *Journal of the Early Republic* 29 (2009): 249–86.

Kashatus, William C., III. *Conflict of Conviction: A Reappraisal of Quaker Involvement in the American Revolution.* Lanham, Md.: University Press of America, 1990.

Katteuha. "Cherokee Women to Governor Benjamin Franklin (September 8, 1787)." In *Transatlantic Feminisms in the Age of Revolutions*, edited by Lisa L. Moore, Joanna Brooks, and Caroline Wigginton, 181–82. New York: Oxford University Press, 2012.

Kaye, Anthony E. *Joining Places: Slave Neighborhoods in the Old South.* Chapel Hill: University of North Carolina Press, 2007.

Keen, Paul. *The Crisis of Literature in the 1790s: Print Culture and the Public Sphere.* New York: Cambridge University Press, 1999.

Kelley, Mary. *Learning to Stand and Speak: Women, Education, and Public Life in America's Republic.* Chapel Hill: University of North Carolina Press, 2006.

Kerber, Linda K. *Women of the Republic: Intellect and Ideology in Revolutionary America.* Chapel Hill: University of North Carolina Press, 1980.

Kidwell, Clara Sue. "Indian Women As Cultural Mediators." *Ethnohistory* 39, no. 2 (1992): 97–107.

Klepp, Susan E. "Benjamin Franklin and Women." In *Companion to Benjamin Franklin*, edited by David Waldstreicher, 237–51. Malden, Mass: Wiley-Blackwell.

———. *Revolutionary Conceptions: Women, Fertility, and Family Limitation in America, 1760–1820.* Chapel Hill: University of North Carolina Press, 2009.

Klepp, Susan E., and Karin A. Wulf. Introduction to *The Diary of Hannah Callender Sansom: Sense and Sensibility in the Age of the American Revolution,* edited by Karin A. Wulf and Susan E. Klepp, 1–24. Ithaca: Cornell University Press, 2010.

Knott, Sarah. *Sensibility and the American Revolution.* Chapel Hill: University of North Carolina Press, 2009.

Krüger-Kahloula, Angelika. "Homage and Hegemony: African American Grave Inscription and Decoration." In *Slavery in the Americas,* edited by Genevieve Fabre and Robert O'Malley, 317–35. New York: Oxford University Press, 1994.

Kujawa, Sheryl A. "'The Path of Duty Plain': Samuel Hopkins, Sarah Osborn, and Revolutionary Newport." *Rhode Island History* 58, no. 3 (2000): 75–89.

———. "Religion, Education, and Gender in Eighteenth Century Rhode Island: Sarah Haggar Wheaten Osborn, 1714–1796." Ph.D. diss., Columbia University Teachers College, 1993.

Kuncio, Robert C. "Some Unpublished Poems of Phillis Wheatley." *New England Quarterly* 43, no. 2 (1970): 287–97.

Lacey, Barbara A. "The Bonds of Friendship: Sarah Osborn of Newport and the Reverend Joseph Fish of North Stonington, 1743–1779." *Rhode Island History* 45, no. 4 (1986): 127–36.

Landes, Joan B. *Women and the Public Sphere in the Age of the French Revolution.* Ithaca: Cornell University Press, 1988.

Landes, Ruth. *The Ojibwa Woman.* Lincoln: University of Nebraska Press, 1997.

Lankford, George E. "Red and White: Some Reflections on Southeastern Symbolism." *Southern Folklore* 50, no. 1 (1993): 53–80.

Larkin, Edward. *Thomas Paine and the Literature of Revolution.* New York: Cambridge University Press, 2005.

Larson, Rebecca. *Daughters of Light: Quaker Women Preaching and Prophesying in the Colonies and Abroad, 1700–1775.* New York: Knopf, 1999.

Latour, Bruno. *Reassembling the Social: An Introduction to Actor-Network-Theory.* Oxford: Oxford University Press, 2005.

LeMaster, Michele. *Brothers Born of One Mother: British-Native American Relations in the Colonial Southeast.* Charlottesville: University of Virginia Press, 2012.

Lemay, J. A. Leo. *The Life of Benjamin Franklin.* Vol. 1. Philadelphia: University of Pennsylvania Press, 2006.

León-Portilla, Miguel, ed. *The Broken Spears: The Aztec Account of the Conquest of Mexico,* translated by Angel Maria Garibay K. and Lysander Kemp. Rev. ed. Boston: Beacon, 1992.

Letters among Hannah Griffitts, Hannah Harrison, and Mary Norris, circa 1760s. Vol. 4 of Dickinson family papers, 1676–1885. Historical Society of Pennsylvania, Philadelphia.

Letter to Milcah Martha Moore, "6th day afternoon," 1776. In Thomas Stewardson's letters. Historical Society of Pennsylvania, Philadelphia.

Levernier, James A. "Style As Protest in the Poetry of Phillis Wheatley." *Style* 27, no. 2 (1993): 172–94.

Levis, H. C. *Baziliωlogia: A Booke of Kings: Notes on a Rare Series of Engraved English Royal Portraits from William the Conqueror to James I, Published Under the Above Title in 1618.* New York: Grolier Club, 1913.

Library Company of Philadelphia. *Benjamin Franklin: Writer and Printer,* 2006. www.librarycompany.org.

Locke, John. *The Works of John Locke.* Vol. 2. London: Routledge/Thoemmes, 1997.

Lockridge, Kenneth A. *On the Sources of Patriarchal Rage: The Commonplace Books of William Byrd and Thomas Jefferson and the Gendering of Power in the Eighteenth Century.* New York: New York University Press, 1992.

Logan, Deborah Norris. *The Norris House.* Philadelphia: Fair-Hill Press, 1867.

Logan, James. "Selections from the Correspondence of the Honourable James Logan." Vol. 1 of mss. B.L82. American Philosophical Society, Philadelphia.

Lokken, Roy N. "The Social Thought of James Logan." *William and Mary Quarterly* 3rd ser. 27, no. 1 (1970): 68–89.

Looby, Christopher. *Voicing America: Language, Literary Form, and the Origins of the United States.* Chicago: University of Chicago Press, 1996.

Loughran, Trish. *The Republic in Print: Print Culture in the Age of U.S. Nation Building, 1770–1870.* New York: Columbia University Press, 2007.

Love, Heather. *Feeling Backward: Loss and the Politics of Queer History.* Cambridge: Harvard University Press, 2007.

Luciano, Dana. *Arranging Grief: Sacred Time and the Body in Nineteenth-Century America.* New York: New York University Press, 2007.

Lukasik, Christopher. "Breeding and Reading: Chesterfieldian Civility in the Early Republic." In *A Companion to American Fiction, 1780–1865,* edited by Shirley Samuels, 158–67. Malden, Mass.: Blackwell, 2004.

Lyons, Clare A. *Sex among the Rabble: An Intimate History of Gender and Power in the Age of Revolution, Philadelphia, 1730–1830.* Chapel Hill: University of North Carolina Press, 2006.

Lyons, Scott Richard. *X-Marks: Native Signatures of Assent.* Minneapolis: University of Minnesota Press, 2010.

Mann, Barbara Alice. *Iroquoian Women: The Gantowisas.* Vol. 4 of American Indian Studies series. New York: Lang, 2000.

Marees, Pieter de. *Description and Historical Account of the Gold Kingdom of Guinea,* translated by Albert van Dantzig and Adam Jones. Oxford: Oxford University Press, 1987.

Marietta, Jack D. *The Reformation of American Quakerism, 1748–1783.* Philadelphia: University of Pennsylvania Press, 1984.

Marrant, John. "A Funeral Preached by the Desire of the Deceased, John Lock; the Text Chose by Himself from the Epistle of St. Paul to the Philippians,

Chap. 1 Ver. 21. *1790*." In *"Face Zion Forward": First Writers of the Black Atlantic, 1785–1798*, edited by John Saillant and Joanna Brooks, 161–76. Boston: Northeastern University Press, 2002.

———. "A Narrative of the Lord's Wonderful Dealings with John Marrant, a Black. *1785*." In *"Face Zion Forward": First Writers of the Black Atlantic, 1785–1798*, edited by John Saillant and Joanna Brooks, 47–75. Boston: Northeastern University Press, 2002.

Mason, Matthew. *Slavery and Politics in the Early American Republic*. Chapel Hill: University of North Carolina Press, 2006.

Masson, Margaret. "The Typology of the Female As a Model for the Regenerate: Puritan Preaching, 1690–1730." *Signs* 2, no. 2 (1976): 304–15.

Mather, Cotton. *A Glorious Espousal: A Brief Essay. . . .* Boston: Kneeland, 1719.

———. *The Negro Christianized: An Essay to Excite and Assist That Good Work, the Instruction of Negro-Servants in Christianity*. Boston: Green, 1706.

———. *The Wonders of the Invisible World. Observations as Well Historical as Theological, upon the Nature, the Number, and the Operations of the Devils*. Boston: Printed by Benj. Harris for Sam Phillips, 1693.

Mattes, Mark Alan. "Penman's Devil: The Chirographic and Typographic Urgency of Race in *The Letters of the Late Ignatius Sancho, An African*." *Early American Literature* 48, no. 3 (2013): 577–612.

McCallum, James Dow, ed. *The Letters of Wheelock's Indians*. Hanover, N.H.: Dartmouth College Publications, 1932.

McCaskie, Thomas C. "Death and the Asantehene: A Historical Meditation." *Journal of African History* 30, no. 3 (1989): 417–44.

McClure, Norman Egbert, ed. *The Letters of John Chamberlain*. Vol. 2. Philadelphia: American Philosophical Society, 1939.

McDowell, William L., ed. *Documents Relating to Indian Affairs: May 21, 1750–August 7, 1754. Colonial Records of South Carolina*. Columbia: South Carolina Archives Department, 1958.

McHenry, Elizabeth. *Forgotten Readers: Recovering the Lost History of African American Literary Societies*. Durham, N.C.: Duke University Press, 2002.

McLuhan, Marshall. *Understanding Media: The Extensions of Man*. Cambridge: MIT Press, 1994.

McMullen, Ann. "Looking for People in Woodsplint Basketry Decoration." In *A Key into the Language of Woodsplint Baskets*, edited by Ann McMullen and Russell G. Handsman, 103–23. Washington, Conn.: American Indian Archaeological Institute, 1987.

Mekeel, Arthur J. "The Relation of the Quakers to the American Revolution." *Quaker History* 65, no. 1 (1976): 3–18.

Melish, Joanne Pope. *Disowning Slavery: Gradual Emancipation and "Race" in New England, 1780–1860*. Ithaca: Cornell University Press, 1998.

Merrell, James H. *Into the American Woods: Negotiators on the Pennsylvania Frontier*. New York: Norton, 1999.

Michelson, Gunther. "Iroquoian Terms for Wampum." *International Journal of American Linguistics* 57, no. 1 (1991): 108–31.

Mihesuah, Devon Abbott. *Indigenous American Women: Decolonization, Empowerment, Activism.* Lincoln: University of Nebraska Press, 2003.

Miller, Susan. *Assuming the Positions: Cultural Pedagogy and the Politics of Commonplace Writing.* Pittsburgh: University of Pittsburgh Press, 1998.

Minkema, Kenneth P., and Harry S. Stout. "The Edwardsean Tradition and the Antislavery Debate, 1740–1865." *Journal of American History* 92, no. 1 (2005): 47–74.

Minutes of the Monthly Meeting of Women's Friends in Philadelphia (PWMM), 1768–81. Haverford College Library, Quaker Collection, Haverford, Pennsylvania.

Monaghan, E. Jennifer. *Learning to Read and Write in Colonial America.* Amherst: University of Massachusetts Press, 2005.

Mooney, James. *Calendar History of the Kiowa Indians.* Washington: Smithsonian Institution, 1979.

Moore, Lisa L. *Sister Arts: The Erotics of Lesbian Landscapes.* Minneapolis: University of Minnesota Press, 2011.

Moore, Lisa L., Joanna Brooks, and Caroline Wigginton, eds. *Transatlantic Feminisms in the Age of Revolutions.* New York: Oxford University Press, 2012.

Moore, Milcah Martha. Devotional book, [1776]. Ms. 975B. Haverford College Library, Quaker Collection, Haverford, Pennsylvania.

———. Letter, 22 March 1785. Edward Wanton Smith Collection, box 955. Haverford College Library, Quaker Collection, Haverford, Pennsylvania.

———. Letter to Hannah Moore, [1778]. Edward Wanton Smith Collection, box 955. Haverford College Library, Quaker Collection, Haverford, Pennsylvania.

———. *Milcah Martha Moore's Book: A Commonplace Book from Revolutionary America,* edited by Catherine La Courreye Blecki and Karin A. Wulf. University Park: Pennsylvania State University Press, 1997.

———, ed. *Miscellanies, Moral and Instructive, in Prose and Verse; Collected from Various Authors, for the Use of Schools, and Improvement of Young Persons of Both Sexes.* Philadelphia: James, 1787.

———. Testimony book. Ms. 975A. Haverford College Library, Quaker Collection, Haverford, Pennsylvania.

Morgan, Edmund. "The Puritan's Marriage with God." *South Atlantic Quarterly* 48, no. 1 (1949): 107–12.

Morgan, Jennifer L. *Laboring Women: Reproduction and Gender in New World Slavery.* Philadelphia: University of Pennsylvania Press, 2004.

Moss, Ann. *Printed Commonplace-Books and the Structuring of Renaissance Thought.* Oxford: Clarendon, 1996.

Moulder, M. Amanda. "'By Women, You Were Brought Forth into This World': Cherokee Women's Oratorical Education in the Late Eighteenth Century."

In *Rhetoric, History, and Women's Oratorical Education: American Women Learn to Speak,* edited by David Gold and Catherine L. Hobbs, 19–37. New York: Routledge, 2013.

Mower, C. Leiren. "Bodies in Labor: Sole Proprietorship and the Labor of Conduct in *The Coquette.*" *American Literature* 74, no. 2 (2002): 315–44.

Mueller, Pamela Bauer. *An Angry Drum Echoed: Mary Musgrove, Queen of the Creeks.* Saint Simon's Island, Ga.: Piñata, 2007.

Murray, David. *Indian Giving: Economies of Power in Indian-White Exchanges.* Amherst: University of Massachusetts Press, 2000.

Nash, Gary B. "Slaves and Slaveholders in Colonial Philadelphia." *William and Mary Quarterly* 3rd ser. 30, no. 2 (1973): 223–56.

Nelson, Dana D. *National Manhood: Capitalist Citizenship and the Imagined Fraternity of White Men.* Durham, N.C.: Duke University Press, 1998.

Newman, Andrew. *On Records: Delaware Indians, Colonists, and the Media of History and Memory.* Lincoln: University of Nebraska Press, 2012.

Norris, John. *A Collection of Miscellanies: Consisting of Poems, Essays, Discourses and Letters, Occasionally Written.* 9th ed. London: Parker, 1740.

Norris papers, ms. box 12, Historical Society of Pennsylvania, Philadelphia.

Norton, Mary Beth. *Liberty's Daughters: The Revolutionary Experience of American Women, 1750–1800.* Ithaca: Cornell University Press, 1996.

———. "'My Resting Reaping Times': Sarah Osborn's Defense of Her 'Unfeminine' Activities, 1767." *Signs* 2, no. 2 (1976): 515–29.

Ong, Walter J. *Orality and Literacy: The Technologizing of the Word.* 30th anniv. ed. New York: Routledge, 2012.

Osborn, Sarah. Diary, 28 April 1761–18 February 1762. Osborn-Anthony papers. Yale University, Beinecke Rare Book and Manuscript Library, New Haven, Connecticut.

———. Letter to Joseph Fish, 16 May 1754. Osborn letters, mss. boxes O. American Antiquarian Society, Worcester, Massachusetts.

———. Letter to Joseph Fish, 4 June 1754. Osborn letters, mss. boxes O. American Antiquarian Society, Worcester, Massachusetts.

———. Letter to Joseph Fish, 1 November 1754. Osborn letters, mss. boxes O. American Antiquarian Society, Worcester, Massachusetts.

———. Letter to Joseph Fish, 10 December 1755. Osborn letters, mss. boxes O. American Antiquarian Society, Worcester, Massachusetts.

———. Letter to Joseph Fish, 17 December 1756. Osborn letters, mss. boxes O. American Antiquarian Society, Worcester, Massachusetts.

———. Letter to Joseph Fish, 3 May 1759. Osborn letters, mss. boxes O. American Antiquarian Society, Worcester, Massachusetts.

———. Letter to Joseph Fish, 10 May 1761. Osborn letters, mss. boxes O. American Antiquarian Society, Worcester, Massachusetts.

———. Letter to Joseph Fish, 21 April 1765. Osborn letters, mss. boxes O. American Antiquarian Society, Worcester, Massachusetts.

———. Letter to Joseph Fish, 28 February–7 March 1767. Osborn letters, mss. boxes O. American Antiquarian Society, Worcester, Massachusetts.

———. Letter to Joseph Fish, 29 July 1769. Simon Gratz Collection. Historical Society of Pennsylvania, Philadelphia.

———. Letter to Joseph Fish, 26 October 1769. Simon Gratz Collection. Historical Society of Pennsylvania, Philadelphia.

———. *Memoirs of the Life of Mrs. Sarah Osborn, Who Died at Newport, Rhodeisland, on the Second Day of August, 1796. In the Eighty Third Year of Her Age,* edited by Samuel Hopkins. Worcester: Leonard Worcester, 1799.

———. *The Nature, Certainty and Evidence of True Christianity in a Letter from a Gentlewoman in New-England, to Another Her Dear Friend, in Great Darkness, Doubt and Concern of a Religious Nature.* Boston: Kneeland, 1755.

Osborn, Sarah, and Susanna Anthony. *Familiar Letters, Written by Mrs. Sarah Osborn and Miss Susanna Anthony, Late of Newport, Rhode-Island.* Newport, R.I.: *Newport Mercury,* 1807.

Ousterhout, Anne M. *The Most Learned Woman in America: A Life of Elizabeth Graeme Fergusson.* University Park: Pennsylvania State University Press, 2004.

Paine, Thomas. *Common Sense; Addressed to the Inhabitants of America.* Philadelphia: Bradford, 1776.

Park, Edwards A. *Memoir of the Life and Character of Samuel Hopkins, D.D.* 2nd ed. Boston: Doctrinal Tract and Book Society, 1854.

Parrish, Susan Scott. "Women's Nature: Curiosity, Pastoral, and the New Science in British America." *Early American Literature* 37, no. 2 (2002): 195–238.

Patterson, Orlando. *Slavery and Social Death: A Comparative Study.* Cambridge: Harvard University Press, 1982.

Pearce, Susan M. *On Collecting: An Investigation into Collecting in the European Tradition.* London: Routledge, 1995.

Pearse, Edward. *The Best Match: Or, The Soul's Espousal to Christ.* 10th ed. Boston: Green, 1708.

Perdue, Theda. *Cherokee Women: Gender and Cultural Change, 1700–1835.* Lincoln: University of Nebraska Press, 1999.

Pettit, Florence H. *America's Indigo Blues: Resist-Printed and Dyed Textiles of the Eighteenth-Century.* New York: Hastings House, 1974.

"PHILADELPHIA, May 7, CIVIC FESTIVAL." *Pennsylvania Gazette,* 7 May 1794, n.p.

Philadelphia Women's Yearly Meeting Minutes (PWYM), 1681–1814. Haverford College Library, Quaker Collection, Haverford, Pennsylvania.

Philadelphia Yearly Meeting of the Religious Society of Friends, Meeting for Sufferings. *The Ancient Testimony and Principles of the People Called Quakers.* Philadelphia, 1776.

Phillippo, James M. *Jamaica: Its Past and Present State.* London: Snow, 1843.

Piersen, William D. *Black Yankees: The Development of an Afro-American Subculture in Eighteenth-Century New England.* Amherst: University of Massachusetts Press, 1988.

Piker, Joshua. *Okfuskee: A Creek Indian Town in Colonial America.* Cambridge: Harvard University Press, 2004.

Pinckney, Eliza Lucas. *The Letterbook of Eliza Lucas Pinckney, 1739–1762,* edited by Elise Pinckney and Marvin R. Zahniser. Columbia: University of South Carolina Press, 1997.

Plato, Ann. *Essays: Including Biographies and Miscellaneous Pieces, in Prose and Poetry.* New York: Oxford University Press, 1988.

Pope, Alexander. *The Poems of Alexander Pope: A Reduced Version of the Twickenham Text,* edited by John Butt. New Haven: Yale University Press, 1963.

Porterfield, Amanda. *Female Piety in Puritan New England: The Emergence of Religious Humanism.* New York: Oxford University Press, 1992.

Povinelli, Elizabeth A. *The Empire of Love: Toward a Theory of Intimacy, Genealogy, and Carnality.* Durham, N.C.: Duke University Press, 2006.

Pruitt, Bettye Hobbs, ed. *The Massachusetts Tax Valuation List of 1771.* Boston: Hall, 1978.

Ramsay, David. *The History of the American Revolution.* Vol. 1. London, 1790.

Rasmussen, Birgit Brander. *Queequeg's Coffin: Indigenous Literacies and Early American Literature.* Durham, N.C.: Duke University Press, 2012.

Rath, Richard Cullen. "Hearing Wampum: The Senses, Mediation, and the Limits of Analogy." In *Colonial Mediascapes: Sensory Worlds of the Early Americas,* edited by Matt Cohen and Jeffrey Glover, 290–321. Lincoln: University of Nebraska Press, 2014.

Reinberger, Mark, and Elizabeth McLean. "Isaac Norris's Fairhill: Architecture, Landscape, and Quaker Ideals in a Philadelphia Colonial Country Seat." *Winterthur Portfolio,* 1 December 1997, 243–74.

Remer, Rosalind. *Printers and Men of Capital: Philadelphia Book Publishers in the New Republic.* Philadelphia: University of Pennsylvania Press, 1996.

Report of the Record Commissioners of the City of Boston, Containing the Boston Records from 1700 to 1728. Boston Record Commissioners' Reports, no. 8. Boston: Rockwell and Churchill, 1883.

Report of the Record Commissioners of the City of Boston, Containing the Records of Boston Selectmen, 1716 to 1736. Boston Record Commissioners' Reports, no. 13. Boston: Rockwell and Churchill, 1885.

Report of the Record Commissioners of the City of Boston, Containing the Boston Town Records, 1742 to 1757. Boston Record Commissioners' Reports, no. 14. Boston: Rockwell and Churchill, 1885.

Rezek, Joseph. "The Orations on the Abolition of the Slave Trade and the Uses of Print in the Early Black Atlantic." *Early American Literature* 45, no. 3 (2010): 655–82.

Richter, Daniel K. *The Ordeal of the Longhouse: Peoples of the Iroquois League in the Era of Colonization.* Chapel Hill: University of North Carolina Press, 1992.

Rigsby, Gregory. "Form and Content in Phillis Wheatley's Elegies." *CLA Journal* 9, no. 4 (1975): 248–57.

Ring, Betty. *Let Virtue Be a Guide to Thee: Needlework in the Education of Rhode Island Women, 1730–1830.* Providence: Rhode Island Historical Society, 1983.

Roach, Joseph. *Cities of the Dead: Circum-Atlantic Performance.* New York: Columbia University Press, 1996.

Robertson, Claire. "Africa into the Americas? Slavery and Women, the Family, and the Gender Division of Labor." In *More Than Chattel: Black Women and Slavery in the Americas,* edited by David Barry Gaspar and Darlene Clarke Hine, 3–40. Bloomington: Indiana University Press, 1996.

Robinson, William H. "Phyllis Wheatley: Colonial Quandary." *CLA Journal* 9, no. 1 (1965): 25–38.

Robinson, W. Stitt, ed. *Virginia Treaties, 1607–1722.* Vol. 4 of *Early American Indian Documents: Treaties and Laws, 1607–1789.* Frederick, Md.: University Publications of America, 1983.

Rosenberg, Karen. "On Being a Woman, from Cradle to Grave." *New York Times,* 13 February 2010, C1.

Rosenthal, Debra J. "The White Blackbird: Miscegenation, Genre, and the Tragic Mulatta in Howells, Harper, and the 'Babes of Romance.'" *Nineteenth-Century Literature* 56, no. 4 (2002): 495–517.

Round, Phillip H. *Removable Type: Histories of the Book in Indian Country, 1663–1880.* Chapel Hill: University of North Carolina Press, 2010.

Rountree, Helen C. "Pocahontas: The Hostage Who Became Famous." In *Sifters: Native American Women's Lives,* edited by Theda Perdue, 13–28. New York: Oxford University Press, 2001.

———. *Pocahontas, Powhatan, Opechancanough: Three Indian Lives Change by Jamestown.* Charlottesville: University of Virginia Press, 2005.

Routley, Erik. "Charles Wesley and Matthew Henry." *Congregational Quarterly* 33 (1955): 345–51.

Rowe, John. *Letters and Diary of John Rowe, Boston Merchant, 1759–1762, 1764–1779,* edited by Anne Rowe Cunningham. Boston: Clarke, 1903.

Rush, Benjamin. "An Account of the Life and Character of Mrs. Elizabeth Ferguson." *Port Folio* 1 (1809): 520–27.

Ryan, Mary P. "Gender and Public Access: Women's Politics in Nineteenth-Century America." In *Habermas and the Public Sphere,* edited by Craig Calhoun, 259–88. Cambridge: MIT Press, 1992.

Sacks, Peter M. *The English Elegy: Studies in the Genre from Spenser to Yeats.* Baltimore: Johns Hopkins University Press, 1985.

Saillant, John, and Joanna Brooks. Introduction to *"Face Zion Forward": First Writers of the Black Atlantic, 1785–1798,* edited by John Saillant and Joanna Brooks, 3–33. Boston: Northeastern University Press, 2002.

Sanford, Enoch. *History of the Town of Berkley, Mass., Including Sketches of the Lives of the Two First Ministers, Rev. Samuel Tobey, and Rev. Thomas Andros, Whose United Ministry Continued Ninety-One Years.* New York: Kilbourne Tompkins, 1872.

Sansom, Hannah Callender. *The Diary of Hannah Callender Sansom: Sense and Sensibility in the Age of the American Revolution,* edited by Karin A. Wulf and Susan E. Klepp. Ithaca: Cornell University Press, 2010.

Sarris, Greg. *Keeping Slug Woman Alive: A Holistic Approach to American Indian Texts.* Berkeley: University of California Press, 1993.

Schaefer, Elizabeth Meg. *Wright's Ferry Mansion.* 2 vols. Columbia: Von Hess Foundation, 2005.

Scheick, William J. *Authority and Female Authorship in Colonial America.* Lexington: University Press of Kentucky, 1998.

———. "Tombless Virtue and Hidden Text: New England Puritan Funeral Elegies." In *Puritan Poets and Poetics: Seventeenth-Century American Poetry in Theory and Practice,* edited by Peter White, 286–302. University Park: Pennsylvania State University Press, 1985.

Schenck, Celeste M. "Feminism and Deconstruction: Re-Constructing the Elegy." *Tulsa Studies in Women's Literature* 5, no. 1 (1986): 13–27.

Schmidt, Leigh Eric. "'The Grand Prophet,' Hugh Bryan: Early Evangelicalism's Challenge to the Establishment and Slavery in the Colonial South." *South Carolina Historical Magazine* 87 (1986): 238–50.

Schneider, Gary. *The Culture of Epistolarity: Vernacular Letters and Letter Writing in Early Modern England, 1500–1700.* Newark: University of Delaware Press, 2005.

Schoelwer, Susan P., and Kate Steinway. *Connecticut Needlework: Women, Art, and Family, 1740–1840.* Hartford: Connecticut Historical Society, 2010.

Schweitzer, Ivy. *Perfecting Friendship: Politics and Affiliation in Early American Literature.* Chapel Hill: University of North Carolina Press, 2007.

———. *The Work of Self-Representation: Lyric Poetry in Colonial New England.* Chapel Hill: University of North Carolina Press, 1991.

Scott, Darieck. *Extravagant Abjection: Blackness, Power, and Sexuality in the African American Literary Imagination.* New York: New York University Press, 2010.

Seeman, Erik R. *Death in the New World: Cross-Cultural Encounters, 1492–1800.* Philadelphia: University of Pennsylvania Press, 2010.

———. *Pious Persuasions: Laity and Clergy in Eighteenth-Century New England.* Baltimore: Johns Hopkins University Press, 1999.

Shea, Daniel B., Jr. *Spiritual Autobiography in Early America.* Princeton: Princeton University Press, 1968.

Shields, David S. *Civil Tongues and Polite Letters in British America.* Chapel Hill: University of North Carolina Press, 1997.

Shields, John C. "Phillis Wheatley's Struggle for Freedom in Her Poetry and Prose." In *The Collected Works of Phillis Wheatley,* edited by John C. Shields, 229–70. New York: Oxford University Press, 1988.

Shoemaker, Nancy. Introduction to *Negotiators of Change: Historical Perspectives on Native American Women,* edited by Nancy Shoemaker, 1–25. London: Routledge, 1995.

———. "The Rise or Fall of Iroquois Women." *Journal of Women's History* 2, no. 3 (1991): 39–57.

Shurtleff, Nathaniel B. *A Topographical and Historical Description of Boston.* Boston: Boston City Council, 1871.

Smallwood, Stephanie. *Saltwater Slavery: A Middle Passage from Africa to American Diaspora.* Cambridge: Harvard University Press, 2007.

Smith, John. *Writings with Other Narratives of Roanoke, Jamestown, and the First English Settlement of America.* New York: Library of America, 2007.

Smith, John J., ed. *Letters of Doctor Richard Hill and His Children: Or, The History of a Family, as Told by Themselves.* Philadelphia: Collins, 1854.

Smith-Rosenberg, Carroll. "Domesticating Virtue: Coquettes and Revolutionaries in Young America." In *American Literary Studies: A Methodological Reader,* edited by Michael A. Elliott and Claudia Stokes, 21–40. New York: New York University Press, 2002.

Snyderman, George S. "The Functions of Wampum." *Proceedings of the American Philosophical Society* 98, no. 6 (1954): 469–94.

Soderlund, Jean R., ed. *William Penn and the Founding of Pennsylvania: A Documentary History.* Philadelphia: University of Pennsylvania Press, 1983.

Spady, James O'Neil. "Colonialism and the Discursive Antecedents of *Penn's Treaty with the Indians.*" In *Friends and Enemies in Penn's Woods: Indians, Colonists, and the Racial Construction of Pennsylvania,* edited by William Pencak and Daniel K. Richter, 19–40. University Park: Pennsylvania State University Press, 2004.

Stabile, Susan M. Introduction to *The Most Learned Woman in America: A Life of Elizabeth Graeme Fergusson,* by Anne M. Ousterhout, 1–27. University Park: Pennsylvania State University Press, 2004.

———. *Memory's Daughters: The Material Culture of Remembrance in Eighteenth-Century America.* Ithaca: Cornell University Press, 2004.

Starr, Paul. *The Creation of the Media: Political Origins of Modern Communications.* New York: Basic Books, 2004.

Stewart, Susan. *On Longing: Narratives of the Miniature, the Gigantic, the Souvenir, the Collection.* Baltimore: Johns Hopkins University Press, 1984.

Stockton, Annis Boudinot. *Only for the Eye of a Friend: The Poems of Annis Boudinot Stockton,* edited by Carla Mulford. Charlottesville: University of Virginia Press, 1995.

Straub, Kristina. *Domestic Affairs: Intimacy, Eroticism, and Violence between Servants and Masters in Eighteenth-Century Britain.* Baltimore: Johns Hopkins University Press, 2009.

Sturtevant, William C. "The Cherokee Frontiers, the French Revolution, and William Augustus Bowles." In *The Cherokee Indian Nation: A Troubled History,* edited by Duane H. King, 61–91. Knoxville: University of Tennessee Press, 1979.

Sweet, James H. *Recreating Africa: Culture, Kinship, and Religion in the African-*

Portuguese World, 1441–1770. Chapel Hill: University of North Carolina Press, 2003.

Sweet, John Wood. "'More Than Tears': The Ordeal of Abolition in Revolutionary New England." *Explorations in Early American Culture* 5 (2001): 118–72.

Sweet, Julie Anne. *Negotiating for Georgia: British-Creek Relations in the Trustee Era, 1733–1752.* Athens: University of Georgia Press, 2005.

Szasz, Margaret Connell. *Indian Education in the American Colonies, 1607–1783.* Albuquerque: University of New Mexico Press, 1988.

Tantaquidgeon, Gladys, and Jayne G. Fawcett. "Symbolic Motifs on Painted Baskets of the Mohegan-Pequot." In *A Key into the Language of Woodsplint Baskets,* edited by Ann McMullen and Russell G. Handsman, 95–101. Washington, Conn.: American Indian Archaeological Institute, 1987.

Teute, Frederika J. "The Loves of the Plants; or, the Cross-Fertilization of Science and Desire at the End of the Eighteenth Century." *Huntington Library Quarterly* 63, no. 3 (2000): 319–45.

Teuton, Christopher B. *Deep Waters: The Textual Continuum in American Indian Literature.* Norman: University of Nebraska Press, 2010.

Thomas, Isaiah. *The History of Printing in America. With a Biography of Printers, and an Account of Newspapers.* Vol. 1. Worcester: Thomas, 1810.

Thorn, Jennifer. "Seduction, Juvenile Death Literature, and Phillis Wheatley's Child Elegies." In *Atlantic Worlds in the Long Eighteenth Century: Seduction and Sentiment,* edited by Toni Bowers and Tita Chico, 189–203. New York: Palgrave Macmillan, 2012.

Todd, Helen. *Mary Musgrove, Indian Princess.* Marietta, Ga.: Larlin, 1981.

Todd, Janet M. *Women's Friendship in Literature.* New York: Columbia University Press, 1980.

Tolles, Frederick B. *James Logan and the Culture of Provincial America,* edited by Oscar Handlin. Boston: Little, Brown, 1957.

"THE Town of Boston affords a recent and melancholy Demonstration. . . ." *Boston Gazette, and Country Journal,* 12 March 1770, [2].

Townsend, Camilla. *Pocahontas and the Powhatan Dilemma: An American Portrait.* New York: Hill and Wang, 2004.

Tyerman, Luke. *The Oxford Methodists: Memoirs of the Rev. Messrs. Clayton, Ingham, Gambold, Hervey, and Broughton, with Biographical Notices of Others.* New York: Harper, 1873.

Ulrich, Laurel Thatcher. *The Age of Homespun: Objects and Stories in the Creation of an American Myth.* New York: Knopf, 2001.

———. *Good Wives: Image and Reality in the Lives of Women in Northern New England, 1650–1750.* New York: Knopf, 1982.

Valdez, Amanda. "In Conversation with Kiki Smith." *Dossier,* 5 April 2010. http://dossierjournal.com.

Van Kirk, Sylvia. *Many Tender Ties: Women in Fur-Trade Society, 1670–1870.* Norman: University of Oklahoma Press, 1980.

———. "Thanadelthur." *Beaver* 304, no. 4 (1974): 40–45.

Veldman, Ilja M. *Crispijn de Passe and His Progeny (1564–1670): A Century of Print Production,* translated by Michael Hoyle. Rotterdam: Sound and Vision, 2001.

Vietto, Angela. *Women and Authorship in Revolutionary America.* Burlington, Vt.: Ashgate, 2005.

Vincens, Simone. *Madame Montour and the Fur Trade (1667–1752),* translated by Ruth Bernstein. Bloomington, Ind.: Xlibris, 2011.

Wardi, Anissa Janine. *Death and the Arc of Mourning in African American Literature.* Gainesville: University Press of Florida, 2003.

Warkentin, Germaine. "In Search of the Word of the Other." *Book History* 2 (1999): 1–27.

Warner, Michael. *The Letters of the Republic: Publication and the Public Sphere in Eighteenth-Century America.* Cambridge: Harvard University Press, 1990.

———. *Publics and Counterpublics.* New York: Zone, 2002.

Waselkov, Gregory A. "Indian Maps of the Colonial Southeast: Archaeological Implications and Prospects." In *Cartographic Encounters: Perspectives on Native American Mapmaking and Map Use,* edited by G. Malcolm Lewis, 205–21. Chicago: University of Chicago Press, 1998.

Waterman, Bryan. "Coquetry and Correspondence in Revolutionary-Era Connecticut: Reading Elizabeth Whitman's Letters." *Early American Literature* 46, no. 3 (2011): 541–63.

Wells, Robert V. "A Tale of Two Cities: Epidemics and Rituals of Death in Eighteenth-Century Boston and Philadelphia." In *Mortal Remains: Death in Early America,* edited by Nancy Isenberg and Andrew Burstein, 56–67. Philadelphia: University of Pennsylvania Press, 2003.

Wesley, John, and Charles Wesley. *Hymns and Sacred Poems.* Philadelphia: Bradford, 1740.

Wharton, Anne Hollingsworth. *Salons Colonial and Republican.* Philadelphia: Lippincott, 1900.

Wheatley, Phillis. *Complete Writings,* edited by Vincent Carretta. New York: Penguin, 2001.

———. *Thoughts on Various Subjects, Religious and Moral.* London: Bell, 1773.

Whitfield, James Monroe. *The Works of James M. Whitfield: America and Other Writings by a Nineteenth-Century African American Poet,* edited by Robert S. Levine and Ivy G. Wilson. Chapel Hill: University of North Carolina Press, 2011.

Wigginton, Caroline. "A Late Night Vindication: Annis Boudinot Stockton's Reading of Mary Wollstonecraft's *A Vindication of the Rights of Woman.*" *Legacy* 25, no. 2 (2008): 225–38.

———. "Letters from a Woman in Pennsylvania, or, Elizabeth Graeme Fergusson Dreams of John Dickinson." In *Community without Consent: New Perspectives on the Stamp Act,* edited by Zachary McLeod Hutchins. Hanover, N.H.: Dartmouth College Press, 2016.

———. "Vexing Motherhood and Interracial Intimacy in Sarah Osborn's Spiritual Diary." *Early American Literature* 47, no. 1 (2012): 115–42.

Williams, Eliphalet. *The Duty of a People, under Dark Providences, or Symptoms of Approaching Evils, to Prepare to Meet Their God.* New London, Conn.: Green, 1756.

Willis, Patricia C. "Phillis Wheatley, George Whitefield, and the Countess of Huntingdon in the Beinecke Library." *Yale University Library Gazette* 80 (April 2006): 161–76.

Winchester, Angus J. L. "Samuel Fothergill (1715–1772)." In *Oxford Dictionary of National Biography,* edited by H. C. G. Matthew and Brian Harrison. New York: Oxford University Press, 2004.

Wolf, Edwin. *The Library of James Logan of Philadelphia, 1674–1751.* Philadelphia: Library Company of Philadelphia, 1974.

———. "The Romance of James Logan's Books." *William and Mary Quarterly* 3rd ser. 13, no. 3 (1956): 342–53.

Womack, Craig S. *Red on Red: Native Literary Separatism.* Minneapolis: University of Minnesota Press, 1999.

Woodward, Grace Steele. *The Cherokees.* Norman: University of Oklahoma Press, 1963.

Woolman, John. *Some Considerations on the Keeping of Negroes. Recommended to the Professors of Christianity of Every Denomination.* Philadelphia: Chattin, 1754.

Worster, Donald. *The Wealth of Nature: Environmental History and the Ecological Imagination.* New York: Oxford University Press, 1993.

Wulf, Karin A. "*Milcah Martha Moore's Book:* Documenting Culture and Connection in the Revolutionary Era." In *Milcah Martha Moore's Book: A Commonplace Book from Revolutionary America,* by Milcah Martha Moore, edited by Catherine La Courreye Blecki and Karin A. Wulf, 1–57. University Park: Pennsylvania State University Press, 1997.

———. *Not All Wives: Women of Colonial Philadelphia.* Ithaca: Cornell University Press, 2000.

Wyss, Hilary E. "Writing Back to Wheelock: One Young Woman's Response to Colonial Christianity." In *Early Native Literacies in New England: A Documentary and Critical Anthology,* edited by Kristina Bross and Hilary E. Wyss, 96–104. Amherst: University of Massachusetts Press, 2008.

Zboray, Ronald J., and Mary Saracino Zboray. *Everyday Ideas: Socioliterary Experience among Antebellum New Englanders.* Knoxville: University of Tennessee Press, 2006.

Ziff, Larzer. *Writing in the New Nation: Prose, Print, and Politics in the Early United States.* New Haven: Yale University Press, 1991.

Žižek, Slavoj, Eric L. Santner, and Kenneth Reinhard. *The Neighbor: Three Inquiries in Political Theology.* Chicago: University of Chicago Press, 2005.

Zobel, Hiller B. *The Boston Massacre.* New York: Norton, 1970.

INDEX

Caroline Wigginton is a native of Ohio. She attended The Ohio State University, where she received undergraduate degrees in English and Biochemistry. After working several years in technology and manufacturing consulting, she returned to school and received her doctorate in English from the University of Texas at Austin. She is assistant professor of English at the University of Mississippi. Along with Joanna Brooks and Lisa L. Moore, she is the coeditor of *Transatlantic Feminisms in the Age of Revolutions* (Oxford, 2012).